Mogadishu, Somalia

Sam Night

Contents

Articles

Overview of Somalia **1**

Somalia 1

History of Somalia 43

Geography of Somalia 73

Politics of Somalia 80

Economy of Somalia 89

Culture of Somalia 97

Hannassa 102

Maduna 102

Overview of Mogadishu **103**

Mogadishu 103

Banaadir 112

History of Mogadishu **113**

History of Mogadishu 113

Cities and Towns Nearby to Visit **120**

Kismayo 120

Afgooye 125

Dinsoor 127

Jamaame 128

Xuddur 130

Wajid, Somalia 131

Jilib 133

Barawa 134

Mandera 136
Merca 140
Jowhar 142
Hobyo 146
Hargeisa 149

Attractions In and Around the City **156**

Mogadishu Cathedral 156
Mosque of Islamic Solidarity 157
Fakr ad-Din Mosque 159
Villa Somalia 160
Gezira Beach 161
Shebelle River 162
National Library of Somalia 164
Bakaara Market 164
Istunka 167
Gelbis 169
Badbaado 170
Banadir Stadium 171
Mogadiscio Stadium 172

Music and Cuisine **173**

Music of Somalia 173
Somali cuisine 177

Transportation **182**

Aden Adde International Airport 182
Mogadishu-Villabruzzi Railway 185

References

Article Sources and Contributors 189
Image Sources, Licenses and Contributors 191

Overview of Somalia

Somalia

Republic of Somalia

Jamhuuriyadda Soomaaliya

جمهورية الصومال

Jumhūriyyat as-Sūmāl

Anthem: *Soomaaliyeey Toosoow*
Somalia, Wake Up

Capital (and largest city)	Mogadishu 2°02′N 45°21′E
Official language(s)	Somali, Arabic
Ethnic groups	Somalis (85%), Benadiri, Bantus and other non-Somalis (15%)
Demonym	Somali; Somalian
Government	Coalition government

-	President	Sharif Ahmed
-	Acting Prime Minister	Abdiwahid Elmi Gonjeh
Formation		
-	Warsangali Sultanate	13th century
-	Adal Sultanate	14th century
-	Ajuuraan Empire	15th century
-	Gobroon Dynasty	17th century
-	Sultanate of Hobyo	19th century
-	Dervish State	20th century
-	Union of protectorate and trust territory	1 July 1960
Area		
-	Total	637,657 km^2 (43rd) 246,200 sq mi
Population		
-	2010 estimate	9,359,000 (87th)
GDP (PPP)		2009 estimate
-	Total	$5.731 billion (155th)
-	Per capita	$600 (224th)
HDI (2009)		N/A (Not ranked)
Currency		Somali shilling (SOS)
Time zone		EAT (UTC+3)
-	Summer (DST)	not observed (UTC+3)
Drives on the		right
ISO 3166 code		SO
Internet TLD		.so
Calling code		252
1	Transitional Federal Charter of the Somali Republic	

Somalia (pronounced /soʊˈmɑːliə/ *soh-MAH-lee-ə*; Somali: *Soomaaliya*; Arabic: الصومال *aṣ-Ṣūmāl*), officially the **Republic of Somalia** (Somali: *Jamhuuriyadda Soomaaliya*, Arabic: جمهورية الصومال *Jumhūriyyat aṣ-Ṣūmāl*) and formerly known as the Somali Democratic Republic under communist rule, is a country located in the Horn of Africa. It is bordered by Djibouti to the northwest, Kenya to the southwest, the Gulf of Aden with Yemen to the north, the Indian Ocean to the east, and Ethiopia to the west. With the longest coastline on the continent, its terrain consists mainly of plateaus, plains and highlands.

In antiquity, Somalia was an important center for commerce with the rest of the ancient world. Its sailors and merchants were the main suppliers of frankincense, myrrh and spices, items which were considered valuable luxuries by the Ancient Egyptians, Phoenicians, Mycenaeans and Babylonians with whom the Somali people traded. According to most scholars, Somalia is most likely where the ancient Kingdom of Punt was situated. The ancient Puntites were a nation of people that had close relations with Pharaonic Egypt during the times of Pharaoh Sahure and Queen Hatshepsut. The pyramidal structures, temples and ancient houses of dressed stone littered around the country are said to date from this period. During the Middle Ages, several powerful Somali empires dominated the regional trade, including the Ajuuraan State, the Sultanate of Adal, the Warsangali Sultanate and the Gobroon Dynasty.

Somalia was never formally colonized. Muhammad Abdullah Hassan's Dervish State successfully repulsed the British Empire four times and forced it to retreat to the coastal region. Due to these successful expeditions, the Dervish State was recognized as an ally by the Ottoman and German Empires. The Turks also named Hassan Emir of the Somali nation, and the Germans promised to officially recognize any territories the Dervishes were to acquire. After a quarter of a century of holding the British at bay, the Dervishes were finally defeated in 1920 as a direct consequence of Britain's new policy of aerial bombardment. As a result of this bombardment, former Dervish territories were turned into a protectorate of Britain. Italy faced similar opposition from Somali Sultans and armies, and did not acquire full control of parts of modern Somalia until the Fascist era in late 1927. This occupation lasted until 1941, and was replaced by a British military administration. Northern Somalia would remain a protectorate, while southern Somalia became a trusteeship. The Union of the two regions in 1960 formed the Somali Republic. A civilian government was formed, and on July 20, 1961, through a popular referendum, a new constitution that had first been drafted the year before was ratified.

Due to its longstanding ties with the Arab world, Somalia was accepted in 1974 as a member of the Arab League. During the same year, the nation's former socialist administration also chaired the Organization of African Unity, the predecessor of the African Union. In 1991, the Somali Civil War broke out, which saw the collapse of the federal government. Somalia's inhabitants subsequently reverted to local forms of conflict resolution, either secular, Islamic or customary law, with a provision for appeal of all sentences. As with other previously nationalized sectors, informal providers stepped in to fill the void and replaced the former government monopoly over healthcare, with access to facilities witnessing a significant increase and general living conditions improving. Through similar grass-roots initiatives, many educational institutions were restored and newer ones were developed; several are now ranked among the 100 best universities in Africa. Additionally, a Transitional Federal Government was created in 2004, which saw the restoration of numerous national institutions, including the Military of Somalia. While it still has room for improvement, the interim government continues to reach out to both Somali and international stakeholders to help grow the administrative capacity of the Transitional Federal Institutions and to work toward eventual national elections in 2011. According to the CIA and the recently re-established Central Bank of Somalia, despite experiencing civil unrest, Somalia has also maintained a healthy informal economy, based mainly on livestock, remittance/money transfer companies, and telecommunications. Libertarian economist Peter T. Leeson attributes this increased economic activity to the Somali traditional law (referred to as *Xeer*), which provides a stable environment to conduct business in.

History

Main articles: History of Somalia and Maritime history of Somalia

History of Somalia

Ancient
Laas Geel Culture
Kingdom of Punt
Malaoites · Oponeans
Mosyllonians
Medieval
Kingdom of Ifat
Adal Sultanate
Ajuuraan Empire
Gobroon Dynasty
Gerad Dynasty
Modern
Sultanate of Hobyo
Dervish State
Italian Somaliland

British Somaliland
Aden Adde Administration
Shermarke Administration
Communist rule
Recent History
Somali maritime history

Prehistory

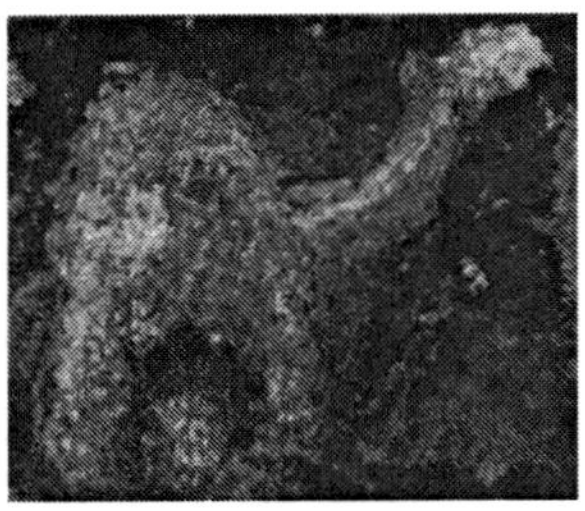

Ancient rock art depicting a camel.

Somalia has been inhabited by humans since the Paleolithic period. Cave paintings dating back as far as 9000 BC have been found in the northern part of the country. The most famous of these is the Laas Geel complex, which contains some of the earliest known rock art on the African continent. Inscriptions have been found beneath each of the rock paintings, but archaeologists have so far been unable to decipher this form of ancient writing. During the Stone age, the Doian culture and the Hargeisan culture flourished here with their respective industries and factories.

The oldest evidence of burial customs in the Horn of Africa comes from cemeteries in Somalia dating back to the 4th millennium BC. The stone implements from the *Jalelo* site in northern Somalia are said to be the most important link in evidence of the universality in Paleolithic times between the East and the West.

Antiquity and classical era

Main article: Architecture of Somalia

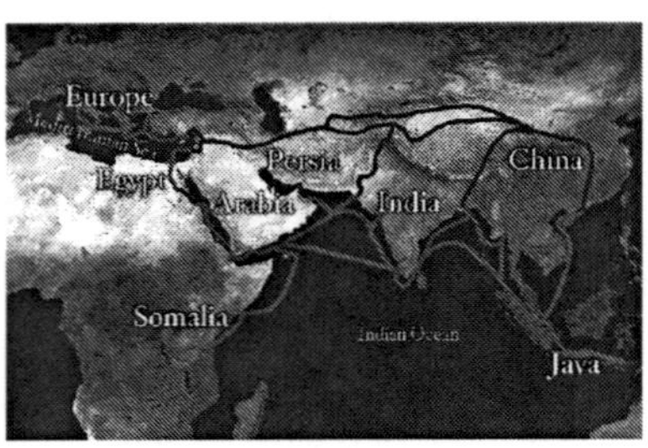

The Silk Road extending from southern Europe through Arabia, Somalia, Egypt, Persia, India and Java until it reaches China.

Ancient pyramidal structures, tombs, ruined cities and stone walls such as the Wargaade Wall littered in Somalia are evidence of an ancient sophisticated civilization that once thrived in the Somali peninsula. The findings of archaeological excavations and research in Somalia show that this civilization had an ancient writing system that remains undeciphered, and enjoyed a lucrative trading relationship with Ancient Egypt and Mycenaean Greece since at least the second millennium BC, which supports evidence of Somalia being the ancient Kingdom of Punt. The Puntites "traded not only in their own produce of incense, ebony and short-horned cattle, but also in goods from other neighboring regions, including gold, ivory and animal skins." According to the temple reliefs at Deir el-Bahari, the Land of Punt was ruled at that time by King Parahu and Queen Ati.

Ancient Somalis domesticated the camel somewhere between the third millennium and second millennium BC from where it spread to Ancient Egypt and North Africa. In the classical period, the city states of Mossylon, Opone, Malao, Mundus and Tabae in Somalia developed a lucrative trade network connecting with merchants from Phoenicia, Ptolemaic Egypt, Greece, Parthian Persia, Saba, Nabataea and the Roman Empire. They used the ancient Somali maritime vessel known as the *beden* to transport their cargo.

Ruins of Qa'ableh.

After the Roman conquest of the Nabataean Empire and the Roman naval presence at Aden to curb piracy, Arab and Somali merchants by agreement barred Indian ships from trading in the free port cities of the Arabian peninsula to protect the interests of Somali and Arab merchants in the extremely lucrative ancient Red Sea–Mediterranean Sea commerce. However, Indian merchants continued to trade in the port cities of the Somali peninsula, which was free from Roman interference.

The Indian merchants for centuries brought large quantities of cinnamon from Sri Lanka and Indonesia to Somalia and Arabia. This is said to have been the best kept secret of the Arab and Somali merchants in their trade with the Roman and Greek world. The Romans and Greeks believed the source of cinnamon to have been the Somali peninsula, but in reality, the highly valued product was brought to Somalia by way of Indian ships. Through collusive agreement by Somali and Arab traders, Indian/Chinese cinnamon was also exported for far higher prices to North Africa, the Near East and Europe, which made the cinnamon trade a very profitable revenue generator, especially for the Somali merchants through whose hands large quantities were shipped across ancient sea and land routes.

Birth of Islam & the Middle Ages

Main articles: Adal Sultanate, Ajuuraan State, and Warsangali Sultanate

The history of Islam in the Horn of Africa is as old as the religion itself. The early persecuted Muslims fled to the Axumite port city of Zeila in modern day Somalia to seek protection from the Quraysh at the court of the Axumite Emperor in present day Ethiopia. Some of the Muslims that were granted protection are said to have settled in several parts of the Horn of Africa to promote the religion.

Ruins of the Adal Sultanate in Zeila.

The victory of the Muslims over the Quraysh in the 7th century had a significant impact on Somalia's merchants and sailors, as their Arab trading partners had then all adopted Islam, and the major trading routes in the Mediterranean and the Red Sea came under the sway of the Muslim Caliphs. Through commerce, Islam spread amongst the Somali population in the coastal cities of Somalia. Instability in the Arabian peninsula saw several migrations of Arab families to Somalia's coastal cities, who then contributed another significant element to the growing popularity of Islam in the Somali peninsula.

13th century Fakr ad-Din mosque

Mogadishu became the center of Islam on the East African coast, and Somali merchants established a colony in Mozambique to extract gold from the Monomopatan mines in Sofala. In northern Somalia, Adal was in its early stages a small trading community established by the newly converted Horn African Muslim merchants, who were predominantly Somali according to Arab and Somali chronicles.

The century between 1150 and 1250 marked a decisive turn in the role of Islam in Somali history. Yaqut al-Hamawi and later Ibn Said noted that the Berbers (Somalis) were a prosperous Muslim nation during that period. The Adal Sultanate was now the center of a commercial empire stretching from Cape Guardafui to Hadiya. The Adalites then came under the influence of the expanding Horn African Ifat Sultanate, and prospered under its patronage.

The capital of Ifat was Zeila, situated in northern present-day Somalia, from where the Ifat army marched to conquer the ancient Kingdom of Shoa in 1270. This conquest ignited a rivalry for supremacy between the Christian Solomonids and the Muslim Ifatites that resulted in several devastating wars, and ultimately ended in a Solomonic victory over the Kingdom of Ifat after the death of the popular Sultan Sa'ad ad-Din II in Zeila by Dawit II. Sa'ad ad-Din II's family was subsequently given safe haven at the court of the King of Yemen, where his sons regrouped and planned their revenge on the Solomonids.

During the Age of the Ajuuraans, the sultanates and republics of Merca, Mogadishu, Barawa, Hobyo and their respective ports flourished and had a lucrative foreign commerce, with ships sailing to and coming from Arabia, India, Venetia, Persia, Egypt, Portugal and as far away as China. Vasco da Gama, who passed by Mogadishu in the 15th century, noted that it was a large city with houses several storeys high and large palaces in its centre, in addition to many mosques with cylindrical minarets.

Model of a medieval Mogadishan ship.

In the 16th century, Duarte Barbosa noted that many ships from the Kingdom of Cambaya in modern-day India sailed to Mogadishu with cloth and spices, for which they in return received gold, wax and ivory. Barbosa also highlighted the abundance of meat, wheat, barley, horses, and fruit on the coastal markets, which generated enormous wealth for the merchants. Mogadishu, the center of a thriving textile industry known as *toob benadir* (specialized for the markets in Egypt, among other places), together with Merca and Barawa, also served as a transit stop for Swahili merchants from Mombasa and Malindi and for the gold trade from Kilwa. Jewish merchants from the Hormuz brought their Indian textile and fruit to the Somali coast in exchange for grain and wood.

Trading relations were established with Malacca in the 15th century, with cloth, ambergris and porcelain being the main commodities of the trade. Giraffes, zebras and incense were exported to the Ming Empire of China, which established Somali merchants as leaders in the commerce between the Asia and Africa and influenced the Chinese language with the Somali language in the process. Hindu merchants from Surat and Southeast African merchants from Pate, seeking to bypass both the Portuguese blockade and Omani meddling, used the Somali ports of Merca and Barawa (which were out of the two powers' jurisdiction) to conduct their trade in safety and without interference.

Early modern era & the Scramble for Africa

Main articles: Dervish State, Gobroon Dynasty, and Sultanate of Hobyo

In the early modern period, successor states of the Adal and Ajuuraan empires began to flourish in Somalia. These were the Gerad Dynasty, the Bari Dynasties and the Gobroon Dynasty. They continued the tradition of castle-building and seaborne trade established by previous Somali empires.

17th century mosque in Hafun, Somalia.

Sultan Yusuf Mahamud Ibrahim, the third Sultan of the House of Gobroon, started the golden age of the Gobroon Dynasty. His army came out victorious during the Bardheere Jihad, which restored stability in the region and revitalized the East African ivory trade. He also received presents from and had cordial relations with the rulers of neighboring and distant kingdoms such as the Omani, Witu and Yemeni Sultans.

Sultan Ibrahim's son Ahmed Yusuf succeeded him and was one of the most important figures in 19th century East Africa, receiving tribute from Omani governors and creating alliances with important Muslim families on the East African coast. In northern Somalia, the Gerad Dynasty conducted trade with Yemen and Persia and competed with the merchants of the Bari Dynasty. The Gerads and the Bari Sultans built impressive palaces, castles and fortresses and had close relations with many different empires in the Near East.

Somali soldiers board a British naval batilla.

In the late 19th century, after the Berlin conference, European powers began the Scramble for Africa, which inspired the Dervish leader Muhammad Abdullah Hassan to rally support from across the Horn of Africa and begin one of the longest colonial resistance wars ever. In several of his poems and speeches, Hassan emphasized that the British "have destroyed our religion and made our children their children" and that the Christian Ethiopians in league with the British were bent upon plundering the political and religious freedom of the Somali nation. He soon emerged as "a champion of his country's political and religious freedom, defending it against all Christian invaders."

Hassan issued a religious ordinance stipulating that any Somali national who did not accept the goal of unity of Somalia and would not fight under his leadership would be considered as kafir or *gaal*. He soon acquired weapons from Turkey, Sudan, and other Islamic and/or Arabian countries, and appointed ministers and advisers to administer different areas or sectors of Somalia. In addition, he gave a clarion call for Somali unity and independence, in the process organizing his forces.

Hassan's Dervish movement had an essentially military character, and the Dervish state was fashioned on the model of a Salihiya brotherhood. It was characterized by a rigid hierarchy and centralization. Though Hassan threatened to drive the Christians into the sea, he executed the first attack by launching his first major military offensive with his 1500 Dervish equipped with 20 modern rifles on the British soldiers stationed in the region.

Taleex was the capital of the Dervish State.

He repulsed the British in four expeditions and had relations with the Central Powers of the Ottomans and the Germans. In 1920, the Dervish state collapsed after intensive aerial bombardments by Britain, and Dervish territories were subsequently turned into a protectorate.

The dawn of fascism in the early 1920s heralded a change of strategy for Italy, as the north-eastern sultanates were soon to be forced within the boundaries of *La Grande Somalia* according to the plan of Fascist Italy. With the arrival of Governor Cesare Maria De Vecchi on 15 December 1923, things began to change for that part of Somaliland known as Italian Somaliland. Italy had access to these areas under the successive protection treaties, but not direct rule.

The Fascist government had direct rule only over the Benadir territory. Fascist Italy, under Benito Mussolini, attacked Abyssinia (Ethiopia) in 1935, with an aim to colonize it. The invasion was condemned by the League of Nations, but little was done to stop it or to liberate occupied Ethiopia. On August 3, 1940, Italian troops, including Somali colonial units, crossed from Ethiopia to invade British Somaliland, and by August 14, succeeded in taking Berbera from the British.

A British force, including troops from several African countries, launched the campaign in January 1941 from Kenya to liberate British Somaliland and Italian-occupied Ethiopia and conquer Italian Somaliland. By February, most of Italian Somaliland was captured and in March, British Somaliland was retaken from the sea. The British Empire forces operating in Somaliland comprised three divisions of South African, West and East African troops. They were assisted by Somali forces led by Abdulahi Hassan with Somalis of the Isaaq, Dhulbahante, and Warsangali clans prominently participating. After World War II, the number of the Italian colonists started to decrease; their numbers had dwindled to less than 10,000 in 1960.

Post-World War II

Main article: Greater Somalia

Following World War II, Britain retained control of both British Somaliland and Italian Somaliland as protectorates. In November 1949, the United Nations granted Italy trusteeship of Italian Somaliland, but only under close supervision and on the condition — first proposed by the Somali Youth League (SYL) and other nascent Somali political organizations, such as Hizbia Digil Mirifle Somali (HDMS) (which later became Hizbia Dastur Mustaqbal Somali) and the Somali National League (SNL), that were then agitating for independence — that Somalia achieve independence within ten years. British Somaliland remained a protectorate of Britain until 1960.

Somali Youth League monument

To the extent that Italy held the territory by UN mandate, the trusteeship provisions gave the Somalis the opportunity to gain experience in political education and self-government. These were advantages that British Somaliland, which was to be incorporated into the new Somali state, did not have. Although in the 1950s British colonial officials attempted, through various development efforts, to make up for past neglect, the protectorate stagnated. The disparity between the two territories in economic development and political experience would cause serious difficulties when it came time to integrate the two parts.

Meanwhile, in 1948, under pressure from their World War II allies and to the dismay of the Somalis, the British "returned" the Haud (an important Somali grazing area that was presumably 'protected' by British treaties with the Somalis in 1884 and 1886) and the Ogaden to Ethiopia, based on a treaty they signed in 1897 in which the British ceded Somali territory to the Ethiopian Emperor Menelik in exchange for his help against plundering by Somali clans.

Britain included the proviso that the Somali nomads would retain their autonomy, but Ethiopia immediately claimed sovereignty over them. This prompted an unsuccessful bid by Britain in 1956 to buy back the Somali lands it had turned over. Britain also granted administration of the almost exclusively Somali-inhabited Northern Frontier District (NFD) to Kenyan nationalists despite an informal plebiscite demonstrating the overwhelming desire of the region's population to join the newly formed Somali Republic.

A referendum was held in neighboring Djibouti (then known as French Somaliland) in 1958, on the eve of Somalia's independence in 1960, to decide whether or not to join the Somali Republic or to remain with France. The referendum turned out in favour of a continued association with France, largely due to a combined yes vote by the sizable Afar ethnic group and resident Europeans. However, the majority of those who voted no were Somalis who were strongly in favour of joining a united Somalia as had been proposed by Mahmoud Harbi, Vice President of the Government Council. Harbi was killed in a plane crash two years later. Djibouti finally gained its independence from France in 1977 and Hassan Gouled Aptidon, a French-groomed Somali who campaigned for a yes vote in the referendum of 1958, eventually wound up as Djibouti's first president (1977–1991).

British Somaliland became independent on June 26, 1960, and the former Italian Somaliland followed suit five days later. On July 1, 1960, the two territories united to form the Somali Republic, albeit within boundaries drawn up by Italy and Britain. A government was formed by Abdullahi Issa, with Aden Abdullah Osman Daar as President and Abdirashid Ali Shermarke as Prime Minister, later to become President (from 1967–1969). On July 20, 1961 and through a popular referendum, the Somali people ratified a new constitution, which was first drafted in 1960. In 1967, Muhammad Haji Ibrahim Egal became Prime Minister, a position to which he was appointed by Shermarke. Egal would later become the President of the autonomous Somaliland region in northwestern Somalia.

In late 1969, following the assassination of President Shermarke, a military government assumed power in a coup d'état led by Major General Salaad Gabeyre Kediye, General Siad Barre and Chief of Police Jama Korshel. Barre became President and Korshel vice-president. The revolutionary army established large-scale public works programs and successfully implemented an urban and rural literacy campaign, which helped dramatically increase the literacy rate. In addition to a nationalization program of industry and land, the new regime's foreign policy placed an emphasis on Somalia's traditional and religious links with the Arab world, eventually joining the Arab League (AL) in 1974. That same year, Barre also served as chairman of the Organization of African Unity (OAU), the predecessor of the African Union (AU).

In July 1976 the Somali Revolutionary Socialist Party (Xisbiga Hantiwadaagga Kacaanka Soomaaliyeed, XHKS) was founded. This party ruled Somalia until the fall of the military government in December 1990 – January 1991. It was violently overthrown by the combined armed revolt of the Somali Salvation Democratic Front (Jabhadda Diimuqraadiga Badbaadinta Soomaaliyeed, SSDF), United Somali Congress (USC), Somali National Movement (SNM), and the Somali Patriotic Movement (SPM) together with the non-violent political oppositions of the Somali Democratic Movement (SDM), the Somali Democratic Alliance (SDA) and the Somali Manifesto Group (SMG). The country was renamed the Somali Democratic Republic.

In July 1977, the Ogaden War broke out after Barre's government sought to incorporate the predominantly Somali-inhabited Ogaden region into a Pan-Somali Greater Somalia. In the first week of the conflict, Somali armed forces took southern and central Ogaden and for most of the war, the Somali army scored continuous victories on the Ethiopian army and followed them as far as Sidamo. By September 1977, Somalia controlled 90% of the Ogaden and captured strategic cities such as Jijiga and put heavy pressure on Dire Dawa, threatening the train route from the latter city to Djibouti. After the siege of Harar, a massive unprecedented Soviet intervention consisting of 20,000 Cuban forces and several thousand Soviet experts came to the aid of Ethiopia's communist Derg regime. By 1978, the Somali troops were ultimately pushed out of the Ogaden. This shift in support by the Soviet Union motivated the Barre government to seek allies elsewhere. It eventually settled on Russia's Cold War arch-rival, the United States, which had been courting the Somali government for some time. All in all, Somalia's initial friendship with the Soviet Union and later partnership with the United States enabled it to build the largest army in Africa.

By 1978, the moral authority of Barre's government had collapsed. Many Somalis had become disillusioned with life under military dictatorship. The regime was weakened further in the 1980s as the Cold War drew to a close and Somalia's strategic importance was diminished. The government became increasingly totalitarian, and resistance movements, encouraged by Ethiopia, sprang up across the country, eventually leading to the Somali Civil War.

During 1990, in the capital city of Mogadishu, the residents were prohibited from gathering publicly in groups greater than three or four. Fuel shortages caused long lines of cars at petrol stations. Inflation had driven the price of pasta, (ordinary dry Italian noodles, a staple at that time), to five U.S. dollars per kilogram. The price of khat, imported daily from Kenya, was also five U.S. dollars per standard bunch. Paper currency notes were of such low value that several bundles were needed to pay for simple restaurant meals. Coins were scattered on the ground throughout the city being too low in value to be used.

A thriving black market existed in the centre of the city as banks experienced shortages of local currency for exchange. At night, the city of Mogadishu lay in darkness. The generators used to provide electricity to the city had been sold off by the government. Close monitoring of all visiting foreigners was in effect. Harsh exchange control regulations were introduced to prevent export of foreign currency and access to it was restricted to official banks, or one of three government-operated hotels.

Although no travel restrictions were placed on foreigners, photographing many locations was banned. During the day in Mogadishu, the appearance of any government military force was extremely rare. Alleged late-night operations by government authorities, however, included "disappearances" of individuals from their homes.

Somali Civil War

Main article: Somali Civil War

1991 was a time of great change for Somalia. President Barre was ousted by combined northern and southern clan-based forces, all of whom were backed and armed by Ethiopia. And following a meeting of the Somali National Movement and northern clans' elders, the northern former British portion of the country declared its independence as Somaliland in May 1991; although de facto independent and relatively stable compared to the tumultuous south, it has not been recognized by any foreign government.

In January 1991, President Ali Mahdi Muhammad was selected by the manifesto group as an interim state president until a conference between all stakeholders to be held in Djibouti the following month to select a national leader. However, United Somali Congress military leader General Mohamed Farrah Aidid, the Somali National Movement leader Abdirahman Ahmed Ali Tuur and the Somali Patriotic Movement leader Col Jess refused to recognize Mahdi as president.

This caused a split between the SNM, USC and SPM and the armed groups Manifesto, Somali Democratic Movement (SDM) and Somali National Alliance (SNA) on the one hand and within the USC forces. This led efforts to remove Barre who still claimed to be the legitimate president of Somalia. He and his armed supporters remained in the south of the country until mid 1992, causing further escalation in violence, especially in the Gedo, Bay, Bakool, Lower Shabelle, Lower Juba, and Middle Juba regions. The armed conflict within the USC devastated the Mogadishu area.

Prior to the civil war, Mogadishu was known as the *"White pearl of the Indian Ocean"*.

The civil war disrupted agriculture and food distribution in southern Somalia. The basis of most of the conflicts was clan allegiances and competition for resources between the warring clans. James Bishop, the United States last ambassador to Somalia, explained that there is "competition for water, pasturage, and... cattle. It is a competition that used to be fought out with arrows and sabers... Now it is fought out with AK-47s." The resulting famine (about 300,000 dead) caused the United Nations Security Council in 1992 to authorise the limited peacekeeping operation United Nations Operation in Somalia I (UNOSOM I). UNOSOM's use of force was limited to self-defense and it was soon disregarded by the warring factions.

In reaction to the continued violence and the humanitarian disaster, the United States organized a military coalition with the purpose of creating a secure environment in southern Somalia for the conduct of humanitarian operations. This coalition, (Unified Task Force or UNITAF) entered Somalia in December 1992 on Operation Restore Hope and was successful in restoring order and alleviating the famine. In May 1993, most of the United States troops withdrew and UNITAF was replaced by the United Nations Operation in Somalia II (UNOSOM II).

However, Mohamed Farrah Aidid saw UNOSOM II as a threat to his power and in June 1993 his militia attacked Pakistan Army troops, attached to UNOSOM II, (see Somalia (March 1992 to February 1996)) in Mogadishu inflicting over 80 casualties. Fighting escalated until 19 American troops and more than 1,000 civilians and militia were killed in a raid in Mogadishu during October 1993. The UN withdrew Operation United Shield in 3 March 1995, having suffered significant casualties, and with the rule of government still not restored. In August 1996, Aidid was killed in Mogadishu.

Following the outbreak of the civil war, many of Somalia's residents left the country in search of asylum. At the end of 2009, about 678,000 were under the responsibility of the UNHCR, constituting the third largest refugee group after war-afflicted Iraq and Afghanistan, respectively. Due to renewed fighting in the southern half of the country, an estimated 132,000 people left in 2009, and another 300,000 were displaced internally.

From 1800 to 1890, between 25,000–50,000 Bantu slaves from Mozambique and Tanzania are thought to have been sold from the slave market of Zanzibar to the Somali coast. Bantus are ethnically, physically, and culturally distinct from Somalis, and have remained marginalized ever since their arrival in Somalia. The number of Bantu in Somalia before the civil war is thought to be about 900,000. Since 2003, more than 12,000 Bantu refugees have been resettled in the United States. The Tanzanian government has also begun granting Bantus citizenship and land in areas of Tanzania where their ancestors are known to have been removed from.

A consequence of the collapse of governmental authority that accompanied the civil war has been the emergence of a significant problem with piracy in the waters off of the coast of Somalia. Piracy arose as a response by local fishermen from littoral towns such as Eyl, Kismayo and Harardhere to illegal fishing by foreign trawlers. An upsurge in piracy in the Gulf of Aden and the Indian Ocean has also been attributed to the effects of the December 26, 2004 tsunami that devastated local fishing fleets and washed ashore containers filled with toxic waste that had been dumped by European fishing vessels. In August 2008, a multinational coalition took on the task of combating the piracy by establishing a Maritime Security Patrol Area (MSPA) within the Gulf of Aden. Additionally, the regional Puntland government in northeastern Somalia committed itself to eradicating piracy and has so far made progress in its campaign, having apprehended numerous pirates in 2010, including a prominent leader. The autonomous region's security forces also reportedly managed to force out the pirate gangs from their traditional safe havens such as Eyl and Gar'ad, with the pirates now operating from only one main town, Harardhere. By the first half of 2010, these increased policing efforts by Puntland government authorities on land along with international naval vessels at sea reportedly contributed to a drop in pirate attacks in the Gulf of Aden from 86 a year prior to 33, forcing pirates to shift attention to other areas such as the Somali Basin and the wider Indian Ocean.

Politics

Main article: Politics of Somalia

Overview

See also: Battle of Mogadishu (2006), Rise of the Islamic Courts Union (2006), War in Somalia (2006–2009), War in Somalia (2009–), and 2009 timeline of the War in Somalia

The Transitional Federal Government (TFG) is the current internationally recognized federal government of Somalia. It was established as one of the Transitional Federal Institutions (TFIs) of government as defined in the Transitional Federal Charter (TFC) adopted in November 2004 by the Transitional Federal Parliament (TFP). The Charter outlines a five-year mandate leading toward the establishment of a new constitution and a transition to a representative government after national elections. The TFG is the most recent attempt to restore national institutions to Somalia after the 1991 collapse of the Siad Barre regime and the ensuing Somali Civil War.

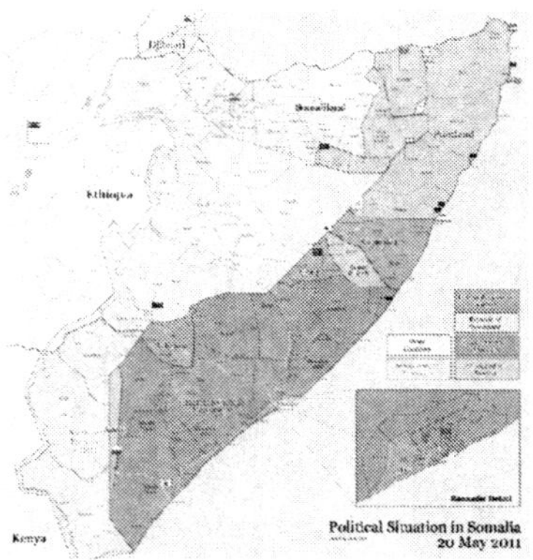

Current political situation in Somalia.

In 2006, the Islamic Courts Union (ICU), an Islamist organization, assumed control of much of the southern part of the country and promptly imposed Shari'a law. The Transitional Federal Government sought to reestablish its authority, and, with the assistance of Ethiopian troops, African Union peacekeepers and air support by the United States, managed to drive out the rival ICU and solidify its rule.

Following this defeat, the Islamic Courts Union splintered into several different factions. Some of the more radical elements, including Al-Shabaab, regrouped to continue their insurgency against the TFG and oppose the Ethiopian military's presence in Somalia. Throughout 2007 and 2008, Al-Shabaab scored military victories, seizing control of key towns and ports in both central and southern Somalia. At the end of 2008, the group had captured Baidoa but not Mogadishu. By January 2009, Al-Shabaab and other militias had managed to force the Ethiopian troops to withdraw from the country, leaving behind an under-equipped African Union peacekeeping force to assist the Transitional Federal Government's troops.

Abdullahi Yusuf Ahmed, one of the founders of the Transitional Federal Government.

On December 29, 2008, Abdullahi Yusuf Ahmed announced before a united parliament in Baidoa his resignation as President of Somalia. In his speech, which was broadcast on national radio, Yusuf expressed regret at failing to end the country's seventeen year conflict as his government had mandated to do. He also blamed the international community for its failure to support the government, and said that the speaker of parliament would succeed him in office per the charter of the Transitional Federal Government.

Over the next few months, a new President was elected from amongst the more moderate Islamists, and Omar Abdirashid Ali Sharmarke, the son of slain former President Abdirashid Ali Sharmarke, was selected as the nation's new Prime Minister. The Transitional Federal Government, with the help of a small team of African Union troops, also began a counteroffensive in February 2009 to retake control of the southern half of the country. To solidify its control of southern Somalia, the TFG formed an alliance with the Islamic Courts Union, other members of the Alliance for the Re-liberation of Somalia, and Ahlu Sunna Waljama'a, a moderate Sufi militia. Furthermore, Al-Shabaab and Hizbul Islam, the two main Islamist groups in opposition, began to fight amongst themselves in mid-2009.

As a truce, in March 2009, Somalia's newly established coalition government announced that it would re-implement Shari'a as the nation's official judicial system. However, conflict continues in the southern and central parts of the country between government troops and extremist Islamist militants with links to al-Qaeda.

In 2009, Transparency International ranked Somalia in last place on its annual Corruption Perceptions Index (CPI), a metric that purports to show the prevalence of corruption in a country's public sector. In the decade since its launch, the CPI has drawn increasing criticism, specifically with regard to the methodologies it uses to obtain its averages; the varying definitions of corruption that are employed; the reliance on the views of a small number of people to obtain data; the inclusion of up to three years of data, which serve to obscure more recent reductions in corruption; the inability of the index to take into account recent anti-corruption reforms, the latter of which can take a while to take effect; and the reliability of the actual sources on which the CPI's rankings are based. These various shortcomings have significantly limited the usefulness and accuracy of the index, and lead to calls for it to be abandoned.

Embassy of Somalia in Paris, France.

In 2010, the UN International Monitoring Group (IMG) published a report accusing the Somali government's security forces of being ineffective and corrupt, and claimed that up to half of the food aid that was destined for the conflict-stricken parts of the country were being misdirected. It also accused Somali officials of collaborating with pirates, UN contractors of helping insurgents, and the Eritrean government of still supporting rebel groups in southern Somalia despite earlier sanctions imposed on the former. Somalia's government and local businessmen, as well as United Nations officials and the Eritrean government all emphatically rejected the report's claims. Additionally, the government of the autonomous Puntland region in northeastern Somalia indicated that the writers of the report drafted it without ever having actually traveled to the region, a fact which was also confirmed by the paper's authors. Puntland's president also stated that the report was "politically motivated" and an attempt "to discredit Puntland as a way of achieving another hidden goal" -- an apparent reference to the report's principal author who has familial ties with the dominant clan in Somaliland, a secessionist region in northwestern Somalia for which the author is known to have actively sought diplomatic recognition. This was echoed in an official press release by the region's Ministry of Information, Communication, Culture and Heritage, which indicated that the charges were "made by certain elements in the IMG" with a history of making such claims "in other organizations in the past but [who] now have infiltrated this UN mission (International Monitoring Group)." The Ministry also enumerated a number of reforms that Puntland's administration has recently enacted as a part of its officially declared anti-piracy campaign, including the arrest, trial and conviction of pirate gangs, as well as raids on suspected pirate hideouts and confiscation of weapons and equipment; ensuring the adequate coverage of the regional authority's anti-piracy efforts by both local and international media; sponsoring a social campaign led by Islamic scholars and community activists aimed at discrediting piracy and highlighting its negative effects; and partnering with the NATO alliance to combat pirates at sea.

Reforms

Somalia's new coalition government has enacted numerous political reforms since taking office in 2009, with an emphasis on transparency and accountability. One of its first changes involved ensuring that all government institutions, which had previously been spread out in various areas throughout the country, were now based in Mogadishu, the nation's capital. The Central Bank of Somalia was also re-established, and a national plan as well as an effective anti-corruption commission were put into place. In July 2009, Somalia's Transitional Federal Government hired Pricewaterhousecoopers (PwC), one of the world's largest professional services companies and the largest of the Big Four auditing firms, to monitor development funding, with PwC now serving as a trustee of an account in Mogadishu earmarked for the security, healthcare and education sectors. This was followed in November of that year with a $2 million agreement between the government and the African Development Bank (AfDB), which saw Somalia re-engage with the AfDB after nearly two decades of interruption. The grant is aimed at providing financial and technical assistance; specifically, to develop a sound legal framework for monetary and fiscal institutions and human and institutional capacity building, as well as to establish public financial systems that are transparent. While its institutions still have room for improvement, the Transitional Federal Government continues to reach out to both Somali and international stakeholders to help grow the administrative capacity of the Transitional Federal Institutions and to work toward eventual national elections in 2011, when the interim government's mandate expires.

Similarly, the autonomous Puntland region's new administration, which took office in early 2009, has also implemented numerous reforms such as the expansion and improvement of its security and judicial sectors. According to Garowe Online, to bolster the region's justice system, numerous new prosecutors, judges and other court personnel as well as additional prison guards were hired and trained. In July 2010, the Puntland Council of Ministers unanimously approved a new anti-terrorism law to more efficiently handle terror suspects and their accomplices; a special court is also expected to be established within the region's existing criminal courts system to facilitate the task. Fiscally, a transparent, budget-based public finance system was established, which has reportedly helped increase public confidence in government. In addition, a new regional constitution was drafted and later passed on June 15, 2009, which is believed to represent a significant step toward the eventual introduction of a multi-party political system to the region for the first time; such a system already exists in the adjacent Somaliland region. More modest reforms were also put into motion in the social sector, particularly in the education and healthcare fields. The regional government has hired more healthcare workers and teachers, with major plans underway for school and hospital renovations. One of the most significant new reforms enacted by the incumbent Puntland administration is the launching in May 2009 of the Puntland Agency for Social Welfare (PASWE), the first organization of its kind in Somali history. The agency provides medical, educational and counseling support to vulnerable groups and individuals such as orphans, the disabled and the blind. PASWE is overseen by a Board of Directors, which consists of religious scholars (*ulema*), businesspeople, intellectuals and traditional elders.

Law

Main articles: Transitional Federal Government, Islamic Courts Union, and Xeer

Following the outbreak of the civil war and the ensuing collapse of the central government, Somalia's residents reverted to local forms of conflict resolution, either secular, traditional or Islamic law, with a provision for appeal of all sentences. The legal structure in Somalia is thus divided along three lines: civil law, religious law and customary law.

Civil law

While Somalia's formal judicial system was largely destroyed after the fall of the Siad Barre regime, it has been rebuilt and is now administered under different regional governments such as the autonomous Puntland and Somaliland macro-regions. In the case of the Transitional Federal Government, a new interim judicial structure was formed through various international conferences.

Despite some significant political differences between them, all of these administrations share similar legal structures, much of which are predicated on the judicial systems of previous Somali administrations. These similarities in civil law include: a) a charter which affirms the primacy of Muslim shari'a or religious law, although in practice shari'a is applied mainly to matters such as marriage, divorce, inheritance, and civil issues. The charter guarantees respect for universal standards of human rights to all subjects of the law. It also assures the independence of the judiciary, which in turn is protected by a judicial committee; b) a three-tier judicial system including a supreme court, a court of appeals, and courts of first instance (either divided between district and regional courts, or a single court per region); and c) the laws of the civilian government which were in effect prior to the military coup d'état that saw the Barre regime into power remain in force until the laws are amended.

Shari'a

Islamic shari'a has traditionally played a significant part in Somali society. In theory, it has served as the basis for all national legislation in every Somali constitution. In practice, however, it only applied to common civil cases such as marriage, divorce, inheritance and family matters. This changed after the start of the civil war, when a number of new shari'a courts began to spring up in many different cities and towns across the country. These new shari'a courts serve three functions; namely, to pass rulings in both criminal and civil cases, to organize a militia capable of arresting criminals, and to keep convicted prisoners incarcerated.

The shari'a courts, though structured along simple lines, feature a conventional hierarchy of a chairman, vice-chairman and four judges. A police force that reports to the court enforces the judges' rulings, but also helps settle community disputes and apprehend suspected criminals. In addition, the courts manage detention centers where criminals are kept. An independent finance committee is also assigned the task of collecting and managing tax revenue levied on regional merchants by the local authorities.

In March 2009, Somalia's newly established coalition government announced that it would implement shari'a as the nation's official judicial system.

Xeer

Somalis have for centuries practiced a form of customary law, which they call *Xeer*. Xeer is a polycentric legal system where there is no monopolistic institution or agent that determines what the law should be or how it should be interpreted.

The Xeer legal system is assumed to have developed exclusively in the Horn of Africa since approximately the 7th century. There is no evidence that it developed elsewhere or was greatly influenced by any foreign legal system. The fact that Somali legal terminology is practically devoid of loan words from foreign languages suggests that Xeer is truly indigenous.

The Xeer legal system also requires a certain amount of specialization of different functions within the legal framework. Thus, one can find *odayal* (judges), *xeer boggeyaal* (jurists), *guurtiyaal* (detectives), *garxajiyaal* (attorneys), *murkhaatiyal* (witnesses) and *waranle* (police officers) to enforce the law.

Xeer is defined by a few fundamental tenets that are immutable and which closely approximate the principle of *jus cogens* in international law: These precepts include a) payment of blood money (locally referred to as *diya*) for libel, theft, physical harm, rape and death, as well as supplying assistance to relatives; b) assuring good inter-clan relations by treating women justly, negotiating with "peace emissaries" in good faith, and sparing the lives of socially protected groups (e.g. children, women, the pious, poets and guests); c) family obligations such as the payment of dowry, and sanctions for eloping; d) rules pertaining to the management of resources such as the use of pasture land, water, and other natural resources; e) providing financial support to married female relatives and newlyweds; and f) donating livestock and other assets to the poor.

Cities

<table>
<tr><th rowspan="18">Cities of the Republic of Somalia

Mogadishu

Bosaso

Kismayo

Borama</th><th>Rank</th><th>Core City</th><th>Division</th><th>Pop.</th><td rowspan="18">
Hargeisa

Merka

Barawa
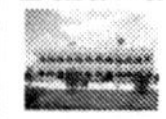
Garowe</td><td></td></tr>
<tr><td>1</td><td>Mogadishu</td><td>Banadir</td><td>Ca. 2,000,000</td><td></td></tr>
<tr><td>2</td><td>Hargeisa</td><td>W.Galbeed</td><td>Ca. 2,000,000</td><td></td></tr>
<tr><td>3</td><td>Bosaso</td><td>Bari</td><td>Ca. 950,000</td><td></td></tr>
<tr><td>4</td><td>Gaalkacyo</td><td>Mudug</td><td>Ca. 545,000</td><td></td></tr>
<tr><td>5</td><td>Berbera</td><td>W.Galbeed</td><td>Ca. 232,500</td><td></td></tr>
<tr><td>6</td><td>Merca</td><td>Shabeellaha Hoose</td><td>Ca. 230,100</td><td></td></tr>
<tr><td>7</td><td>Jamaame</td><td>Jubbada Hoose</td><td>Ca. 224,700</td><td></td></tr>
<tr><td>8</td><td>Kismayo</td><td>Jubbada Hoose</td><td>Ca. 183,300</td><td></td></tr>
<tr><td>9</td><td>Baidoa</td><td>Bay</td><td>Ca. 157,500</td><td></td></tr>
<tr><td>10</td><td>Burao</td><td>Togdheer</td><td>Ca. 120,400</td><td></td></tr>
<tr><td>11</td><td>Afgooye</td><td>Shabeellaha Hoose</td><td>Ca. 79,400</td><td></td></tr>
<tr><td>12</td><td>Beledweyne</td><td>Hiiraan</td><td>Ca. 67,200</td><td></td></tr>
<tr><td>13</td><td>Qoryoley</td><td>Shabeellaha Hoose</td><td>Ca. 62,700</td><td></td></tr>
<tr><td>14</td><td>Garowe</td><td>Nugaal</td><td>Ca. 57,300</td><td></td></tr>
<tr><td>15</td><td>Jowhar</td><td>Shabeellaha Dhexe</td><td>Ca. 57,100</td><td></td></tr>
<tr><td>16</td><td>Bardera</td><td>Gedo</td><td>Ca. 51,300</td><td></td></tr>
<tr><td>17</td><td>Qardho</td><td>Bari</td><td>Ca. 47,400</td><td></td></tr>
</table>

Regions and districts

Main article: Regions and Districts of Somalia

Prior to the civil war, Somalia was divided into eighteen regions (*gobollada*, singular *gobol*), which were in turn subdivided into districts. The regions are:

1 Awdal
2 Bakool
3 Banaadir
4 Bari
5 Bay
6 Galguduud
7 Gedo
8 Hiiraan
9 Jubbada Dhexe
10 Jubbada Hoose
11 Mudug
12 Nugaal
13 Sanaag
14 Shabeellaha Dhexe
15 Shabeellaha Hoose
16 Sool
17 Togdheer
18 Woqooyi Galbeed

On a *de facto* basis, northern Somalia is now divided up among the quasi-independent states of Puntland, Somaliland, and Galmudug. The south is at least nominally controlled by the Transitional Federal Government, although it is in fact controlled by Islamist groups outside Mogadishu. Under the *de facto* arrangements there are now 27 regions.

Geography

Main article: Geography of Somalia

Location and habitat

Somalia is bordered by Djibouti to the northwest, Kenya to the southwest, the Gulf of Aden with Yemen to the north, the Indian Ocean to the east, and Ethiopia to the west. Strategically located at the mouth of the Bab el Mandeb gateway to the Red Sea and the Suez Canal, the country occupies the tip of a region that, due to its resemblance on the map to a rhinoceros' horn, is commonly referred to as the Horn of Africa.

The Cal Madow mountain range in northern Somalia features the nation's highest peak, Shimbiris.

Somalia has the longest coastline on the continent, with a seaboard that stretches 3,025 kilometers. Its terrain consists mainly of plateaus, plains and highlands. The nation has a total area of 637,657 square kilometres (**unknown operator: u',' ** m^2), 627,337 square kilometres (**unknown operator: u',' ** m^2) of which constitutes land, with 10,320 square kilometres (**unknown operator: u',' ** m^2) of water. Somalia's land boundaries extend to about 2,340 kilometres (**unknown operator: u',' ** m); 58 kilometres (58000 m) of that is shared with Djibouti, 682 kilometres (682000 m) with Kenya, and 1,600 kilometres (**unknown operator: u',' ** m) with Ethiopia. Its maritime claims include territorial waters of 200 nautical miles (370 km; 230 mi).

In the north, a scrub-covered, semi-desert plain referred as the *Guban* lies parallel to the Gulf of Aden littoral. With a width of twelve kilometers in the west to as little as two kilometers in the east, the plain is bisected by watercourses that are essentially beds of dry sand except during the rainy seasons. When the rains arrive, the Guban's low bushes and grass clumps transform into lush vegetation. This coastal strip is part of the Ethiopian xeric grasslands and shrublands ecoregion.

The Jubba river.

Cal Madow is a mountain range in the northeastern part of the country. Extending from several kilometers west of the city of Bosaso to the northwest of Erigavo, it features Somalia's highest peak, Shimbiris, which sits at an elevation of about 2416 metres (7927 ft). The rugged east-west ranges of the Karkaar Mountains also lie to the interior of the Gulf of Aden littoral.

In the central regions, the country's northern mountain ranges give way to shallow plateaus and typically dry watercourses that are referred to locally as the *Ogo*. The Ogo's western plateau, in turn, gradually merges into the Haud, an important grazing area for livestock.

Somalia has only two permanent rivers, the Jubba and the Shabele, both of which begin in the Ethiopian highlands. These rivers mainly flow southwards, with the Jubba River entering the Indian Ocean at Kismayo. The Shabele River at one time apparently used to enter the sea near Merca, but now reaches a point just southwest of Mogadishu. After that, it consists of swamps and dry reaches before finally disappearing in the desert terrain east of Jilib, near the Jubba River.

Climate

Due to Somalia's proximity to the equator, there is not much seasonal variation in its climate. Hot conditions prevail year-round along with periodic monsoon winds and irregular rainfall. Mean daily maximum temperatures range from 30 to 40 °C (86 to 104 °F), except at higher elevations and along the eastern seaboard, where the effects of a cold offshore current can be felt. In Mogadishu, for instance, average afternoon highs range from 28 °C (82 °F) to 32 °C (90 °F) in April. Some of the highest mean annual temperatures in the world have been recorded in the country; Berbera on the northwestern coast has an afternoon high that averages more than 38 °C (100 °F) from June through September. Nationally, mean daily minimums usually vary from about 15 to 30 °C (59 to 86 °F). The greatest range in climate occurs in northern Somalia, where temperatures sometimes surpass 45 °C (113 °F) in July on the littoral plains and drop below the freezing point during December in the highlands. In this region, relative humidity ranges from about 40 percent in the mid-afternoon to 85 percent at night, changing somewhat according to the season.

Arabian horses, referred to as *faras*, seen here in the arid plains of Dhahar.

Unlike the climates of most other countries at this latitude, conditions in Somalia range from arid in the northeastern and central regions to semiarid in the northwest and south. In the northeast, annual rainfall is less than 4 inches (100 mm); in the central plateaus, it is about 8 to 12 inches (200 to 300 mm). The northwestern and southwestern parts of the nation, however, receive considerably more rain, with an average of 20 to 24 inches (510 to 610 mm) falling per year. Although the coastal regions are hot and humid throughout the year, the hinterland is typically dry and hot.

There are four main seasons around which pastoral and agricultural life revolve, and these are dictated by shifts in the wind patterns. From December to March is the *Jilal*, the harshest dry season of the year. The main rainy season, referred to as the *Gu*, lasts from April to June. This period is characterized by the southwest monsoons, which rejuvenate the pasture land, especially the central plateau, and briefly transform the desert into lush vegetation. From July to September is the second dry season, the *Xagaa* (pronounced "Hagaa"). The *Dayr*, which is the shortest rainy season, lasts from October to December.

The *tangambili* periods that intervene between the two monsoons (October–November and March–May) are hot and humid.

Climate data for Somalia

Month	Jan	Feb	Mar	Apr	May	Jun	Jul	Aug	Sep	Oct	Nov	Dec	Year
Average high °C (°F)	30 (86)	30 (86)	40 (104)	40 (104)	40 (104)	40 (104)	40 (104)	30 (86)	30 (86)	30 (86)	30 (86)	30 (86)	30 (86)
Average low °C (°F)	15 (59)	15 (59)	15 (59)	15 (59)	15 (59)	15 (59)	15 (59)	15 (59)	15 (59)	15 (59)	15 (59)	15 (59)	15 (59)
Precipitation mm (inches)	40 (1.57)	40 (1.57)	40 (1.57)	40 (1.57)	40 (1.57)	40 (1.57)	50 (1.97)	50 (1.97)	40 (1.57)	40 (1.57)	40 (1.57)	40 (1.57)	500 (19.69)

Source: Country Studies - Somalia

Health

Until the collapse of the federal government in 1991, the organizational and administrative structure of Somalia's healthcare sector was overseen by the Ministry of Health. Regional medical officials enjoyed some authority, but healthcare was largely centralized. The socialist government of former President of Somalia Siad Barre had put an end to private medical practice in 1972. Much of the national budget was devoted to military expenditure, leaving few resources for healthcare, among other services.

Edna Adan Maternity Hospital in Hargeisa, one of Somalia's many new private healthcare facilities.

Although Somalia's public healthcare system was largely destroyed during the ensuing civil war, general living conditions have significantly improved in the intervening years, both in absolute terms and relative to other countries in Africa. As with other previously nationalized sectors, informal providers have filled the vacuum and replaced the former government monopoly over healthcare, with access to facilities witnessing a significant increase. Many new healthcare centers, clinics, hospitals and pharmacies have in the process been established through home-grown Somali initiatives. While the state of medicine remains quite basic, medical consultations in these facilities are very affordable ($0.50/visit).

Comparing the 2000–2005 period with the half-decade just prior to the outbreak of the conflict (1985–1990), life expectancy actually increased from 46 to 48.5 years; by 2010, it had risen to 50 years on average. The number of one-year-olds fully immunized against measles rose 10% from 30% to 40%, and for tuberculosis, it grew nearly 20% from 31% to 50%. In keeping with the trend, the number of infants with low birth weight fell from 16 per 1000 to 0.3 (almost none), a 15% drop in total. Infant mortality per 1,000 births also fell from 152 to 114.9, a 24% improvement; by 2010, it had plummeted to 107.42 deaths/1,000 live births. Significantly, maternal mortality per 100,000 births fell from 1,600 to 1,100, a drop of over 30%. The number of physicians per 100,000 people also rose from 3.4 to 4. Additionally, the percentage of the population with access to sanitation services increased 8% from 18% to 26%, and the percentage of the population with access to at least one health facility almost doubled from 28% to 54.8%.

According to a 2005 World Health Organization estimate, about 97.9% of Somalia's women and girls have undergone female circumcision, a pre-marital custom mainly endemic to Northeast Africa and parts of the Near East that has its ultimate origins in Ancient Egypt. Encouraged by women in the community, it is primarily intended to deter promiscuity and to offer protection from assault. About 93% of Somalia's male population is also reportedly circumcised.

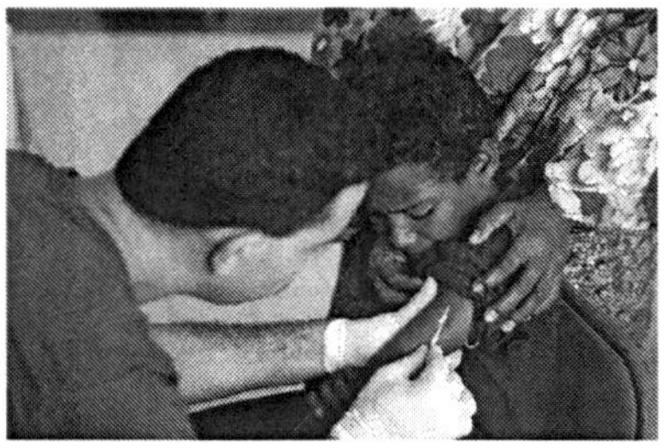

A Somali boy receiving a polio vaccination.

Somalia has one of the lowest HIV infection rates on the continent. This is attributed to the Muslim nature of Somali society and adherence of Somalis to Islamic morals. While the estimated HIV prevalence rate in Somalia in 1987 (the first case report year) was 1% of adults, a more recent estimate from 2007 now places it at only 0.5% of the nation's adult population despite the ongoing civil strife.

Although healthcare is now largely concentrated in the private sector, the country's public healthcare system is in the process of being rebuilt, and is overseen by the Ministry of Health. The current Minister of Health is Qamar Adan Ali. The autonomous Puntland region maintains its own Ministry of Health, which is headed by Dr. Mohamed Bashir Ali Bihi, as does the Somaliland region in northwestern Somalia, with its Ministry of Health led by Osman Bile Ali.

Some of the prominent healthcare facilities in the country are East Bardera Mothers and Children's Hospital, Abudwak Maternity and Children's Hospital, Edna Adan Maternity Hospital and West Bardera Maternity Unit.

Education

Main article: Education in Somalia

New Mogadishu University campus

Following the outbreak of the civil war in 1991, the task of running schools in Somalia was initially taken up by community education committees established in 94% of the local schools. Numerous problems had arisen with regard to access to education in rural areas and along gender lines, quality of educational provisions, responsiveness of school curricula, educational standards and controls, management and planning capacity, and financing. To address these concerns, educational policies are being developed which are aimed at guiding the scholastic process as the nation embarks on the path of reconstruction and economic development. In the autonomous Puntland region, the latter includes a gender sensitive national education policy compliant with world standards, such as those outlined in the Convention on the Rights of the Child (CRC) and the Convention on the Elimination of All Forms of Discrimination against Women (CEDAW). Examples of this and other educational measures at work are the regional government's enactment of legislation aimed at securing the educational interests of girls, promoting the growth of an Early Childhood Development (ECD) program designed to reach parents and care-givers in their homes as well as in the ECD centers for 0-5 year old children, and introducing incentive packages to encourage teachers to work in remote rural areas.

The Ministry of Education is officially responsible for education in Somalia, and oversees the nation's primary, secondary, technical and vocational schools, as well as primary and technical teacher training and non-formal education. About 15% of the government's budget is allocated toward scholastic instruction. The autonomous Puntland and Somaliland macro-regions maintain their own Ministries of Education.

The Hammar Jab Jab School in Mogadishu.

In 2006, Puntland was the second territory in Somalia after Somaliland to introduce free primary schools, with teachers now receiving their salaries from the Puntland administration. From 2005/2006 to 2006/2007, there was a significant increase in the number of schools in Puntland, up 137 institutions from just one year prior. During the same period, the number of classes in the region increased by 504, with 762 more teachers also offering their services. Total student enrollment increased by 27% over the previous year, with girls lagging only slightly behind boys in attendance in most regions. The highest class enrollment was observed in the northernmost Bari region, and the lowest was observed in the under-populated Ayn region. The distribution of classrooms was almost evenly split between urban and rural areas, with marginally more pupils attending and instructors teaching classes in urban areas.

Entrance to Amoud University in Borama.

Higher education in Somalia is now largely private. Several universities in the country, including Mogadishu University, have been scored among the 100 best universities in Africa in spite of the harsh environment, which has been hailed as a triumph for grass-roots initiatives. Other universities also offering higher education in the south include Benadir University, the Somalia National University, Kismayo University and the University of Gedo. In Puntland, higher education is provided by the Puntland State University and East Africa University. In Somaliland, it is provided by Amoud University, the University of Hargeisa, Somaliland University of Technology and Burao University.

Qu'ranic schools (also known as *duqsi*) remain the basic system of traditional religious instruction in Somalia. They provide Islamic education for children, thereby filling a clear religious and social role in the country. Known as the most stable local, non-formal system of education providing basic religious and moral instruction, their strength rests on community support and their use of locally made and widely available teaching materials. The Qu'ranic system, which teaches the greatest number of students relative to other educational sub-sectors, is often the only system accessible to Somalis in nomadic as compared to urban areas. A study from 1993 found, among other things, that about 40% of pupils in Qur'anic schools were girls. To address shortcomings in religious instruction, the Somali government on its own part also subsequently established the Ministry of Endowment and Islamic Affairs, under which Qur'anic education is now regulated.

Economy

Main article: Economy of Somalia

Air Somalia Tupolev Tu-154 in Sharjah, United Arab Emirates. Somalia today has a thriving private airline industry.

According to the CIA and the Central Bank of Somalia, despite experiencing civil unrest, Somalia has maintained a healthy informal economy, based mainly on livestock, remittance/money transfer companies and telecommunications. Due to a dearth of formal government statistics and the recent civil war, it is difficult to gauge the size or growth of the economy. For 1994, the CIA estimated the GDP at $3.3 billion. In 2001, it was estimated to be $4.1 billion. By 2009, the CIA estimated that the GDP had grown to $5.731 billion, with a projected real growth rate of 2.6%. According to a 2007 British Chambers of Commerce report, the private sector also grew, particularly in the service sector. Unlike the pre-civil war period when most services and the industrial sector were government-run, there has been substantial, albeit unmeasured, private investment in commercial activities; this has been largely financed by the Somali diaspora, and includes trade and marketing, money transfer services, transportation, communications, fishery equipment, airlines, telecommunications, education, health, construction and hotels. Libertarian economist Peter T. Leeson attributes this increased economic activity to the Somali customary law (referred to as *Xeer*), which he suggests provides a stable environment to conduct business in.

The Central Bank of Somalia indicates that the country's GDP per capita is $333, which is lower than that of Kenya at $350, but better than that of Tanzania at $280 as well as Eritrea at $190 and Ethiopia at $100. About 43% of the population live on less than 1 US dollar a day, with about 24% of those found in urban areas and 54% living in rural areas.

Cans of *Las Qoray* brand tuna fish made in Las Khorey.

As with neighboring countries, Somalia's economy consists of both traditional and modern production, with a gradual shift in favor of modern industrial techniques taking root. According to the Central Bank of Somalia, about 80% of the population are nomadic or semi-nomadic pastoralists, who keep goats, sheep, camels and cattle. The nomads also gather resins and gums to supplement their income.

Agriculture is the most important economic sector. It accounts for about 65% of the GDP and employs 65% of the workforce. Livestock contributes about 40% to GDP and more than 50% of export earnings. Other principal exports include fish, charcoal and bananas; sugar, sorghum and corn are products for the domestic market. According to the Central Bank of Somalia, imports of goods total about $460 million per year, and have recovered and even surpassed aggregate imports prior to the start of the civil war in 1991. Exports, which total about $270 million annually, have also surpassed pre-war aggregate export levels but still lead to a trade account deficit of about $190 million US dollars per year. However, this trade deficit is far exceeded by remittances sent by Somalis in the diaspora, which have helped sustain the import level.

With the advantage of being located near the Arabian Peninsula, Somali traders have increasingly begun to challenge Australia's traditional dominance over the Gulf Arab livestock and meat market, offering quality animals at very low prices. In response, Gulf Arab states have started to make strategic investments in the country, with Saudi Arabia building livestock export infrastructure and the United Arab Emirates purchasing large farmlands. Somalia is also a major world supplier of frankincense and myrrh.

The modest industrial sector, based on the processing of agricultural products, accounts for 10% of Somalia's GDP. Up to 14 private airline firms operating 62 aircraft now also offer commercial flights to international locations, including Daallo Airlines. With competitively priced flight tickets, these companies have helped buttress Somalia's bustling trade networks.

Bosaso port.

Prior to the outbreak of the civil war in 1991, the roughly 53 state-owned small, medium and large manufacturing firms were foundering, with the ensuing conflict destroying many of the remaining industries. However, primarily as a result of substantial local investment by the Somali diaspora, many of these small-scale plants have re-opened and newer ones have been created. The latter include fish-canning and meat-processing plants in the northern regions, as well as about 25 factories in the Mogadishu area, which manufacture pasta, mineral water, confections, plastic bags, fabric, hides and skins, detergent and soap, aluminum, foam mattresses and pillows, fishing boats, carry out packaging, and stone processing. In 2004, an $8.3 million Coca-Cola bottling plant also opened in the city, with investors hailing from various constituencies in Somalia. The robust private sector has also attracted foreign investment from the likes of General Motors and Dole Fruit.

Payment system

Main articles: Central Bank of Somalia and Somali shilling

The Central Bank of Somalia is the official monetary authority of Somalia. In terms of financial management, it is in the process of assuming the task of both formulating and implementing monetary policy.

Owing to a lack of confidence in the local currency, the US dollar is widely accepted as a medium of exchange alongside the Somali shilling. Dollarization notwithstanding, the large issuance of the Somali shilling has increasingly fueled price hikes, especially for low value transactions. This inflationary environment, however, is expected to come to an end as soon as the Central Bank assumes full control of monetary policy and replaces the presently circulating currency introduced by the private sector.

A Dahabshiil franchise outlet in Columbus, Ohio.

Although Somalia has had no central monetary authority for upwards of 15 years between the outbreak of the civil war in 1991 and the subsequent re-establishment of the Central Bank of Somalia in 2009, the nation's payment system is actually fairly advanced due primarily to the widespread existence of private money transfer operators (MTO) that have acted as informal banking networks.

These remittance firms (*hawalas*) have become a large industry in Somalia, with an estimated $1.6 billion USD annually remitted to the region by Somalis in the diaspora via money transfer companies. Most are credentialed members of the Somali Money Transfer Association (SOMTA), an umbrella organization that regulates the community's money transfer sector, or its predecessor, the Somali Financial Services Association (SFSA). The largest of the Somali MTOs is Dahabshiil, a Somali-owned firm employing more than 2000 people across 144 countries with branches in London and Dubai.

As the reconstituted Central Bank of Somalia fully assumes its monetary policy responsibilities, some of the existing money transfer companies are expected in the near future to seek licenses so as to develop into full-fledged commercial banks. This will serve to expand the national payments system to include formal cheques, which in turn is expected to reinforce the efficacy of the use of monetary policy in domestic macroeconomic management.

Energy

The World Bank reports that electricity is now in large part supplied by local businesses, using generators purchased abroad. By dividing Somalia's cities into specific quarters, the private sector has found a manageable method of providing cities with electricity. A customer is given a menu of choices for electricity tailored to his or her needs, such as evenings only, daytime only, 24 hour-supply or charge per lightbulb.

Somalia has untapped reserves of numerous natural resources, including uranium, iron ore, tin, gypsum, bauxite, copper, salt and natural gas. Due to its proximity to the oil-rich Gulf Arab states such as Saudi Arabia and Yemen, the nation is also believed to contain substantial unexploited reserves of oil. A survey of Northeast Africa by the World Bank and U.N. ranked Somalia second only to Sudan as the top prospective producer. American, Australian and Chinese oil companies, in particular, are excited about the prospect of finding petroleum and other natural resources in the country. An oil group listed in Sydney, Range Resources, anticipates that the Puntland province in the north has the potential to produce 5 billion to 10 billion barrels of oil. As a result of these developments, the Somali Petroleum Company was created by the federal government.

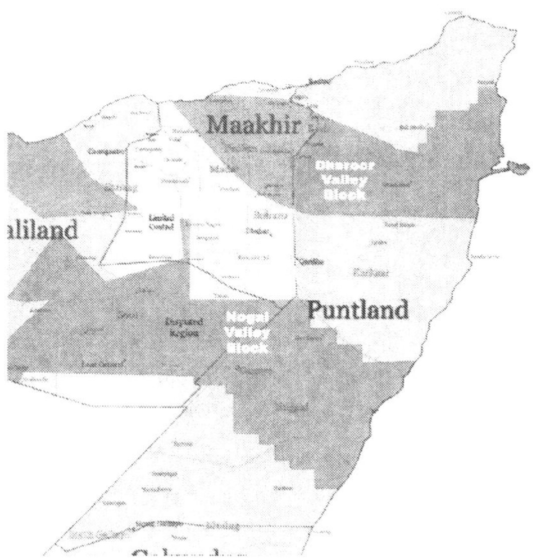

Oil blocks in Puntland.

According to surveys, uranium is also found in large quantities in the Buurhakaba region. A Brazilian company in the 1980s had invested $300 million for a uranium mine in central Somalia, but no long-term mining took place.

Additionally, the Puntland region under the Farole administration has since sought to refine the province's existing oil deal with Range Resources. The Australian oil firm, for its part, indicated that it looked forward to establishing a mutually beneficial and profitable working relationship with the region's new government.

In mid-2010, Somalia's business community also pledged to invest $1 billion in the national gas and electricity industries over the following five years. Abdullahi Hussein, the director of the just-formed Trans-National Industrial Electricity and Gas Company, predicted that the investment strategy would create 100,000 jobs, with the net effect of stimulating the local economy and discouraging unemployed youngsters from turning to vice. The new firm was established through the merger of five Somali companies from the trade, finance, security and telecommunications sectors. The first phase of the project is scheduled to start within six months of the establishment of the company, and will train youth to supply electricity to economic areas and communities. The second phase, which is slated to begin in mid-to-late 2011, will see the construction of factories in specially designated economic zones for the fishing, agriculture, livestock and mining industries.

According to the Central Bank of Somalia, as the nation embarks on the path of reconstruction, the economy is expected to not only match its pre-civil war levels, but also to accelerate in growth and development due to Somalia's untapped natural resources.

Telecommunications and media

Somalia now offers some of the most technologically advanced and competitively priced telecommunications and internet services in the world. After the start of the civil war, various new telecommunications companies began to spring up and compete to provide missing infrastructure. Funded by Somali entrepreneurs and backed by expertise from China, Korea and Europe, these nascent telecommunications firms offer affordable mobile phone and internet services that are not available in many other parts of the continent. Customers can conduct money transfers and other banking activities via mobile phones, as well as easily gain wireless internet access.

The Hormuud Telecom building in Mogadishu.

After forming partnerships with multinational corporations such as Sprint, ITT and Telenor, these firms now offer the cheapest and clearest phone calls in Africa. Installation time for a landline is just three days, while in Kenya to the south, waiting lists are many years long. These Somali telecommunication companies also provide services to every city, town and hamlet in Somalia. There are presently around 25 mainlines per 1,000 persons, and the local availability of telephone lines (*tele-density*) is higher than in neighboring countries; three times greater than in adjacent Ethiopia. Prominent Somali telecommunications companies include Golis Telecom Group, Hormuud Telecom, Somafone, Nationlink, Netco, Telcom and Somali Telecom Group. Hormuud Telecom alone grosses about $40 million a year. Despite their rivalry, several of these companies signed an interconnectivity deal in 2005 that allows them to set prices, maintain and expand their networks, and ensure that competition does not get out of control.

Investment in the telecom industry is one of the clearest signs that Somalia's economy has continued to grow despite the ongoing civil strife in parts of the southern half of the country. Although in need of some regulation, the sector provides invaluable communication services, and in the process, greatly facilitates job creation and income generation.

As of 2005, there were also 20 privately-owned Somali newspapers, 12 radio and television stations, and numerous internet sites offering information to the public. Several local satellite-based television services transmit international news stations, such as CNN. In addition, one of Somalia's upstart media firms recently established a partnership with the BBC.

Military

Main article: Military of Somalia

Prior to the outbreak of the civil war in 1991 and the subsequent disintegration of the Armed Forces, Somalia's friendship with the Soviet Union and later partnership with the United States enabled it to build the largest army in Africa. The creation of the Transitional Federal Government in 2004 saw the re-establishment of the Military of Somalia, which now maintains a force of 10,000 troops.

A Spoon Rest A (P-12) early warning radar unit, part of radar installation operated by Somali troops at the Berbera airport.

The Ministry of Defense is responsible for the Armed Forces. The Somali Navy is also being re-established, with 500 Marines currently training in Mogadishu out of an expected 5,000-strong force. In addition, there are plans for the re-establishment of the Somali Air Force, with six combat and six transport planes already purchased. A new police force was also formed to maintain law and order, with the first police academy to be built in Somalia for several years opening on December 20, 2005 at Armo, 100 kilometers south of Bosaso, the commercial capital of the northeastern Puntland region. Additionally, construction began in May 2010 on a new naval base in the town of Bandar Siyada, located 25 km west of Bosaso. The new naval base is funded by the Puntland administration in conjunction with Saracen International, a UK-based security company. It will include a center for training recruits, and a command post for the naval force.

Environment

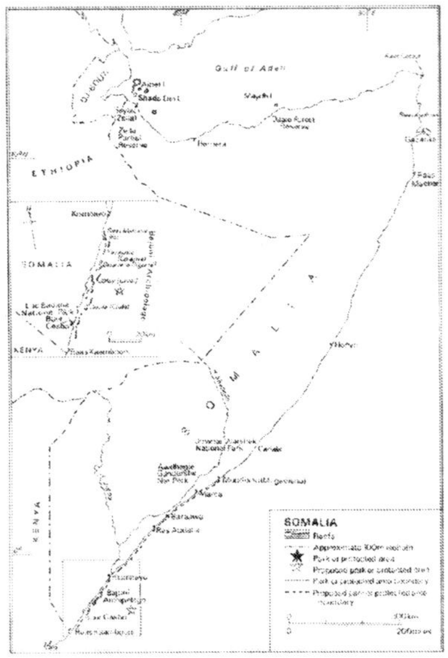

Somalia's coral reefs, ecological parks and protected areas.

Somalia is a semi-arid country with about 1.64% arable land. The first local environmental organizations were ECOTERRA Somalia and the Somali Ecological Society, both of which helped promote awareness about ecological concerns and mobilized environmental programs in all governmental sectors as well as in civil society. From 1971 onwards, a massive tree-planting campaign on a nationwide scale was introduced by the Siad Barre government to halt the advance of thousands of acres of wind-driven sand dunes that threatened to engulf towns, roads and farm land. By 1988, 265 hectares of a projected 336 hectares had been treated, with 39 range reserve sites and 36 forestry plantation sites established. In 1986, the Wildlife Rescue, Research and Monitoring Centre was established by ECOTERRA Intl., with the goal of sensitizing the public to ecological issues. This educational effort led in 1989 to the so-called "Somalia proposal" and a decision by the Somali government to adhere to the Convention on International Trade in Endangered Species of Wild Fauna and Flora (CITES), which established for the first time a worldwide ban on the trade of elephant ivory.

Later, Fatima Jibrell, a prominent Somali environmental activist, mounted a successful campaign to salvage old-growth forests of acacia trees in the northeastern part of Somalia. These trees, which can grow up to 500 years old, were being cut down to make charcoal since this so-called "black gold" is highly in demand in the Arabian Peninsula, where the region's Bedouin tribes believe the acacia to be sacred. However, while being a relatively inexpensive fuel that meets a user's needs, the production of charcoal often leads to deforestation and desertification. As a way of addressing this problem, Jibrell and the Horn of Africa Relief and Development Organization (Horn Relief), an organization of which she is a co-founder and Executive Director, trained a group of adolescents to educate the public on the permanent damage that producing charcoal can create. In 1999, Horn Relief coordinated a peace march in the northeastern Puntland region of Somalia to put an end to the so-called "charcoal wars." As a result of Jibrell's lobbying and education efforts, the Puntland government in 2000 prohibited the exportation of charcoal. The government has also since enforced the ban, which has reportedly led to an 80% drop in exports of the product. Jibrell was awarded the Goldman Environmental Prize in 2002 for her efforts against environmental degradation and desertification. In 2008, she also won the National Geographic Society/Buffett Foundation Award for Leadership in Conservation.

Environmentalist Fatima Jibrell.

Following the massive tsunami of December 2004, there have also emerged allegations that after the outbreak of the Somali Civil War in the late 1980s, Somalia's long, remote shoreline was used as a dump site for the disposal of toxic waste. The huge waves which battered northern Somalia after the tsunami are believed to have stirred up tonnes of nuclear and toxic waste that was illegally dumped in the country by several European firms.

The European Green Party followed up these revelations by presenting before the press and the European Parliament in Strasbourg copies of contracts signed by two European companies — the Italian Swiss firm, Achair Partners, and an Italian waste broker, Progresso — and representatives of the then "President" of Somalia, the faction leader Ali Mahdi Mohamed, to accept 10 million tonnes of toxic waste in exchange for $80 million (then about £60 million).

According to reports by the United Nations Environment Programme (UNEP), the waste has resulted in far higher than normal cases of respiratory infections, mouth ulcers and bleeding, abdominal haemorrhages and unusual skin infections among many inhabitants of the areas around the northeastern towns of Hobyo and Benadir on the Indian Ocean coast — diseases consistent with radiation sickness. UNEP adds that the current situation along the Somali coastline poses a very serious environmental hazard not only in Somalia, but also in the eastern Africa sub-region.

Demographics

Main article: Demographics of Somalia

Somalia has a population of around 10,112,453 inhabitants, about 85% of whom are ethnic Somalis. Civil strife in the early 1990s greatly increased the size of the Somali diaspora, as many of the best educated Somalis left for the Middle East, Europe and North America.

A Somali girl.

Non-Somali ethnic minority groups make up the remainder of the nation's population, and are largely concentrated in the southern regions. They include Benadiri, Bravanese, Bantus, Bajuni, Ethiopians, Indians, Persians, Italians and Britons. Most Europeans left after independence.

The country's population is expanding at a growth rate of 2.809% per annum and a birth rate of 43.33 births/1,000 people. Most local residents are young, with a median age of 17.6 years; about 45% of the population is between the ages of 0–14 years, 52.5% is between the ages of 15–64 years, and only 2.5% is 65 years of age or older. The gender ratio is roughly balanced, with proportionally about as many men as women.

There is little reliable statistical information on urbanization in Somalia. However, rough estimates have been made indicating a rate of urbanization of 4.2% per annum (2005-10 est.), with many towns quickly growing into cities. As of 2008, 37% of the nation's population live in towns and cities, with the percentage rapidly increasing.

Languages

Main article: Languages of Somalia

The Somali language is the official language of Somalia. It is a member of the Cushitic branch of the Afro-Asiatic language family, and its nearest relatives are the Afar and Saho languages. Somali is the best documented of the Cushitic languages, with academic studies of it dating from before 1900.

Somali dialects are divided into three main groups: Northern, Benaadir and Maay. Northern Somali (or Northern-Central Somali) forms the basis for Standard Somali. Benaadir (also known as Coastal Somali) is spoken on the Benadir coast from Cadale to south of Merca, including Mogadishu, as well as in the immediate hinterland. The coastal dialects have additional phonemes which do not exist in Standard Somali. Maay is principally spoken by the Digil and Mirifle (Rahanweyn) clans in the southern areas of Somalia.

The Osmanya writing script

Since Somali had long lost its ancient script, a number of writing systems have been used over the years for transcribing the language. Of these, the Somali alphabet is the most widely used, and has been the official writing script in Somalia since the government of former President of Somalia Siad Barre formally introduced it in October 1972.

The script was developed by the Somali linguist Shire Jama Ahmed specifically for the Somali language, and uses all letters of the English Latin alphabet except *p*, *v* and *z*. Besides Ahmed's Latin script, other orthographies that have been used for centuries for writing Somali include the long-established Arabic script and Wadaad's writing. Indigenous writing systems developed in the 20th century include the Osmanya, Borama and Kaddare scripts, which were invented by Osman Yusuf Kenadid, Sheikh Abdurahman Sheikh Nuur and Hussein Sheikh Ahmed Kaddare, respectively.

In addition to Somali, Arabic is an official national language in Somalia. Many Somalis speak it due to centuries-old ties with the Arab World, the far-reaching influence of the Arabic media, and religious education.

English is also widely used and taught. Italian used to be a major language, but its influence significantly diminished following independence. It is now most frequently heard among older generations. Other minority languages include Bravanese, a variant of Swahili that is spoken along the coast by the Bravanese people.

Religion

Main articles: Islam in Somalia and Christianity in Somalia

With very few exceptions, Somalis are entirely Muslims, the majority belonging to the Sunni branch of Islam and the Shafi`i school of Islamic jurisprudence, although some are also adherents of the Shia Muslim denomination. Sufism, the mystical dimension of Islam, is also well-established, with many local *jama'a* (*zawiya*) or congregations of the various *tariiqa* or Sufi orders. The constitution of Somalia likewise defines Islam as the religion of the Somali Republic, and Islamic sharia as the basic source for national legislation.

Islam entered the region very early on, as a group of persecuted Muslims had, at Prophet Muhammad's urging, sought refuge across the Red Sea in the Horn of Africa. Islam may thus have been introduced into Somalia well before the faith even took root in its place of origin.

Eid celebrations at the Mosque of Islamic Solidarity in Mogadishu (2006).

In addition, the Somali community has produced numerous important Islamic figures over the centuries, many of whom have significantly shaped the course of Muslim learning and practice in the Horn of Africa, the Arabian Peninsula, and well beyond. Among these Islamic scholars is the 14th century Somali theologian and jurist Uthman bin Ali Zayla'i of Zeila, who wrote the single most authoritative text on the Hanafi school of Islam, consisting of four volumes known as the *Tabayin al-Haqa'iq li Sharh Kanz al-Daqa'iq*.

Christianity is a minority religion in Somalia, with no more than 1,000 practitioners in a population of over eight million inhabitants. There is one diocese for the whole country, the Diocese of Mogadishu, which estimates that there were only about 100 Catholic practitioners in Somalia in 2004.

In 1913, during the early part of the colonial era, there were virtually no Christians in the Somali territories, with only about 100-200 followers coming from the schools and orphanages of the few Catholic missions in the British Somaliland protectorate. There were also no known Catholic missions in Italian Somaliland during the same period. In the 1970s, during the reign of Somalia's then Marxist government, church-run schools were closed and missionaries sent home. There has been no archbishop in the country since 1989, and the cathedral in Mogadishu was severely damaged during the civil war.

Some non-Somali ethnic minority groups also practice animism, which represents (in the case of the Bantu) religious traditions inherited from their ancestors in southeastern Africa.

Culture

Main article: Culture of Somalia

Cuisine

Main article: Somali cuisine

The cuisine of Somalia varies from region to region and consists of an exotic mixture of diverse culinary influences. It is the product of Somalia's rich tradition of trade and commerce. Despite the variety, there remains one thing that unites the various regional cuisines: all food is served halal. There are therefore no pork dishes, alcohol is not served, nothing that died on its own is eaten, and no blood is incorporated. *Qaddo* or lunch is often elaborate.

Various types of popular Somali dishes.

Varieties of *bariis* (rice), the most popular probably being basmati, usually serve as the main dish. Spices like cumin, cardamom, cloves, cinnamon and sage are used to aromatize these different rice dishes. Somalis serve dinner as late as 9 pm. During Ramadan, dinner is often served after Tarawih prayers – sometimes as late as 11 pm.

Xalwo or halva is a popular confection served during special occasions such as Eid celebrations or wedding receptions. It is made from sugar, cornstarch, cardamom powder, nutmeg powder and ghee. Peanuts are also sometimes added to enhance texture and flavor. After meals, homes are traditionally perfumed using frankincense (*lubaan*) or incense (*cuunsi*), which is prepared inside an incense burner referred to as a *dabqaad*.

Music

Main article: Music of Somalia

Somalia has a rich musical heritage centered on traditional Somali folklore. Most Somali songs are pentatonic; that is, they only use five pitches per octave in contrast to a heptatonic (seven note) scale such as the major scale. At first listen, Somali music might be mistaken for the sounds of nearby regions such as Ethiopia, Sudan or Arabia, but it is ultimately recognizable by its own unique tunes and styles. Somali songs are usually the product of collaboration between lyricists (*midho*), songwriters (*lahan*) and singers (*'odka* or "voice").

Somali singer Aar Maanta performing with his band.

Literature

Main article: Somali literature

Somali scholars have for centuries produced many notable examples of Islamic literature ranging from poetry to Hadith. With the adoption of the Latin alphabet in 1972 as the nation's standard orthography, numerous contemporary Somali authors have also released novels, some of which have gone on to receive worldwide acclaim. Of these modern writers, Nuruddin Farah is probably the most celebrated. Books such as *From a Crooked Rib* and *Links* are considered important literary achievements, works which have earned Farah, among other accolades, the 1998 Neustadt International Prize for Literature. Farah Mohamed Jama Awl is another prominent Somali writer who is perhaps best known for his Dervish era novel, *Ignorance is the enemy of love*.

Architecture

Main article: Architecture of Somalia

Eyl castle.

Somali architecture is a rich and diverse tradition of engineering and designing multiple different construction types such as stone cities, castles, citadels, fortresses, mosques, temples, aqueducts, lighthouses, towers and tombs during the ancient, medieval and early modern periods in Somalia, as well as the fusion of Somalo-Islamic architecture with Occidental designs in contemporary times.

In ancient Somalia, pyramidical structures known in Somali as *taalo* were a popular burial style, with hundreds of these drystone monuments scattered around the country today. Houses were built of dressed stone similar to the ones in Ancient Egypt, and there are examples of courtyards and large stone walls such as the Wargaade Wall enclosing settlements.

The adoption of Islam in the early medieval era of Somalia's history brought Islamic architectural influences from Arabia and Persia, which stimulated a shift from drystone and other related materials in construction to coral stone, sundried bricks, and the widespread use of limestone in Somali architecture. Many of the new architectural designs such as mosques were built on the ruins of older structures, a practice that would continue over and over again throughout the following centuries.

See also

Main article: Outline of Somalia

- Index of Somalia-related articles

Bibliography

- Abdullahi, Mohamed Diriye, *Culture and Customs of Somalia*, (Greenwood Press: 2001)
- Cassanelli, Lee V., *The shaping of Somali society: reconstructing the history of a pastoral people, 1600-1900*, (University of Pennsylvania Press: 1982)
- Cerulli, Enrico, *Somalia: Scritti Vari Editi ed Inediti*, (Istituto poligrafico dello Stato: 1957)
- Hess, Robert L. *Italian Colonialism in Somalia*, (University of Chicago: 1966)
- Laitin, David D., *Politics, Language, and Thought: The Somali Experience*, (University Of Chicago Press: 1977)
- Lewis, I.M., *Pastoral Democracy: A study on Pastoralism and Politics among the Northern Somali clans*, (Ohio University Press: 1958)
- Van Notten, Michael, *The Law of the Somalis: A Stable Foundation for Economic Development in the Horn of Africa*, First Printing edition, (The Red Sea Press: 2005)

External links

Government

- Official Website of the Transitional Federal Government of Somalia [1]
- Chief of State and Cabinet Members [2]

General information

- Somalia [3] entry at *The World Factbook*
- Somalia [4] from *UCB Libraries GovPubs*
- Somalia [5] at the Open Directory Project
- Wikimedia Atlas of Somalia
- Somalia travel guide from Wikitravel

1. REDIRECT Template:Navboxes

1. REDIRECT Template:Navboxes

ace:Somalia mhr:Сомали pnb:صومالی

History of Somalia

History of Somalia

Ancient
Laas Geel Culture
Kingdom of Punt
Malaoites · Oponeans
Mosyllonians
Medieval
Kingdom of Ifat
Adal Sultanate
Ajuuraan Empire
Gobroon Dynasty
Gerad Dynasty
Modern
Sultanate of Hobyo
Dervish State
Italian Somaliland
British Somaliland
Aden Adde Administration
Shermarke Administration
Communist rule
Recent History
Somali maritime history

Somalia (Somali: *Soomaaliya*; Arabic: الصومال *aṣ-Ṣūmāl*), officially the **Republic of Somalia** (Somali: *Jamhuuriyadda Soomaaliya*, Arabic: جمهورية الصومال *Jumhūriyyat aṣ-Ṣūmāl*) and formerly known as the **Somali Democratic Republic**, is a country located in the Horn of Africa. It is bordered by Djibouti to the northwest, Kenya on its southwest, the Gulf of Aden with Yemen on its north, the Indian Ocean at its east, and Ethiopia to the west.

This article describes its overall history. See Somalia for details of the country as it is today.

Prehistory

Somalia has been inhabited since the Paleaelithic period. Cave paintings said to date back as far as 9000 BC have been found in northern Somalia. The most famous of these is the Laas Geel complex, which contains some of the earliest known rock art on the African continent. Inscriptions have been found beneath each of the rock paintings, but archaeologists have so far been unable to decipher this form of ancient writing. During the Stone age, the Doian culture and the Hargeisan culture flourished here with their respective industries and factories.

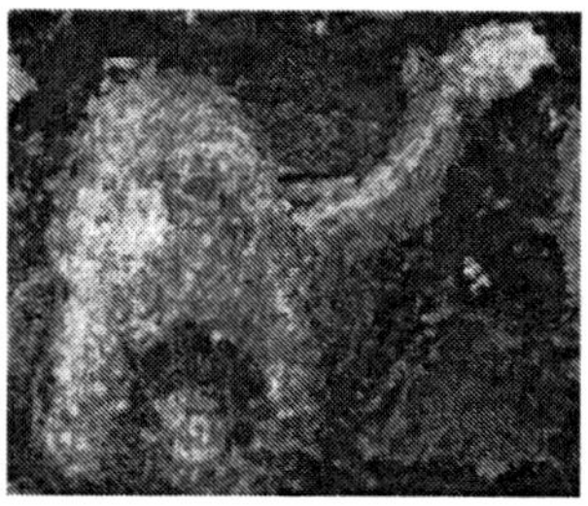
Ancient rock art depicting a camel.

The oldest evidence of burial customs in the Horn of Africa comes from cemeteries in Somalia dating back to 4th millennium BC. The stone implements from the *Jalelo* site in northern Somalia are said to be the most important link in evidence of the universality in palaeolithic times between the East and the West

Ancient

Main articles: Architecture of Somalia and Somali maritime history

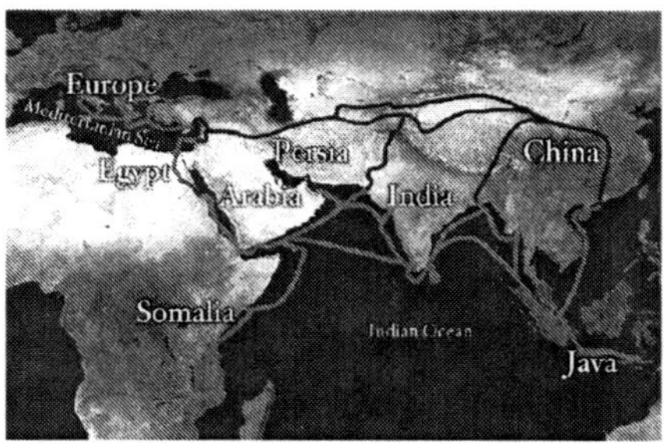

The Silk Road extending from southern Europe through Arabia, Somalia, Egypt, Persia, India and Java until it reaches China.

Ancient pyramidical structures, tombs, ruined cities and stone walls such as the Wargaade Wall littered in Somalia are evidence of an ancient sophisticated civilization that once thrived in the Somali peninsula. The findings of archaeological excavations and research in Somalia show that this ancient civilization had had an ancient writing system that remains undeciphered and enjoyed a lucrative trading relationship with Ancient Egypt and Mycenean Greece since at least the second millennium BC, which supports the view of Somalia being the ancient Kingdom of Punt. The Puntites "traded not only in their own produce of incense, ebony and short-horned cattle, but also in goods from other neighbouring regions, including gold, ivory and animal skins." According to the temple reliefs at Deir el-Bahri, the Land of Punt was ruled at that time by King Parahu and Queen Ati.

Ancient Somalis domesticated the camel somewhere between the third millennium and second millennium BC from where it spread to Ancient Egypt and North Africa.. In the classical period, the city states of Mosylon, Opone, Malao (ancient), Sarapion, Mundus, and Tabae in Somalia developed a lucrative trade network connecting with merchants from Phoenicia, Ptolemic Egypt, Greece, Parthian Persia, Saba, Nabataea and the Roman Empire. They used the ancient Somali maritime vessel known as the beden to transport their cargo. After the Roman conquest of the Nabataean Empire and the Roman naval presence at Aden to curb piracy, Arab merchants barred Indian merchants from trading in the free port cities of the Arabian peninsula because of the nearby Roman presence. However, they continued to trade in the port cities of the Somali peninsula, which was free from any Roman threat or spies. The reason for barring Indian ships from entering the wealthy Arabian port cities was to protect and hide the exploitative trade practices of the Somali and Arab merchants in the extremely lucrative ancient Red Sea-Mediterranean Sea commerce. The Indian merchants for centuries brought large quantities of cinnamon from Ceylon and the Far East to Somalia and Arabia. This is said to have been one of the most remarkable secrets of the Red Sea port cities of Arabia and the Horn of Africa in their trade with the Roman and Greek world. The Romans and Greeks believed the source of cinnamon to have been the Somali peninsula but in reality, the highly valued product was brought to Somalia by way of Indian ships. Through Somali and Arab traders, Indian/Chinese cinnamon was also exported for far higher prices to North Africa, the Near East and Europe, which made the cinnamon trade a very profitable revenue maker, especially for the Somali merchants through whose hands the large quantities were shipped across the ancient sea and land routes. [*citation needed*]

Ruins of Qa'ableh.

Medieval

Main articles: Adal Sultanate, Ajuuraan State, and Warsangali Sultanate

History of Islam in the Horn of Africa is as old as the religion itself. The early persecuted Muslims fled to the Axumite port city of Zeila in Modern Somalia to seek protection from the Quraish at the court of the Axumite Emperor in modern Ethiopia. Some of the Muslims that were granted protection are said to have settled in several parts of the Horn of Africa to promote the religion. The victory of the Muslims over the Quraish in the 7th century

Ruins of the Sultanate of Adal in Zeila, Somalia.

had a significant impact on Somalia's merchants and sailors, as their Arab trading partners had now all adopted Islam and the major trading routes in the Mediterranean and the Red Sea now became part of a trade network known as Pax Islamica. Through commerce, Islam spread amongst the Somali population in the coastal cities of Somalia. Instability in the Arabian peninsula saw several migrations of Arab families to Somalia's coastal cities, who then contributed another significant element to the growing popularity of Islam in the Somali peninsula.

13th century Fakr ad-Din mosque

Mogadishu became the center of Islam on the East African coast, and Somali merchants established a colony in Mozambique to extract gold from the Monomopatan mines in Sofala. In northern Somalia, Adal was in its early stages a small trading community established by the newly-converted Horn African Muslim merchants, who were predominantly Somali according to Arab and Somali chronicles. The century between 1150 and 1250 marked a decisive turn in the role of Islam in Somali history. Following his visit to the city, the 12th century Syrian historian Yaqut al-Hamawi wrote that Mogadishu was inhabited by dark-skinned Berbers, the ancestors of the modern Somalis. The Adal Sultanate was now a center of a commercial empire stretching from Cape Guardafui to Hadiya. The Adalites then came under the influence of the expanding Horn African Kingdom of Ifat, and prospered under its patronage. The capital of the Ifat was Zeila, situated in in northern present-day Somalia, from where the Ifat army marched to conquer the ancient Kingdom of Shoa in 1270.

The Muslim and Christian communities of modern Somalia and Ethiopia enjoyed friendly relations for centuries. The conquest of Shoa ignited a rivalry for supremacy between the Christian Solomonids and the Muslim Ifatites which resulted in several devastating wars and ultimately ended in a Solomonic victory over the Kingdom of Ifat. Parts of northwestern Somalia came under the rule of the Solomonids in medieval times, especially during the reign of Amda Seyon I (r. 1314-1344). In 1403 or 1415 (under Emperor Dawit I or Emperor Yeshaq I, respectively) measures were taken against the Muslim Sultanate of Adal. The Emperor eventually captured King Sa'ad ad-Din II in Zeila and had him executed. The Walashma Chronicle, however, records the date as 1415, which would make the Ethiopian victor Emperor Yeshaq I. After the war, the reigning king had his minstrels compose a song praising his victory, which contains the first written record of the word "Somali". Sa'ad ad-Din II's family was subsequently given safe haven at the court of the King of Yemen, where his sons regrouped and planned their revenge on the Solomonids.

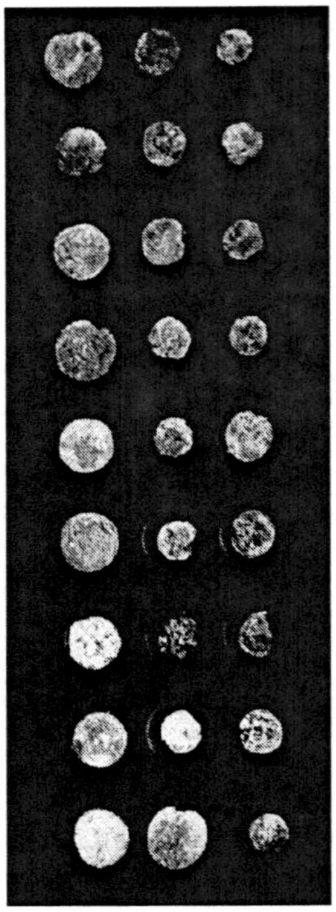
Mogadishan currency - The Kingdom of Mogadishu was an important monetary supporter of Adal.

The oldest son Sabr ad-Din II build a new capital eastwards of Zeila known as *Dakkar* and began referring to himself as the *King of Adal*. He continued the war against the Solomonic Empire. Despite his army's smaller size, he was able to defeat the Solomonids at the battles of *Serjan* and *Zikr Amhara* and consequently pillaged the surrounding areas. Many similar battles were fought between the Adalites and the Solomonids with both sides achieving victory and suffering defeat but ultimately Sultan Sabr ad-Din II successfully managed to drive the Solomonic army out of Adal territory. He died a natural death and was succeeded by his brother Mansur ad-Din who invaded the capital and royal seat of the Solomonic Empire and drove Emperor Dawit II to Yedaya where according to al-Maqrizi, Sultan Mansur destroyed a Solomonic army and killed the Emperor. He then advanced to the mountains of Mokha where he encountered a 30 000 strong Solomonic army. The Adalite soldiers surrounded their enemies and for two months besieged the trapped Solomonic soldiers until a truce was declared in Mansur's favour.

Later on in the campaign, the Adalites were struck by a catastrophe when Sultan Mansur and his brother Muhammad were captured in battle by the Solomonids. Mansur was immediately succeeded by the youngest brother of the family Jamal ad-Din II. Sultan Jamal reorganized the army into a formidable force and defeated the Solomonic armies at Bale,Yedeya and Jazja. Emperor Yeshaq responded by gathering a large army and invaded the cities of Yedeya and Jazja but was repulsed by the soldiers of Jamal. Following this success, Jamal organized another successful attack against the Solomonic forces and inflicted heavy casualties in what was reportedly the largest Adalite army ever fielded. As a result, Yeshaq was forced to withdraw towards the Blue Nile over the next five months, while Jamal ad Din's forces pursued them and looted much gold on the way, although no engagement ensued.

Almnara Tower Somalia.

After returning home, Jamal sent his brother Ahmad with the Christian battle-expert *Harb Jaush* to successfully attack the province of Dawaro. Despite his losses, Emperor Yeshaq was still able to continue field armies against Jamal. Sultan Jamal continued to advance further into the Abyssinian heartland. However Jamal upon hearing of Yeshaq's plan to sent several large armies to attack three different areas of Adal, including the capital returned back to Adal where he fought the Solomonic forces at *Harjai* and according to al-Maqrizi this is where the Emperor Yeshaq died in battle. The young Sultan Jamal ad-Din II at the end of his reign had outperformed his brothers and forefathers in the war arena and became the most successful ruler of Adal to date. Within a few years, however, Jamal was assassinated by either disloyal friends or cousins around 1432 or 1433, and was succeeded by his brother Badlay ibn Sa'ad ad-Din. Sultan Badlay continued the campaigns of his younger brother and began several successful expeditions against the christian empire. He recovered the Kingdom of Bali and began preparations of a major Adalite offensive into the Ethiopian Highlands. He successfully collected funding from surrounding Muslim Kingdoms as far away as the Kingdom of Mogadishu. These ambitious plans however were thrown out the war chamber when King Badlay died during the invasion of Dawaro. He was succeeded by his son Muhammad ibn Badlay who sent envoys to the Sultan of Mamluk Egypt to gather support and arms in the continuing war against the Christian empire. The Adalite ruler Muhammad and the Solomonic ruler Baeda Maryam agreed to a truce and both states in the following decades saw an unprecedent period of peace and stability.

Ahmed Gurey monument in Mogadishu.

Sultan Muhammad was succeeded by his son Shams ad Din while Emperor Baeda Maryam was succeeded by his son Eskender. During this time period warfare broke out again between the two states and Emperor Eskender invaded *Dakkar* where he was stopped by a large Adalite army who destroyed the Solomonic army to such an extent that no further expeditions were carried out for the remaining of Eskender's reign. Adal however continued to raid the Christian empire unabated under the General Mahfuz, the leader of the Adalite war machine who annually invaded the Christian territories. Eskender was succeeded by Emperor Na'od who tried to defend the Christians from General Mahfuz but he too was also killed in battle by the Adalite army in Ifat.

Ahmed Gurey's pioneering use of cannons supplied by the Ottomans figured prominently in his Conquest of Ethiopia.

At the turn of the 16th century Adal regrouped and around 1527 under the charismatic leadership of Imam Ahmad ibn Ibrihim al-Ghazi (*Gurey* in Somali, *Gragn* in Amharic, both meaning "left-handed), Adal invaded Ethiopia. Adalite armies with Ottoman support and arms marched into Ethiopia and caused considerable damage on the Highland state. Many historic Churches, manuscripts and settlements were looted and burned during the campaigns. Adal's use of firearms, still only rarely used in Ethiopia, allowed the conquest of well over half of Ethiopia, reaching as far north as Tigray. The complete conquest of Ethiopia was averted by the timely arrival of a Portuguese expedition led by Cristovão da Gama, son of the famed navigator Vasco da Gama. The Portuguese had been in the area earlier in early 16th centuries (in search of the legendary priest-king Prester John), and although a diplomatic mission from Portugal, led by *Rodrigo de Lima*, had failed to improve relations between the countries, they responded to the Ethiopian pleas for help and sent a military expedition to their fellow Christians. A Portuguese fleet under the command of Estêvão da Gama was sent from India and arrived at Massawa in February 1541. Here he received an ambassador from the Emperor beseeching him to send help against the Muslims, and in July following a force of 400 musketeers, under the command of Christovão da Gama, younger brother of the admiral, marched into the interior, and being joined by Ethiopian troops they were at first successful against the Muslims but they were subsequently defeated at the Battle of Wofla (28 August 1542), and their commander captured and executed. On February 21, 1543, however, a joint Portuguese-Ethiopian force defeated the Muslim army at the Battle of Wayna Daga, in which Ahmed Gurey was killed and the war won. Ahmed Gurey's widow married his nephew Nur ibn Mujahid, in return for his promise to avenge Ahmed's death, who succeeded Ahmed Gurey, and continued hostilities against his northern adversaries until he killed the Ethiopian Emperor in his second invasion of Ethiopia

Barawa city, was an important medieval centre of Somali enterprise.

During the Age of the Ajuuraans, the sultanates and republics of Merca, Mogadishu, Barawa, Hobyo and their respective ports flourished and had a lucrative foreign commerce with ships sailing to and coming from Arabia, India, Venetia, Persia, Egypt, Portugal and as far away as China. Vasco Da Gama, who passed by Mogadishu in the 15th century, noted that it was a large city with houses of four or five storeys high and big palaces in its centre and many mosques with cylindrical minarets. In the 16th century, Duarte Barbosa noted that many ships from the Kingdom of Cambaya in India sailed to Mogadishu with cloths and spices, for which they in return received gold, wax and ivory. Barbaso also highlighted the abundance of meat, wheat, barley, horses, and fruit on the coastal markets, which generated enormous wealth for the merchants.

Model of a medieval Mogadishan ship.

Mogadishu, the center of a thriving weaving industry known as *toob benadir* (specialized for the markets in Egypt and Syria), together with Merca and Barawa also served as transit stops for Swahili merchants from Mombasa and Malindi and for the gold trade from Kilwa. Jewish merchants from the Hormuz brought their Indian textile and fruit to the Somali coast in exchange for grain and wood, Trading relations were established with Malacca in the 15th century with cloth, ambergris and porcelain being the main commodities of the trade. Giraffes, zebras and incense were exported to the Ming Empire of China, which established Somali merchants as leaders in the commerce between the Asia and Africa and influenced the Chinese language with the Somali language in the process. Hindu merchants from Surat and Southeast African merchants from Pate, seeking to bypass both the Portuguese blockade and Omani meddling, used the Somali ports of Merca and Barawa (which were out of the two powers' jurisdiction) to conduct their trade in safety and without interference.

In 1660, the Portuguese in Mombasa surrendered to a joint Somali-Omani force.

The 16th century Somali-Portuguese wars in East Africa meant that geopolitical tensions would remain high and the increased contact between Somali sailors and Ottoman corsairs worried the Portuguese who send a punitive expedition against Mogadishu under Joao de Sepuvelda, which was unsuccessful. Ottoman-Somali cooperation against the Portuguese in the Indian Ocean reached a high point in the 1580s when Ajuuraan clients of the Somali coastal cities began to symphatize with the Arabs and Swahilis under Portuguese rule and sent an envoy to the Turkish corsair Mir Ali Bey for a joint expedition against the Portuguese. He agreed and was joined by a Somali fleet, which began attacking Portuguese colonies in Southeast Africa. The Somali-Ottoman offensive managed to drive out the Portuguese from several important cities such as Pate, Mombasa and Kilwa. However, the Portuguese governor sent envoys to India requesting a large Portuguese fleet. This request was answered and it reversed the previous offensive of the Muslims into one of defense. The Portuguese armada managed to re-take most of the lost cities and began punishing their leaders, but they refrained from attacking Mogadishu.

Early modern

Main articles: Dervish State, Gobroon Dynasty, and Sultanate of Hobyo

Eyl Castle, Somalia.

In the early modern period, successor states of the Adal and Ajuuraan empires began to flourish in Somalia. These were the Warsangali Sultanate, the Bari Dynasties and the Gobroon Dynasty. They continued the tradition of castle-building and seaborne trade established by previous Somali empires. Sultan Yusuf Mahamud Ibrahim, the third Sultan of the House of Gobroon, started the Golden age of the Gobroon Dynasty. His army came out victorious during the Bardheere Jihad, which restored stability in the region and revitalized the East African ivory trade. He also received presents and had cordial relations with the rulers of neighbouring and distant kingdoms such as the Omani, Witu and Yemeni Sultans. Sultan Ibrahim's son Ahmed Yusuf succeeded him and was one of the most important figures in 19th century East Africa, receiving tribute from Omani governors and creating alliances with important Muslim families on the East African coast. In northern Somalia, the Gerad Dynasty conducted trade with Yemen and Persia and competed with the merchants of the Bari Dynasty. The Gerads and the Bari Sultans built impressive palaces, castles and fortresses and had close relations with many different empires in the Near East.

Muhammad Abdullah Hassan, leader of the Dervishes.

In the late 19th century, after the Berlin conference, European powers began the Scramble for Africa, which inspired the Dervish leader Muhammad Abdullah Hassan to rally support from across the Horn of Africa and begin one of the longest colonial resistance wars ever. In several of his poems and speeches, Hassan emphasized that the British "have destroyed our religion and made our children their children" and that the Christian Ethiopians in league with the British were bent upon plundering the political and religious freedom of the Somali nation. He soon emerged as "a champion of his country's political and religious freedom, defending it against all Christian invaders." Hassan issued a religious ordinance that any Somali national who did not accept the goal of unity of Somalia and would not fight under his leadership would be considered as kafir or *gaal*. He soon acquired weapons from Turkey, Sudan, and other Islamic and/or Arabian countries, and appointed ministers and advisers to administer different areas or sectors of Somalia. In addition, Hassan gave a clarion call for Somali unity and independence, in the process organizing his follower-warriors. His Dervish movement had an essentially military character, and the Dervish State was fashioned on the model of a *Salihiya* brotherhood. It was characterized by a rigid hierarchy and centralization. Though Hassan threatened to drive the Christians into the sea, he committed the first attack by launching his first major military offensive with his 1500 Dervish equipped with 20 modem rifles on the British soldiers stationed in the region.

He repulsed the British in four expeditions and had relations with the central powers of the Ottomans and the Germans. In 1920, the Dervish state collapsed after intensive British arial bombardments, and Dervish territories were subsequently turned into a protectorate. The dawn of fascism in the early 1920s heralded a change of strategy for Italy, as the north-eastern sultanates were soon to be forced within the boundaries of *La Grande Somalia* according to the plan of Fascist Italy. With the arrival of Governor Cesare Maria De Vecchi on 15 December 1923, things began to change for that part of Somaliland. Italy had access to these areas under the successive protection treaties, but not direct rule. The Fascist government had direct rule only over the Benadir territory. Given the defeat of the Dervish movement in the early 1920s and the rise of fascism in Europe, on 10 July 1925 Mussolini gave the green light to De Vecchi to start the takeover of the north-eastern sultanates. Everything was to be changed and the treaties abrogated.

Taleex was the capital of the Dervish State.

Governor De Vecchi's first plan was to disarm the sultanates. But before the plan could be carried out there should be sufficient Italian troops in both sultanates. To make the enforcement of his plan more viable, he began to reconstitute the old Somali police corps, the Corpo Zaptié, as a colonial force.

In preparation for the plan of invasion of the sultanates, the Alula Commissioner, E. Coronaro received orders in April 1924 to carry out a reconnaissance on the territories targeted for invasion. In spite of the forty year Italian relationship with the sultanates, Italy did not have adequate knowledge of the geography. During this time, the Stefanini-Puccioni geological survey was scheduled to take place, so it was a good opportunity for the expedition of Coronaro to join with this.

Coronaro's survey concluded that the Ismaan Sultanate depended on sea traffic, therefore, if this were blocked any resistance which could be mounted came after the invasion of the sultanate would be minimal. As the first stage of the invasion plan Governor De Vecchi ordered the two Sultanates to disarm. The reaction of both sultanates was to object, as they felt the policy was in breach of the protectorate agreements. The pressure engendered by the new development forced the two rival sultanates to settle their differences over Nugaal possession, and form a united front against their common enemy.

Yusuf Ali Kenadid, a prominent Somali anti-imperialist leader and the founder of the Sultanate of Hobyo.

The Sultanate of Hobyo was different from that of Majeerteen in terms of its geography and the pattern of the territory. It was founded by Yusuf Ali Keenadid in the middle of the 19th century in central Somalia. Its jurisdiction stretched from Ceeldheer through to *Dusamareeb* in the south-west, from *Galladi* to Galkacyo in the west, from Jerriiban to Garaad in the north-east, and the Indian Ocean in the east.

By 1 October, De Vecchi's plan was to go into action. The operation to invade Hobyo started in October 1925. Columns of the new Zaptié began to move towards the sultanate. Hobyo, Ceelbuur, Galkayo, and the territory between were completely overrun within a month. Hobyo was transformed from a sultanate into an administrative region. Sultan Yusuf Ali surrendered. Nevertheless, soon suspicions were aroused as Trivulzio, the Hobyo commissioner, reported movement of armed men towards the borders of the sultanate before the takeover and after. Before the Italians could concentrate on the Majeerteen, they were diverted by new setbacks. On 9 November, the Italian fear was realized when a mutiny, led by one of the military chiefs of Sultan Ali Yusuf, Omar Samatar, recaptured El-Buur. Soon the rebellion expanded to the local population. The region went into revolt as El-Dheere also came under the control of Omar Samatar. The Italian forces tried to recapture El-Buur but they were repulsed. On 15 November the Italians retreated to Bud Bud and on the way they were ambushed and suffered heavy casualties.

While a third attempt was in the last stages of preparation, the operation commander, Lieutenant-Colonel Splendorelli, was ambushed between Bud Bud and *Buula Barde*. He and some of his staff were killed. As a consequence of the death of the commander of the operations and the effect of two failed operations intended to overcome the El-Buur mutiny, the spirit of Italian troops began to wane. The Governor took the situation seriously, and to prevent any more failure he requested two battalions from Eritrea to reinforce his troops, and assumed lead of the operations. Meanwhile, the rebellion was gaining sympathy across the country, and as far afield as Western Somalia.

Somali soldiers board a British naval batilla.

The fascist government was surprised by the setback in Hobyo. The whole policy of conquest was collapsing under its nose. The El-Buur episode drastically changed the strategy of Italy as it revived memories of the Adwa fiasco when Italy had been defeated by Abyssinia. Furthermore, in the Colonial Ministry in Rome, senior officials distrusted the Governor's ability to deal with the matter. Rome instructed De Vecchi that he was to receive the reinforcement from Eritrea, but that the commander of the two battalions was to temporarily assume the military command of the operations and De Vecchi was to stay in Mogadishu and confine himself to other colonial matters. In the case of any military development, the military commander was to report directly to the Chief of Staff in Rome.

While the situation remained perplexing, De Vecchi moved the deposed sultan to Mogadishu. Fascist Italy was poised to re-conquer the sultanate by whatever means. To maneuver the situation within Hobyo, they even contemplated the idea of reinstating Ali Yusuf. However, the idea was dropped after they became pessimistic about the results.

To undermine the resistance, however, and before the Eritrean reinforcement could arrive, De Vecchi began to instill distrust among the local people by buying the loyalty of some of them. In fact, these tactics had better results than had the military campaign, and the resistance began gradually to wear down. Given the anarchy which would follow, the new policy was a success.

On the military front, on 26 December 1925 Italian troops finally overran El-Buur, and the forces of Omar Samatar were compelled to retreat to Western Somaliland.

By neutralising Hobyo, the fascists could concentrate on the Majeerteen. In early October 1924, E. Coronaro, the new Alula commissioner, presented Boqor (king) Osman with an ultimatum to disarm and surrender. Meanwhile, Italian troops began to pour into the sultanate in anticipation of this operation. While landing at Haafuun and Alula, the sultanate's troops opened fire on them. Fierce fighting ensued and to avoid escalating the conflict and to press the fascist government to revoke their policy, Boqor Osman tried to open a dialogue. However, he failed, and again fighting broke out between the two parties. Following this disturbance, on 7 October the Governor instructed Coronaro to order the Sultan to surrender; to intimidate the people he ordered the seizure of all merchant boats in the Alula area. At Hafun, Arimondi bombarded and destroyed all the boats in the area.

On 13 October Coronaro was to meet Boqor Osman at Baargaal to press for his surrender. Under siege already, Boqor Osman was playing for time. However, on 23 October, Boqor Osman sent an angry response to the Governor defying his order. Following this a full scale attack was ordered in November. Baargaal was bombarded and destroyed to the ground. This region was ethnically compact, and was out of range of direct action by the fascist government of Muqdisho. The attempt of the colonizers to suppress the region erupted into explosive confrontation. The Italians were meeting fierce resistance on many fronts. In December 1925, led by the charismatic leader Hersi Boqor, son of Boqor Osman, the sultanate forces drove the Italians out of Hurdia and Haafuun, two strategic coastal towns. Another contingent attacked and destroyed an Italian communications centre at Cape Guardafui, at the tip of the Horn. In retaliation the Bernica and other warships were called on to bombard all main coastal towns of the Majeerteen. After a violent confrontation Italian forces captured Ayl (Eil), which until then had remained in the hands of Hersi Boqor. In response to the unyielding situation, Italy called for reinforcements from their other colonies, notably Eritrea. With their arrival at the closing of 1926, the Italians began to move into the interior where they had not been able to venture since their first seizure of the coastal towns. Their attempt to capture Dharoor Valley was resisted, and ended in failure.

De Vecchi had to reassess his plans as he was being humiliated on many fronts. After one year of exerting full force he could not yet manage to gain a result over the sultanate. In spite of the fact that the Italian navy sealed the sultanate's main coastal entrance, they could not succeed in stopping them from receiving arms and ammunition through it. It was only early 1927 when they finally succeeded in shutting the northern coast of the sultanate, thus cutting arms and ammunition supplies for the Majeerteen. By this time, the balance had tilted to the Italians' side, and in January 1927 they began to attack with a massive force, capturing Iskushuban, at the heart of the Majeerteen. Hersi Boqor unsuccessfully attacked and challenged the Italians at Iskushuban. To demoralise the resistance, ships were ordered to target and bombard the sultanate's coastal towns and villages. In the interior the Italian troops confiscated livestock. By the end of the 1927 the Italians had nearly taken control of the sultanate. Defeated and Hersi Boqor and his top staff were forced to retreat to Ethiopia in order to rebuild the forces. However, they had an epidemic of cholera which frustrated all attempts to recover his force.

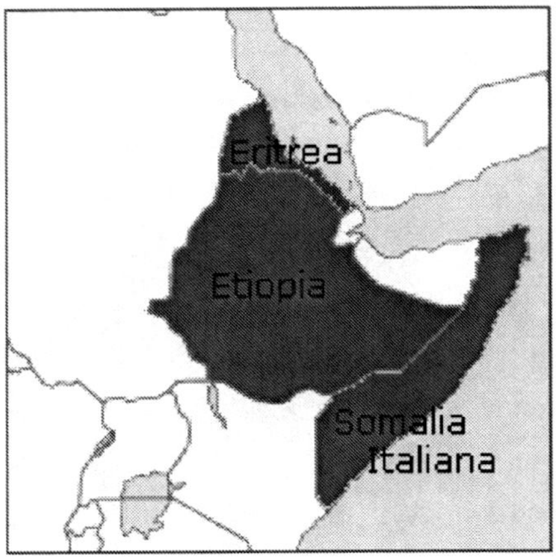

Map of Italian East Africa (Africa Orientale Italiana)

With the elimination of the north-eastern sultanates and the breaking of the Benaadir resistance, from this period henceforth, Italian Somaliland was to become a reality.

By 1935, the British were ready to cut their losses in "British Somaliland". The dervishes refused to accept any negotiations. Even after they had been soundly defeated in 1920, sporadic violence continued for the entire duration of British occupation. To make matters worse, Italy invaded and conquered Ethiopia in 1936, whom the British had been using to help their effort to put down the Somali uprisings. Now with Ethiopia unavailable, the British were faced with the option of doing the dirty work themselves, or packing up and looking for friendlier territory.

By this time many thousand Italian immigrants were living in Romanesque villas on extensive plantations in the south. Conditions for natives were very prosperous under fascist Italian rule, and the southern Somalis never violently resisted. It had become obvious then that Italy had won the horn of Africa, and Britain left upon Mussolini's insistence, with little protest.

Meanwhile the French colony had faded to obsolescence with Britain's dwindling control, and it too was neglected. The Italians then enjoyed sole dominance of the entire East African region including recently occupied Ethiopia.

On May 9, 1936, Mussolini proclaimed the creation of the Italian Empire, calling it the "Africa Orientale Italiana" (A.O.I.) and formed by Ethiopia, Eritrea and Italian Somalia. Many investments in infrastructure were made by the Italians in their Empire, like the *Strada Imperiale* ("imperial road") between Addis Abeba and Mogadishu.

World War II

Italian hegemony of Somalia was short-lived, because of World War II. At the start of the war, Mussolini realized he would have to concentrate his resources primarily on the home front to survive the Allied onslaught.

The Italians conquered the British Somaliland in August 1940, but the British were able to totally reconquer Somalia by 1941. Italian officers organized an Italian guerrilla with Italian colonial troops, that lasted in Somalia from the end of 1941 to spring 1943.

During the war years, Somalia was directly ruled by a British military administration and martial law was in place, especially in the north where bitter memories of past bloodshed still lingered.

Unfortunately these policies were as ill-advised as they were previously. The irregular bandits and militias of the Somali outback received a windfall in weaponry, thanks to the world wide surge in arms production from the war. The Italian settlers and other anti-British elements made sure the rebels got as many guns as they needed to cause trouble. Despite a fresh Somali thorn in their side, the British protectorate lasted until 1949, and actually made some progress in economic development. The British established their capital in the northern city of Hargeisa, and wisely allowed local Muslim judges to try most cases, rather than impose alien British military justice on the populace.

The British allowed almost all the Italians to stay, except for a few too risky for their security, and regularly employed them as civil servants and in the educated professions. The fact that 9 out of 10 of the Italians were loyal to Mussolini, and probably actively spying on the Italian Army's behalf during World War II, was tolerated due to Somalia's relative strategic irrelevance to the larger war effort. Indeed, considering that they were technically citizens of an enemy power, the British lent considerable leeway to the Italian residents, even allowing them to form their own political parties in direct competition with British authority.

Post-War period

After the war, the British gradually relaxed military control of Somalia, and attempted to introduce democracy, and numerous native Somalian political parties sprang into existence, the first being the Somali Youth League (SYL) in 1945. The Potsdam conference was unsure of what to do with Somalia, whether to allow Britain to continue its occupation, to return control to the Italians, who actually had a significant number of people living there, or grant full independence. This question was hotly debated in the Somalian political scene for the next several years. Many wanted outright independence, especially the rural citizens in the west and north. Southerners enjoyed the economic prosperity brought by the Italians, and preferred their leadership. A smaller faction appreciated the British attempt to maintain order.

SYL Monument.

Ogaden granted to Ethiopia

In 1948 a commission led by representatives of the victorious Allied nations wanted to decide the Somali question once and for all. They made one particular decision, granting Ogaden to Ethiopia, which would spark war decades later. After months of vacillations and eventually turning the debate over to the United Nations, in 1949 it was decided that in recognition of its genuine economic improvements to the country, Italy would retain a nominal trusteeship of Somalia for the next 10 years, after which it would gain full independence. The SYL, Somalia's first and most powerful party, strongly opposed this decision, preferring immediate independence, and would become a source of unrest in the coming years.

Despite the SYL's misgivings the 1950s were something of a golden age for Somalia. With UN aid money pouring in, and experienced Italian administrators who had come to see Somalia as their home, infrastructural and educational development bloomed. This decade passed relatively without incident and was marked by positive growth in virtually all parts of Somali life. As scheduled, in 1960, Somalia was granted independence, and power transferred from the Italian administrators to the well developed Somali political culture.

Independence

The freshly independent Somalis loved politics. Every nomad had a radio to listen to political speeches, and although remarkable for an African Muslim country, women were also active participants. There were only mild mumblings from the more conservative sectors of society. Despite this promising start, there were significant underlying problems, most notably the north/south economic divide and the Ogaden issue. Also, long held distrust of Ethiopia and the deeply ingrained belief that Ogaden was rightfully part of Somalia, should have been properly addressed prior to independence. The north and south spoke different languages (English vs Italian respectively) and had different currencies.

Hawo Takowas a remarkable woman who had played a significant role in Somalia's struggle for independence. .

Starting in the early 1960s, troubling trends began to emerge when the north started to reject referendums that had won a majority of votes, based on an overwhelming southern favoritism. This came to a head in 1961 when northern paramilitary organizations revolted when placed under southerners' command. The north's second largest political party began openly advocating secession. Attempts to mend these divides with the formation of a

Pan-Somalian party were ineffectual; one opportunistic party attempted to unite the bickering regions by rallying them against their common enemy Ethiopia and the cause of reconquering Ogaden. Other nationalistic party platforms included the independence of the northern Kenyan holdings of the Italian colony, from Kenya proper. These regions were largely inhabited by ethnic Somalis who had become accustomed to Italian rule, and were distressed by the different regime they faced in Kenya.

Greater Somalia

Main article: Greater Somalia

Somali people in the Horn of Africa are divided among different territories that were artificially and arbitrarily partitioned by the former Imperial powers. Besides Somalia proper, other historically and almost exclusively Somali-inhabited areas of the Horn of Africa now find themselves administered by neighboring countries, such as the Somali Region in Ethiopia and the North Eastern Province (NFD) in Kenya. Pan Somalism was and is an ideology that advocates the unification of all ethnic Somalis under one flag and one nation. This led to a series of cross border raids by Somali insurgents and violent crackdowns by Ethiopian troops from 1960 to 1964, when open conflict erupted between Ethiopia and Somalia. This lasted a few months until a cease fire was signed in the same year. In the aftermath, Ethiopia and Kenya signed a mutual defense pact to protect their newly acquired territories from the Somali separatists.

Although Somalis were, to some extent, politically influenced in the post-war period by the British and the Italians, the socialist parties rejected the European's advice whole cloth, and preferred association with the like-minded Soviet Union and the People's Republic of China. By the middle of the 1960s, the Somalis had initiated a formal military relationship with the Soviet Union whereby the Soviets provided extensive material and training to the Somali armed forces in exchange for use of the Somali naval bases. They also had an exchange program in which several hundred soldiers from one country went to the others to train or be trained. As a result of their contact with the Soviet military, many Somali officers gained a distinctly Marxist worldview. China supplied a lot of non-military industrial funding for various projects. Italy, for its part, continued to support its expatriate citizens in the Horn of Africa. The relationship between the rapidly communizing Somali government and the Italian government also remained cordial. The Somalis, however, were increasingly becoming jaded with the United States, which had been sending substantial military aid to their hostile neighbor, Ethiopia, and thanks to incessant anti-Western indoctrination at the hands of their new Russian friends.

By the late 1960s, the Somali democracy that had gotten off to such an enthusiastic start just ten years prior, was beginning to crumble. In the 1967 election, due to a complicated web of clan loyalties, the winner was not properly recognized and instead a new secret vote was taken by already elected National Assemblymen (senators). The central election issue was whether or not to use military force to bring about the long lived dream of pan-Somalism, which would mean war with Ethiopia and Kenya and possibly Djibouti. In 1968 there seemed to be a brief respite from ominous developments when a telecommunications and trade treaty was worked out with Ethiopia, which was very profitable for both countries, and especially for residents on the border who had been living in a de facto state of emergency since the 1964 cease fire.

1969 was a tumultuous year for Somali politics with even more party defections, collusions, betrayals and collaborations than normal. In a major upset, the SYL and its various closely allied supporting parties, which had previously enjoyed a near monopoly of 120 out of 123 seats in the Assembly, saw their power slashed to only 46 seats. This resulted in angry accusations of election fraud from the displaced SYLers, and their remaining members still had the clout to do something about it. Particularly unsettling was that the military was a strong supporter of the SYL, since that party had always been supportive about invading Ethiopia and Kenya, thus giving the military a reason to exist.

Barre regime

1969 coup d'etat

Major General Salaad Gabeyre Kediye led the Bloodless revolution of 1969.

The stage was set for a coup d'état, but the event that precipitated the coup was unplanned. On 15 October 1969, a bodyguard killed president Shermarke while prime minister Igaal was out of the country. (The assassin, a member of a lineage said to have been badly treated by the president, was subsequently tried and executed by the revolutionary government.) Igaal returned to Mogadishu to arrange for the selection of a new president by the National Assembly. His choice was, like Shermarke, a member of the Daarood clan-family (Igaal was an Isaaq). Government critics, particularly a group of army officers, saw no hope for improving the country's situation by this means. Critics also saw the process as extremely corrupt with votes for the presidency being actively bid on, the highest offer being 55,000 Somali Shillings (approximately $8,000) per vote by Hagi Musa Bogor. On 21 October 1969, when it became apparent that the assembly would support Igaal's choice, army units, with the cooperation of the police, took over strategic points in Mogadishu and rounded up government officials and other prominent political figures.

Although not regarded as the author of the military takeover, army commander Major General Salad Gabeire Kediye and Mahammad Siad Barre assumed leadership of the officers who deposed the civilian government. The new governing body, the Supreme Revolutionary Council leader Salad Gabeire, installed Siad Barre as its president. The SRC arrested and detained at the presidential palace leading members of the democratic regime, including Igaal. The SRC banned political parties, abolished the National Assembly, and suspended the constitution. The new regime's goals included an end to "tribalism, nepotism, corruption, and misrule". Existing treaties were to be honored, but national liberation movements and Somali unification were to be supported. The country was renamed the

Somali Democratic Republic.

Supreme Revolutionary Council (SRC)

The SRC also gave priority to rapid economic and social development through "crash programs", efficient and responsive government, and creation of a standard written form of Somali as the country's single official language. The régime pledged continuance of regional détente in its foreign relations without relinquishing Somali claims to disputed territories.

The SRC's domestic program, known as the First Charter of the Revolution, appeared in 1969. Along with Law Number 1, an enabling instrument promulgated on the day of the military takeover, the First Charter provided the institutional and ideological framework of the new regime. Law Number 1 assigned to the SRC all functions previously performed by the president, the National Assembly, and the Council of Ministers, as well as many duties of the courts. The role of the twenty-five-member military junta was that of an executive committee that made decisions and had responsibility to formulate and execute policy. Actions were based on majority vote, but deliberations rarely were published. SRC members met in specialized committees to oversee government operations in given areas. A subordinate fourteen-man secretariat—the Council of the Secretaries of State (CSS)--functioned as a cabinet and was responsible for day-to-day government operation, although it lacked political power. The CSS consisted largely of civilians, but until 1974 several key ministries were headed by military officers who were concurrently members of the SRC. Existing legislation from the previous democratic government remained in force unless specifically abrogated by the SRC, usually on the grounds that it was "incompatible… with the spirit of the Revolution." In February 1970, the democratic constitution of 1960, suspended at the time of the coup, was repealed by the SRC under powers conferred by Law Number 1.

Although the SRC monopolized executive and legislative authority, Siad Barre filled a number of executive posts: titular head of state, chairman of the CSS (and thereby head of government), commander in chief of the armed forces, and president of the SRC. His titles were of less importance, however, than was his personal authority, to which most SRC members deferred, and his ability to manipulate the clans.

Military and police officers, including some SRC members, headed government agencies and public institutions to supervise economic development, financial management, trade, communications, and public utilities. Military officers replaced civilian district and regional officials. Meanwhile, civil servants attended reorientation courses that combined professional training with political indoctrination, and those found to be incompetent or politically unreliable were fired. A mass dismissal of civil servants in 1974, however, was dictated in part by economic pressures.

The legal system functioned after the coup, subject to modification. In 1970 special tribunals, the National Security Courts (NSC), were set up as the judicial arm of the SRC. Using a military attorney as prosecutor, the courts operated outside the ordinary legal system as watchdogs against activities considered to be counterrevolutionary. The first cases that the courts dealt with involved Shermaarke's assassination and charges of corruption leveled by the SRC against members of the democratic regime. The NSC subsequently heard cases with and without political content. A uniform civil code introduced in 1973 replaced predecessor laws inherited from the Italians and British and also imposed restrictions on the activities of sharia courts. The new regime subsequently extended the death penalty and prison sentences to individual offenders, formally eliminating collective responsibility through the payment of *diyya* or blood money.

The SRC also overhauled local government, breaking up the old regions into smaller units as part of a long-range decentralization program intended to destroy the influence of the traditional clan assemblies and, in the government's words, to bring government "closer to the people." Local councils, composed of military administrators and representatives appointed by the SRC, were established under the Ministry of Interior at the regional, district, and village levels to advise the government on local conditions and to expedite its directives. Other institutional innovations included the organization (under Soviet direction) of the National Security Service (NSS), directed initially at halting the flow of professionals and dissidents out of the country and at counteracting attempts to settle disputes among the clans by traditional means. The newly formed Ministry of Information and National Guidance set up local political education bureaus to carry the government's message to the people and used Somalia's print and broadcast media for the "success of the socialist, revolutionary road." A censorship board, appointed by the ministry, tailored information to SRC guidelines.

The SRC took its toughest political stance in the campaign to break down the solidarity of the lineage groups. Tribalism was condemned as the most serious impediment to national unity. Siad Barre denounced clanism in a wider context as a "disease" obstructing development not only in Somalia, but also throughout the Third World. The government meted out prison terms and fines for a broad category of proscribed activities classified as clanism. Traditional headmen, whom the democratic government had paid a stipend, were replaced by reliable local dignitaries known as "peacekeepers" (*nabod doan*), appointed by Mogadishu to represent government interests. Community identification rather than lineage affiliation was forcefully advocated at orientation centers set up in every district as the foci of local political and social activity. For example, the SRC decreed that all marriage ceremonies should occur at an orientation center. Siad Barre presided over these ceremonies from time to time and contrasted the benefits of socialism to the evils he associated with clanism.

To increase production and control over the nomads, the government resettled 140,000 nomadic pastoralists in farming communities and in coastal towns, where the erstwhile herders were encouraged to engage in agriculture and fishing. By dispersing the nomads and severing their ties with the land to which specific clans made collective claim, the government may also have undercut clan solidarity. In many instances, real improvement in the living conditions of resettled nomads was evident, but despite government efforts to eliminate it, clan consciousness as well as a desire to return to the nomadic life persisted. Concurrent SRC attempts to improve the status of Somali women were unpopular in a traditional Muslim society, despite Siad Barre's argument that such reforms were consistent with Islamic principles.

Siad Barre and scientific socialism

Somalia's adherence to socialism became official on the first anniversary of the military coup when Siad Barre proclaimed that Somalia was a socialist state, despite the fact that the country had no history of class conflict in the Marxist sense. For purposes of Marxist analysis, therefore, clanism was equated with class in a society struggling to liberate itself from distinctions imposed by lineage group affiliation. At the time, Siad Barre explained that the official ideology consisted of three elements: his own conception of community development based on the principle of self-reliance, a form of socialism based on Marxist principles, and Islam. These were subsumed under "scientific socialism," although such a definition was at variance with the Soviet and Chinese models to which reference was frequently made. The theoretical underpinning of the state ideology combined aspects of the Qur'an with the influences of Marx, Lenin, and Mao, but Siad Barre was pragmatic in its application. "Socialism is not a religion," he explained; "It is a political principle" to organize government and manage production. Somalia's alignment with communist states, coupled with its proclaimed adherence to scientific socialism, led to frequent accusations that the country had become a Soviet satellite. For all the rhetoric extolling scientific socialism, however, genuine Marxist sympathies were not deep-rooted in Somalia. But the ideology was acknowledged—partly in view of the country's economic and military dependence on the Soviet Union—as the most convenient peg on which to hang a revolution introduced through a military coup that had supplanted a Western-oriented parliamentary democracy.

More important than Marxist ideology to the popular acceptance of the revolutionary regime in the early 1970s were the personal power of Siad Barre and the image he projected. Styled the "Victorious Leader" (Guulwaadde), Siad Barre fostered the growth of a personality cult. Portraits of him in the company of Marx and Lenin festooned the streets on public occasions. The epigrams, exhortations, and advice of the paternalistic leader who had synthesized Marx with Islam and had found a uniquely Somali path to socialist revolution were widely distributed in Siad Barre's little blue-and-white book. Despite the revolutionary regime's intention to stamp out the clan politics, the government was commonly referred to by the code name MOD. This acronym stood for Marehan (Siad Barre's clan), Ogaden (the clan of Siad Barre's mother), and Dulbahante (the clan of Siad Barre son-in-law Colonel Ahmad Sulaymaan Abdullah, who headed the NSS). These were the three clans whose members formed the government's inner circle. In 1975, for example, ten of the twenty members of the SRC were from the Daarood clan-family, of which these three clans were a part, while the Digil and Rahanweyn, sedentary interriverine clan-families, were totally unrepresented.

The language and literacy issue

The Osmanya script for the Somali language

One of the principal objectives of the revolutionary regime was the adoption of a standard orthography of the Somali language. Such a system would enable the government to make Somali the country's official language. Since independence Italian and English had served as the languages of administration and instruction in Somalia's schools. All government documents had been published in the two European languages. Indeed, it had been considered necessary that certain civil service posts of national importance be held by two officials, one proficient in English and the other in Italian. During the Husseen and Igaal governments, when a number of English-speaking northerners were put in prominent positions, English had dominated Italian in official circles and had even begun to replace it as a medium of instruction in southern schools. Arabic—or a heavily arabized Somali—also had been widely used in cultural and commercial areas and in Islamic schools and courts. Religious traditionalists and supporters of Somalia's integration into the Arab world had advocated that Arabic be adopted as the official language, with Somali as a vernacular. A few months after independence, the Somali Language Committee was appointed to investigate the best means of writing Somali. The committee considered nine scripts, including Arabic, Latin, and various indigenous scripts. Its report, issued in 1962, favored the Latin script, which the committee regarded as the best suited to represent the phonemic structure of Somali and flexible enough to be adjusted for the dialects. Facility with a Latin system, moreover, offered obvious advantages to those who sought higher education outside the country. Modern printing equipment would also be more easily and reasonably available for Latin type. Existing Somali grammars prepared by foreign scholars, although outdated for modern teaching methods, would give some initial advantage in the preparation of teaching materials. Disagreement had been so intense among opposing factions, however, that no action was taken to adopt a standard script, although successive governments continued to reiterate their intention to resolve the issue.

On coming to power, the SRC made clear that it viewed the official use of foreign languages, of which only a relatively small fraction of the population had an adequate working knowledge, as a threat to national unity, contributing to the stratification of society on the basis of language. In 1971 the SRC revived the Somali Language Committee and instructed it to prepare textbooks for schools and adult education programs, a national grammar, and a new Somali dictionary. However, no decision was made at the time concerning the use of a particular script, and each member of the committee worked in the one with which he was familiar. The understanding was that, upon adoption of a standard script, all materials would be immediately transcribed.

On the third anniversary of the 1969 coup, the SRC announced that a Latin script had been adopted as the standard script to be used throughout Somalia beginning January 1, 1973. There were 18 varying scripts brought to the Language Committee. Of these, 11 were new Somali scripts invented by aspiring linguists. Of the remaining seven, 4 were Arabic and 3 Latin. There were over a dozen linguists and Shire Jama Ahmed's Latin version which he already used to print pamphlets won over the council. It is the Somali script or written Af Soomaali used today. The Somali script has 21 consonants and five vowels. As a prerequisite for continued government service, all officials were given three months (later extended to six months) to learn the new script and to become proficient in it. During 1973 educational material written in the standard orthography was introduced in elementary schools and by 1975 was also being used in secondary and higher education.

Somalia's literacy rate was estimated at only 5 percent in 1972. After adopting the new script, the SRC launched a "cultural revolution" aimed at making the entire population literate in two years. The first part of the massive literacy campaign was carried out in a series of three-month sessions in urban and rural sedentary areas and reportedly resulted in several hundred thousand people learning to read and write. As many as 8,000 teachers were recruited, mostly among government employees and members of the armed forces, to conduct the program.

The campaign in settled areas was followed by preparations for a major effort among the nomads that got underway in August 1974. The program in the countryside was carried out by more than 20,000 teachers, half of whom were secondary school students whose classes were suspended for the duration of the school year. The rural program also compelled a privileged class of urban youth to share the hardships of the nomadic pastoralists. Although affected by the onset of a severe drought, the program appeared to have achieved substantial results in the field in a short period of time. Nevertheless, the UN estimate of Somalia's literacy rate in 1990 was only 24 percent.

Creation of the Somali Revolutionary Socialist Party

One of the SRC's first acts was to prohibit the existence of any political association. Under Soviet pressure to create a communist party structure to replace Somalia's military regime, Siad Barre had announced as early as 1971 the SRC's intention to establish a one-party state. The SRC already had begun organizing what was described as a "vanguard of the revolution" composed of members of a socialist elite drawn from the military and the civilian sectors. The National Public Relations Office (retitled the National Political Office in 1973) was formed to propagate scientific socialism with the support of the Ministry of Information and National Guidance through orientation centers that had been built around the country, generally as local selfhelp projects.

The SRC convened a congress of the Somali Revolutionary Socialist Party (SRSP) in June 1976 and voted to establish the Supreme Council as the new party's central committee. The council included the nineteen officers who composed the SRC, in addition to civilian advisers, heads of ministries, and other public figures. Civilians accounted for a majority of the Supreme Council's seventy-three members. On

July 1, 1976, the SRC dissolved itself, formally vesting power over the government in the SRSP under the direction of the Supreme Council.

In theory the SRSP's creation marked the end of military rule, but in practice real power over the party and the government remained with the small group of military officers who had been most influential in the SRC. Decision-making power resided with the new party's politburo, a select committee of the Supreme Council that was composed of five former SRC members, including Siad Barre and his son-in-law, NSS chief Abdullah. Siad Barre was also secretary general of the SRSP, as well as chairman of the Council of Ministers, which had replaced the CSS in 1981. Military influence in the new government increased with the assignment of former SRC members to additional ministerial posts. The MOD circle also had wide representation on the Supreme Council and in other party organs. Upon the establishment of the SRSP, the National Political Office was abolished; local party leadership assumed its functions.

Ogaden War

Main article: Ogaden War

In 1977 the Somali president, Siad Barre, was able to muster 35,000 regulars and 15,000 fighters of the Western Somali Liberation Front. His forces began infiltrating into the Ogaden in May-June 1977, and overt warfare began in July. By September 1977 Mogadishu controlled all of the Ogaden and had followed retreating Ethiopian forces into non-Somali regions of Harerge, Bale, and Sidamo.

After watching Ethiopian events in 1975-76, the Soviet Union concluded that the revolution would lead to the establishment of an authentic Marxist-Leninist state and that, for geopolitical purposes, it was wise to transfer Soviet interests to Ethiopia. To this end, Moscow secretly promised the Derg military aid on condition that it renounce the alliance with the United States. Mengistu Haile Mariam, believing that the Soviet Union's revolutionary history of national reconstruction was in keeping with Ethiopia's political goals, closed down the U.S. military mission and the communications centre in April 1977. In September, Moscow suspended all military aid to Somalia, and began to openly deliver weapons to its new ally, and reassigned military advisers from Somalia to Ethiopia. This Soviet volte-face also gained Ethiopia important support from North Korea, which trained a People's Militia, and from Cuba and the People's Democratic Republic of Yemen, which provided infantry, pilots, and armoured units. Somalia renounced the Treaty of Friendship and Cooperation with the Soviet Union expelled all Soviet advisers, broke diplomatic relations with Cuba, and ejected all Soviet personnel from Somalia

By March 1978, Ethiopia and its allies regained control over the Ogaden. Siad Barre proved unable to return the Ogaden to Somali rule, and the people grew restive; in northern Somalia, rebels destroyed administrative centres and took over major towns. Both Ethiopia and Somalia were unable to surmount droughts and famines that afflicted the Horn during the 1980s. In 1988 Siad and Mengistu agreed to withdraw their armies from further confrontation in the Ogaden.

Somalia, 1980-90

Repression

Faced with shrinking popularity and an armed and organized domestic resistance, Siad Barre unleashed a reign of terror against the Majeerteen, the Hawiye, and the Isaaq, carried out by the Red Berets (Duub Cas), a special unit recruited from the president's Marehan clansmen. Thus, by the beginning of 1986, Siad Barre's grip on power seemed secure, despite the host of problems facing the regime. The president received a severe blow from an unexpected quarter, however. On the evening of May 23, he was severely injured in an automobile accident. Astonishingly, although at the time he was in his early seventies and suffered from chronic diabetes, Siad Barre recovered sufficiently to resume the reins of government following a month's recuperation. But the accident unleashed a power struggle among senior army commandants, elements of the president's Marehan clan, and related factions, whose infighting practically brought the country to a standstill. Broadly, two groups contended for power: a constitutional faction and a clan faction. The constitutional faction was led by the senior vice president, Brigadier General Mahammad Ali Samantar; the second vice president, Major General Husseen Kulmiye; and generals Ahmad Sulaymaan Abdullah and Ahmad Mahamuud Faarah. The four, together with president Siad Barre, constituted the politburo of the SRSP.

Opposed to the constitutional group were elements from the president's Marehan clan, especially members of his immediate family, including his brother, Abdirahmaan Jaama Barre; the president's son, Colonel Masleh Siad, and the formidable Mama Khadiija, Siad Barre's senior wife. By some accounts, Mama Khadiija ran her own intelligence network, had well-placed political contacts, and oversaw a large group who had prospered under her patronage.

In November 1986, the dreaded Red Berets unleashed a campaign of terror and intimidation on a frightened citizenry. Meanwhile, the ministries atrophied and the army's officer corps was purged of competent career officers on suspicion of insufficient loyalty to the president. In addition, ministers and bureaucrats plundered what was left of the national treasury after it had been repeatedly skimmed by the top family.

The same month, the SRSP held its third congress. The Central Committee was reshuffled and the president was nominated as the only candidate for another seven-year term. Thus, with a weak opposition divided along clan lines, which he skillfully exploited, Siad Barre seemed invulnerable well into 1988. The regime might have lingered indefinitely but for the wholesale disaffection engendered by the genocidal policies carried out against important lineages of Somali kinship groupings. These actions were waged first against the Majeerteen clan (of the Darod clan-family), then against the Isaaq clans of the north, and finally against the Hawiye, who occupied the strategic central area of the country, which included the capital. The disaffection of the Hawiye and their subsequent organized armed resistance eventually caused the regime's downfall.

Somali Civil War

Main article: Somali Civil War

With worsening conditions in Somalia, rebels of the United Somali Congress (USC) led by Mohamed Farrah Aidid attacked Mogadishu and on January 26, 1991, Barre's government was taken out of power.

In May 1991, the northernwestern Somaliland region of Somalia declared its independence. This Isaaq-dominated governing zone is not recognized by any major international organization or country, although it has remained more stable and certainly more peaceful than the rest of Somalia, neighboring Puntland notwithstanding.

UN Security Council Resolution 794 was unanimously passed on December 3, 1992, which approved a coalition of United Nations peacekeepers led by the United States to form UNITAF, tasked with ensuring humanitarian aid being distributed and peace being established in Somalia until the humanitarian efforts were transferred to the UN. The UN humanitarian troops landed in 1993 and started a two-year effort (primarily in the south), known as UNOSOM II, to alleviate famine conditions.

US Army helicopter shortly before Battle of Mogadishu in 1993.

Many Somalis opposed the foreign presence. In October, several gun battles in Mogadishu between local gunmen and peacekeepers resulted in the death of 24 Pakistanis and 19 US soldiers (total US deaths were 31). Most of the Americans were killed in the Battle of Mogadishu. The incident later became the basis for the book and movie *Black Hawk Down*. The UN withdrew on March 3, 1995, having suffered more significant casualties. Order in Somalia still has not been restored.

Yet again another secession from Somalia took place in the northeastern region. The self-proclaimed state took the name Puntland after declaring "temporary" independence in 1998, with the intention that it would participate in any Somali reconciliation to form a new central government.

A third secession occurred in 1998 with the declaration of the state of Jubaland. The territory of Jubaland is now encompassed by the state of Southwestern Somalia and its status is unclear.

A fourth self-proclaimed entity led by the Rahanweyn Resistance Army (RRA) was set up in 1999, along the lines of the Puntland. That "temporary" secession was reasserted in 2002. This led to the autonomy of Southwestern Somalia. The RRA had originally set up an autonomous administration over the Bay and Bakool regions of south and central Somalia in 1999.

Recent history

Main articles: Anarchy in Somalia, Transitional Federal Government, Islamic Courts Union, Harakat al-Shabaab Mujahideen, War in Somalia (2006–2009), and War in Somalia (2009–)

The various Somali militias had at that point developed into security agencies for hire. Due to that development, security had much improved and an economic rebound occurred. Somalia was then arguably partly in a state of anarcho-capitalism, where all services were provided by private ventures. According to the CIA, Somalia's telecommunication firms provide wireless services in most major cities and offer the lowest international call rates on the continent.

In 2000, Abdiqasim Salad Hassan was selected to lead the Transitional National Government (TNG).

This was followed in 2004 by the establishment of the Transitional Federal Government (TFG) of the Republic of Somalia, the most recent attempt to restore national institutions to the nation after the 1991 collapse of the Barre regime and the ensuing civil war. On October 10, 2004, Somali parliament members elected Abdullahi Yusuf Ahmed, the former President of Puntland, to be the next president and head of the TFG. The other institutions adopted at this time were the Transitional Federal Charter and the selection of a 275-member Transitional Federal Parliament.

Though internationally recognized, the TFG's support in Somalia was waning until the United States-backed 2006 intervention by the Ethiopian military, which helped drive out the rival Islamic Courts Union (ICU) in Mogadishu and solidify the TFG's rule. Following this defeat, the ICU splintered into several different factions. Some of the more radical elements, including Al-Shabaab, regrouped to continue their insurgency against the TFG and oppose the Ethiopian military's presence in Somalia. Throughout 2007 and 2008, Al-Shabaab scored military victories, seizing control of key towns and ports in both central and southern Somalia. At the end of 2008, the group had captured Baidoa but not Mogadishu. By January 2009, Al-Shabaab and other militias had managed to force the Ethiopian troops to withdraw from the country, leaving behind an underequipped African Union (AU) peacekeeping force.

Over the next few months, a new President was elected from amongst the more moderate Islamists, and the Transitional Federal Government, with the help of a small team of African Union troops, began a counteroffensive in February 2009 to retake control of the southern half of the country. To solidify its control of southern Somalia, the TFG formed an alliance with the Islamic Courts Union and other members of the Alliance for the Re-liberation of Somalia. Furthermore, Al-Shabaab and Hizbul Islam, the two main Islamist groups in opposition, began to fight amongst themselves in mid 2009.

As a truce, in March 2009, Somalia's newly established coalition government announced that it would implement shari'a as the nation's official judicial system.

Timelines

Ancient

- **c. 2350 BC:** Egyptians establish trade with the Land of Punt
- **1st century AD:** Ports on the Somali coast are active in commerce trading with Greek, and later Roman merchants.

Muslim era

- **700 - 1000 AD:** the Port cities in Somalia trade with Arab merchants and adopt Islam
- **1300 - 1400 AD:** Mogadishu and other prosperous Somali city-states are visited by Ibn Battuta and Zheng he
- **1500 - 1660:** the rise and fall of the Adal Sultanate
- **1528 - 1535:** Jihad against Ethiopia led by Ahmad ibn Ibrihim al-Ghazi (also called Ahmed Gurey and Ahmed Gran; "the Left-handed")
- **1400 - 1700:** the Rise and Fall of the Ajuuraan Dynasty
- **1800 - 1900:** Geledi Sultanate/Hobyo Sultanate

Colonial era

- **20 July 1887 :** British Somaliland protectorate (in the north) subordinated to Aden to 1905.
- **3 August 1889:** Benadir Coast Italian Protectorate (in the northeast), (unoccupied until May 1893).
- **1900:** Mohammed Abdullah Hassan spearheads a Somali war against foreigners
- **16 March 1905:** Italian Somalia (Italian Somaliland) colony (in the northeast and in the south).
- **July 1910:** Italian Somaliland a crown colony.
- **1920:** Mohammed Abdullah Hassan (called "the Mad Mullah" by the British) dies and the longest and bloodiest colonial resistance war in Africa ends.
- **15 January 1935:** Italian Somalia part of Italian East Africa with Italian Eritrea (and from 1936 Ethiopia).
- **1 June 1936:** Part of Italian East Africa (province of Somalia, formed by the merger of the colony and the Ethiopian region of Ogaden; see Ethiopia).

World War II

- **18 August 1940:** Italian occupation of British Somaliland.
- **February 1941:** British administration of Italian Somalia.

Independence and Cold War

- **1 April 1950:** Italian Somalia becomes United Nations trust territory administration and Somalia is promised independence within 10 years.
- **26 June 1960:** Independence of British Somalia to reunite with Italian Somalia.
- **1 July 1960:** Reunification of British Somalia with Italian Somalia to form the Somali Republic.
- **1960 - 1967:** Presidency of Aden Abdullah Osman Daar
- **1967 - 1969:** Presidency of Abdirashid Ali Shermarke; assassinated by one of his own bodyguards.
- **21 October 1969:** Somali Democratic Republic
- **1969 - 1991:** Mohamed Siad Barre Leader of the Supreme Revolutionary Council rises to power.
- **23 July 1977 - 15 March 1978:** Ogaden War

- **1982**: 1982 Ethiopian-Somali Border War

See also

Main articles: Outline of Somalia and Index of Somalia-related articles

- Adal Sultanate
- Ajuuraan State
- Borama script
- Dervish State
- Gobroon Dynasty
- Greater Somalia
- Land of Punt
- Marehan sultanate
- Osmanya script
- Somali maritime history
- Somali people
- Sultanate of Hobyo
- Warsangali Sultanate
- Xeer

References

- Samatar (ed.), Said S. (November 9 2005). "Somalia Country Studies" [2]. *Federal Research Division of Library of Congress.*
- Aidid, Mohammed Farah; Dr. Satya Pal Ruhela (2001). "Somalia: From The Dawn of Civilization To The Modern Times" [3]. Civic Webs Virtual Library. Retrieved 2006-12-20.
- Aidid, Mohammed Farah; Dr. Satya Pal Ruhela (1993). *Somalia: From The Dawn of Civilization To The Modern Times* [3]. India: Vikas Publishing House PVT LTD. ISBN 0-7069-8004-2.

Geography of Somalia

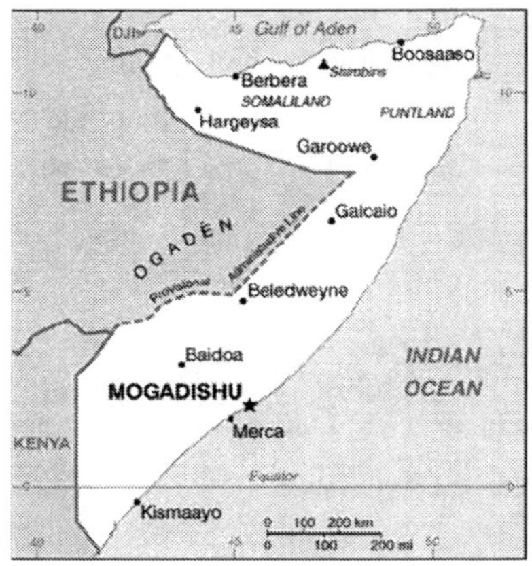

Africa's easternmost country. Somalia has a land area of 637,540 square kilometers. Somalia occupies the tip of a region commonly referred to as the Horn of Africa (because of its resemblance on the map to a rhinoceros' horn) that also includes Ethiopia, Eritrea and Djibouti. Somalia's terrain consists mainly of plateaus, plains, and highlands. In the far north, however, the rugged east-west ranges of the Karkaar Mountains lie at varying distances from the Gulf of Aden coast. The weather is hot throughout the year, except at the higher elevations in the north. Rainfall is sparse, and most of Somalia has a semiarid-to- arid environment suitable only for the nomadic pastoralism practiced by well over half the population. Only in limited areas of moderate rainfall in the northwest, and particularly in the southwest, where the country's two perennial rivers are found, is agriculture practiced to any extent.

The local geology suggests the presence of valuable mineral deposits. Somalia's long coastline (more than 3,300 kilometers) has been of importance chiefly in permitting trade with the Middle East and the rest of the Horn of Africa.

Climate

See also: Climate

Climate is the primary factor in much of Somali life. For the large nomadic population, the timing and amount of rainfall are crucial determinants of the adequacy of grazing and the prospects of relative prosperity. There are some indications that the climate has become drier in the last century and that the increase in the number of people and animals has put a growing burden on water and vegetation.

Somalis recognize four seasons, two rainy (*Du* and *Dayr*) and two dry (*Jiilaal* and *Xagaa*). The *gu* rains begin in April and last until June, producing a fresh supply of pasture and for a brief period turning the desert into a flowering garden. Lush vegetation covers most of the land, especially the central grazing plateau where grass grows tall. Milk and meat abound, water is plentiful, and animals do not require much care. The clans, reprieved from four months' drought, assemble to engage alternately in banter and poetic exchange or in a new cycle of hereditary feuds. They also offer sacrifices to Allah and to the founding clan ancestors, whose blessings they seek. Numerous social functions occur: marriages are contracted, outstanding disputes are settled or exacerbated, and a person's age is calculated in terms of the number of gu he or she has lived. The gu season is followed by the *hagaa* drought (July-September) and the hagaa by the day rains (October-November). Next is *jiilaal* (December-March), the harshest season for pastoralists and their herds.

Most of the country receives less than 500 millimeters (19.7 in) of rain annually, and a large area encompassing the northeast and much of northern Somalia receives as little as 50 to 150 millimeters (1.97 to 5.91 in). Certain higher areas in the north, however, record more than 500 millimeters (19.7 in) a year, as do some coastal sites. The southwest receives 330 to 500 millimeters (13.0 to 19.7 in). Generally, rainfall takes the form of showers or localized torrential rains and is extremely variable.

Mean daily maximum temperatures throughout the country range from 30 to 40 °C (86 to 104 °F), except at higher elevations and along the Indian Ocean coast. Mean daily minimum temperatures vary from 20 °C (68 °F) to more than 30 °C (86 °F). Northern Somalia experiences the greatest temperature extremes, with readings ranging from below freezing in the highlands in December to more than 45 °C (113 °F) in July in the coastal plain skirting the Gulf of Aden. The north's relative humidity ranges from about 40 percent in midafternoon to 85 percent at night, varying somewhat with the season. During the colder months, December to February, visibility at higher elevations is often restricted by fog.

Temperatures in the south are less extreme, ranging from about 20 to 40 °C (68 to 104 °F). The hottest months are February through April. Coastal readings are usually five to ten degrees cooler than those inland. The coastal zone's relative humidity usually remains about 70 percent even during the dry seasons.

Terrain, Vegetation, and Drainage

Satellite image of Somalia, generated from raster graphics data supplied by The Map Library

Physiographically, Somalia is a land of limited contrast. In the north, a maritime semidesert plain parallels the Gulf of Aden coast, varying in width from roughly twelve kilometers in the west to as little as two kilometers in the east. Scrub-covered and generally drab, this plain, known as the Guban (scrub land), is crossed by broad, shallow watercourses that are beds of dry sand except in the rainy seasons. When the rains arrive, the vegetation, which is a combination of low bushes and grass clumps, is quickly renewed, and for a time the guban provides some grazing for nomad livestock. This coastal strip is part of the Ethiopian xeric grasslands and shrublands ecoregion.

Inland from the gulf coast, the plain rises to the precipitous northward-facing cliffs of the dissected highlands. These form the rugged Karkaar mountain ranges that extend from the northwestern border with Ethiopia eastward to the tip of the Horn of Africa, where they end in sheer cliffs at Caseyr. The general elevation along the crest of these mountains averages about 1,800 meters above sea level south of the port town of Berbera, and eastward from that area it continues at 1,800 to 2,100 meters almost to Caseyr. The country's highest point, Shimber Berris, which rises to 2,407 meters, is located near the town of Erigavo.

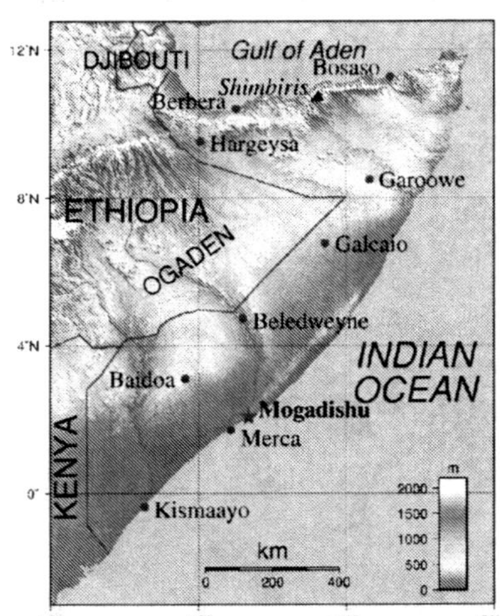

Topography of Somalia

Southward the mountains descend, often in scarped ledges, to an elevated plateau devoid of perennial rivers. This region of broken mountain terrain, shallow plateau valleys, and usually dry watercourses is known to the Somalis as the Ogo.

In the Ogo's especially arid eastern part, the plateau—broken by several isolated mountain ranges—gradually slopes toward the Indian Ocean and in central Somalia constitutes the Mudug Plain. A major feature of this eastern section is the long and broad Nugaal Valley, with its extensive network of intermittent seasonal watercourses. The Nugaal river enters the Indian Ocean at Eyl. The eastern area's population consists mainly of pastoral nomads eking a living in a zone of low and erratic rainfall.

The western part of the Ogo plateau region is crossed by numerous shallow valleys and dry watercourses. Annual rainfall is greater than in the east, and there are flat areas of arable land that provide a home for dryland cultivators. Most important, the western area has permanent wells to which the predominantly nomadic population returns during the dry seasons. The western plateau slopes gently southward and merges imperceptibly into an area known as the Haud, a broad, undulating terrain that constitutes some of the best grazing lands for Somali nomads, despite the lack of appreciable rainfall more than half the year. Enhancing the value of the Haud are the natural depressions that during periods of rain become temporary lakes and ponds.

The Haud zone continues for more than sixty kilometers into Ethiopia, and the vast Somali Plateau, which lies between the northern Somali mountains and the highlands of southeast Ethiopia, extends south and eastward through Ethiopia into central and southwest Somalia. The portion of the Haud lying within Ethiopia was the subject of an agreement made during the colonial era. In 1948, under pressure from their World War II allies and to the dismay of the Somalis, the British "returned" the Haud (an important Somali grazing area that was presumably 'protected' by British treaties with the Somalis in 1884 and 1886) and the Ogaden to Ethiopia, based on a an 1897 treaty in which the British ceded Somali territory to the Ethiopian Emperor Menelik in exchange for his help against plundering by Somali clans. Britain included the proviso that the Somali nomads would retain their autonomy, but Ethiopia immediately claimed sovereignty over them. This prompted an unsuccessful bid by Britain in 1956 to buy back the Somali lands it had turned over. The stretch of land has since been a considerable source of regional strife.

Southwestern Somalia is dominated by the country's only two permanent rivers, the Jubba and the Shabele. With their sources in the Ethiopian highlands, these rivers flow in a generally southerly direction, cutting wide valleys in the Somali Plateau as it descends toward the sea; the plateau's elevation falls off rapidly in this area. The adjacent coastal zone, which includes the lower reaches of the rivers and extends from the Mudug Plain to the Kenyan border, averages 180 meters above sea level.

The Jubba River enters the Indian Ocean at Kismaayo. Although the Shabeelle River at one time apparently also reached the sea near Merca, its course is thought to have changed in prehistoric times. The Shabeelle now turns southwestward near Balcad (about thirty kilometers north of Mogadishu) and parallels the coast for more than eighty-five kilometers. The river is perennial only to a point southwest of Mogadishu; thereafter it consists of swampy areas and dry reaches and is finally lost in the sand east of Jilib, not far from the Jubba River. During the flood seasons, the Shabeelle River may fill its bed to a point near Jilib and occasionally may even break through to the Jubba River farther south. Favorable rainfall and soil conditions make the entire riverine region a fertile agricultural area and the center of the country's largest sedentary population.

In most of northern, northeastern, and north-central Somalia, where rainfall is low, the vegetation consists of scattered low trees, including various acacias, and widely scattered patches of grass. This vegetation gives way to a combination of low bushes and grass clumps in the highly arid areas of the northeast and along the Gulf of Aden.

As elevations and rainfall increase in the maritime ranges of the north, the vegetation becomes denser. Aloes are common, and on the higher plateau areas of the Ogo are woodlands. At a few places above 1,500 meters, the remnants of juniper forests (protected by the state) and areas of Euphorbia candelabrum (a chandelier-type spiny plant) occur. In the more arid highlands of the northeast, *Boswellia* and *Commiphora* trees are sources, respectively, of the frankincense and myrrh for which Somalia has been known since ancient times.

Hargeisa and much of northwestern Somalia is desert or hilly terrain. Here, the Naasa Hablood hills are shown.

A broad plateau encompassing the northern city of Hargeysa, which receives comparatively heavy rainfall, is covered naturally by woodland (much of which has been degraded by overgrazing) and in places by extensive grasslands. Parts of this area have been under cultivation since the 1930s, producing sorghum and maize; in the 1990s it constituted the only significant region of sedentary cultivation outside southwestern Somalia.

The Haud south of Hargeysa is covered mostly by a semiarid woodland of scattered trees, mainly acacias, underlain by grasses that include species especially favored by livestock as forage. There vegetation forms spatially periodic patterns reminiscent of a tiger skin when viewed from above and therefore knowns as "Tiger bush". As the Haud merges into the Mudug Plain in central Somalia, the aridity increases and the vegetation takes on a subdesert character. Farther southward the terrain gradually changes to semiarid woodlands and grasslands as the annual precipitation increases.

The region encompassing the Shabeelle and Jubba rivers is relatively well watered and constitutes the country's most arable zone. The lowland between the rivers supports rich pasturage. It features arid to subarid savanna, open woodland, and thickets that include frequently abundant underlying grasses. There are areas of grassland, and in the far southwest, near the Kenyan border, some dry evergreen forests are found.

Along the Indian Ocean from Hobyo southwestward to near Mogadishu lies a stretch of dry coastal sand dunes, the Hobyo grasslands and shrublands ecoregion. This area is covered with scattered scrub and grass clumps where rainfall is sufficient although unpredictable. Much of this coast is thinly populated but overgrazing, particularly south of Mogadishu, has resulted in the destruction of the protective vegetation cover and the gradual movement of the once-stationary dunes inland. The original flora of this coast contains a number of endemic species and beginning in the early 1970s, efforts were made to stabilize these dunes by replanting. Endemic mammals are the Silver Dik-dik *(Madoqua piacentinii)*, one of the world's smallest antelopes, and the Somali golden mole *(Calcochloris tytonis)*. Other endemic species include two reptiles, a skink *Haackgreerius miopus* and a lizard *Latastia cherchii* and two birds, Ash's Lark *(Mirafra ashi)* and the Obbia Lark *(Spizocorys obbiensis)*. The longterm political strife in Somalia has meant the coast is poorly studied and the state of the habitat unknown.

Other vegetation includes plants and grasses found in the swamps into which the Shabeelle River empties most of the year and in other large swamps in the course of the lower Jubba River. Swamps of East African mangroves are found at points along the coast, particularly from Kismaayo to near the Kenyan border. Uncontrolled exploitation appears to have caused some damage to forests in that area. Other mangroves are located near Mogadishu and at a number of places along the northeastern and northern coasts.

Data

Location: East Africa, bordering the Gulf of Aden and the Indian Ocean, east of Ethiopia

Geographic coordinates: 10°00′N 49°00′E

Map references: Africa

Area:
total: 637,657 km²
land: 627,337 km²
water: 10,320 km²

Area - comparative: slightly smaller than Texas

Land boundaries:
total: 2,366 km
border countries: Djibouti 58 km, Ethiopia 1,626 km, Kenya 682 km

Coastline: 3,300 km

Maritime claims:
territorial sea: 200 nmi (370.4 km; 230.2 mi)

Climate: principally desert; December to February - northeast monsoon, moderate temperatures in north and very hot in south; May to October - southwest monsoon, torrid in the north and hot in the south, irregular rainfall, hot and humid periods (tangambili) between monsoons

Terrain: mostly flat to undulating plateau rising to hills in north

Elevation extremes:
lowest point: Indian Ocean 0 m
highest point: Shimbiris 2,416 m

Natural resources: uranium and largely unexploited reserves of iron ore, tin, gypsum, bauxite, copper, salt

Land use:
arable land: 2%
permanent crops: 0%
permanent pastures: 69%
forests and woodland: 26%
other: 3% (1993 est.)

Irrigated land: 1,800 km² (1993 est.)

Natural hazards: recurring droughts; frequent dust storms over eastern plains in summer; floods during rainy season

Environment - current issues: famine; use of contaminated water contributes to human health problems; deforestation; overgrazing; soil erosion; desertification

Environment - international agreements:
party to: Endangered Species, Law of the Sea
signed, but not ratified: Marine Dumping, Nuclear Test Ban

Geography - note: strategic location on Horn of Africa along southern approaches to Bab el Mandeb and route through Red Sea and Suez Canal

See also

- Somalia
- List of cities in Somalia

References

General references

- Hadden, Robert Lee. 2007. "The Geology of Somalia: A Selected Bibliography of Somalian Geology, Geography and Earth Science." [1] Engineer Research and Development Laboratories, Topographic Engineering Center (now known as the Army Geospatial Center, US Army Corps of Engineers), in Alexandria, VA. Includes data and citations on the geology, geography, water and transportation in Somalia.

Politics of Somalia

Somalia

This article is part of the series:
Politics and government of Somalia

- Transitional Federal Charter

- **Executive**
  - Transitional Federal Government
  - President
    - Sharif Ahmed
  - Acting Prime Minister
    - Abdiwahid Elmi Gonjeh
  - Ministry of Defense
    - Military of Somalia
  - Council of Ministers

- **Legislative**
  - Transitional Federal Parliament
    - List of MPs

- **Judiciary**
  - Judiciary of Somalia

- **States**
  - Puntland
    - Oil exploration in Puntland
  - Galmudug
  - Maakhir
  - Somaliland
    (*de facto* independent state)
    - Politics of Somaliland

- States
- Regions and districts

- Elections
- Political parties

- Foreign relations
- Human Rights

Other countries · Atlas
Politics portal

The **politics of Somalia** are defined by the state of civil war which, since 1991, has divided the country. What started out as various warring entities and autonomist and secessionist regions fighting for control developed into a fragile government fighting an Islamic insurgency. In 1991, Mohammed Siad Barre fell. There was no permanent government until 2004. In 2004, a transitional federal government was formed. This had a 5-year mandate. The transitional federal assembly has 275-seats that has members chosen from various clans. There are 18 administrative regions. Somalia is full of different political parties. Due to the transitional government the political parties make no affect on it.

At the beginning of 2007 Somalia was consolidating under the Transitional Federal Government (TFG), which recently completed a military campaign against the Islamic Courts Union (ICU). The Islamic Courts Union is now part of the TFG, along with the Alliance for the Re-liberation of Somalia The TFG is supported by the United Nations. Until recently, it governed out of an administrative capital in Baidoa. In the last days of 2006, forces of the transitional government supported by Ethiopian forces ousted the ICU from Mogadishu. Peace keeping forces from the African Union are expected to support the transitional government in its bid to control the country.

During the war against the ICU, the autonomous states of Puntland and Galmudug had closely aligned themselves with the TFG and the supporting Ethiopian forces, while other former administrations such as Southwestern Somalia, Hiraanland and the Juba Valley Alliance fully integrated themselves with the TFG.

Somalia became a united independent state on 1 July 1960 upon the merger of British Somaliland, which had become independent from the British five days earlier on 26 June 1960 and Italian Somaliland, which became independent from the Italian-administered United Nations trusteeship on 1 July to form the Somali Republic. The territory that was once British Somaliland is the area that now forms Somaliland.

Political overview

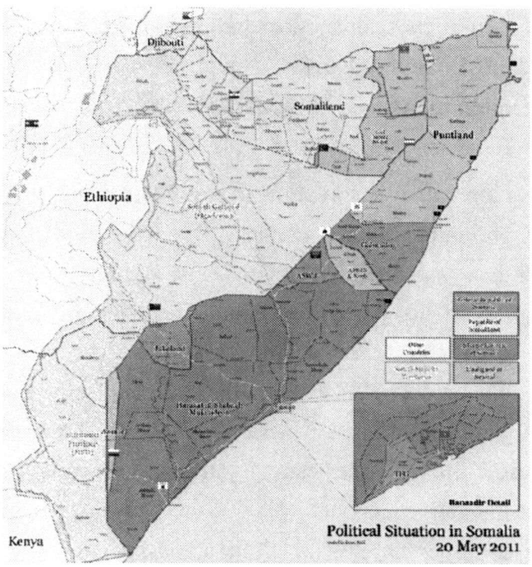

Map of Somalia's autonomous regions

Somalia had a middle functioning government following the United Somali Congress (USC) ouster of Major General Siad Barre in 1991. The political situation of the Somali Civil War has been marked by chaos, interclan fighting, random banditry, internecine warfare between proto-governments and resistance to the state. The breakaway country such as Somaliland and Puntland put together functional regional governance. In the rest of the country there are a wide range of semi-functional governments and anarchic conditions under various warlords (Anarchy in Somalia, 1991-2006).

In 2000, the international community recognised the Transitional National Government, originally headed by Abdulkassim Salat Hassan, as the government for the entire country. The government only recently was able to enter the capital because of the violence occurring within the country(see Fall of Mogadishu).

On October 14, 2004 Somali members of parliament elected warlord Abdullahi Yusuf Ahmed, previously president of Puntland, to be the next president. He appointed a cabinet led by Prime Minister Ali Mohamed Ghedi. Because of the situation in Mogadishu, the election was held in a sports centre in Nairobi, Kenya. Yusuf was elected transitional President by Somalia's transitional parliament. He won 189 of the 275 votes from members of parliament. The session of Parliament was also held in neighbouring Kenya. His government is recognized by most western nations as legitimate, although his actual authority is still limited.

Many other small political organizations exist, some clan-based, others seeking a Somalia free from clan-based politics (such as the United Somali Front). Many of them have come into existence since the new president was chosen.

On June 5, 2006, the Islamic Courts Union (ICU) defeated the Alliance for the Restoration of Peace and Counter-Terrorism (ARPCT) in the Second Battle of Mogadishu, bringing the ICU to power in the capital. The ICU took control of much of southern Somalia, with the goal of restoring law and order and instituting Islamic sharia law. Talks between the ICU and the TFG did not lead to reconciliation or settlement. In September 2006, a proposal by the Inter-Governmental Authority on Development and the African Union to introduce an 8,000 strong peacekeeping force into Somalia was rejected by the ICU (see IGASOM). Islamist leaders threatened to turn the country into a graveyard for foreign soldiers should peacekeepers be introduced.

The Transitional Federal Government has ambassadors in a few countries, including but not limited to Arab League states such as Saudi Arabia, United Arab Emirates, Kuwait, Egypt and Libya. It also represents Somalia in the United Nations, the Organization of African Unity (OAU), the Arab League, IGAD, and other multilateral organizations.

Until the start of 2007 the Islamic Courts Union operated a government in Mogadishu, after consolidating power from factions of warlords that previously shared control. The ICU leaders are Sheikh Sharif Ahmed, head of the executive committee, and Sheikh Hassan Dahir Aweys, head of Shura. The USA accuses Aweys and other ICU leaders of links with terrorism. The Islamic Courts Union (ICU) brought a degree of law and order to Somalia for the first time since the central government collapsed in 1991. It included the implementation of Sharia Islamic law. But they were driven out of Somalia in late 2006 and early 2007 by a joint Ethiopian-American offensive.Thousands of Ethiopian troops poured across the border, backed up by American air strikes and American intelligence. The Islamic Courts Union (ICU) then went underground.

The Transitional Federal Government is not a liberal democracy because it operates not from a Constitution, but from its authority outlined in the Transitional Federal Charter of the Somali Republic which was ratified by the Transitional Federal Parliament (TFP) consisting of mostly *de facto* powers, such as warlords and other closely selected representatives. There were no general elections for parliament. The Parliament also elected President Abdullahi Yusuf Ahmed; he was not elected by popular vote.

Somalia's transitional parliament fired its former speaker Sharif Hassan Sheikh Aden and 30 other lawmakers for failing to attend sessions in recent months on April 17, 2007.

Politics since 1991

The flag of Somalia

In the wake of the collapse of the Somali Government in 1991, factions organized around military leaders took control of Somalia, a form of government referred to as warlordism. The resulting chaos and loss of life provided the context for the international intervention led by the United Nations and the United States (see UNOSOM I, UNITAF and UNOSOM II). Because of local resistance to external interference, culminating in the First Battle of Mogadishu, UN operations in Somalia were curtailed, then finally withdrawn in 1995.

Main article: Factions in the Somali Civil War

Since 1991, there have been fourteen efforts at national reconciliation; to date, none has been successful. Various groupings of Somali factions have sought to control the national territory (or portions thereof) and have fought small wars with one another. Somaliland (Somali: Jamhuuriyadda Soomaaliland, Arabic: أرض الصومال Arḍ aṣ-Ṣūmāl) is a territory located in the Horn of Africa. It is regarded internationally as being an autonomous region of Somalia.[2][3] Although no sovereign state has recognised the independence of Somaliland, Israel and other regional states have expressed this possibility.[4] Since 1991 it has been governed by a secessionist administration as the Republic of Somaliland,[1] which is considered a de facto independent state.[5][6][7]

The breakaway republic, which declared its independence in May 1991,[8][9] remains unrecognised by any state or international organisation.[10][11] Although many foreign governments maintain informal ties with the state, with an increasing number of foreign delegations and embassies having been established in the capital Hargeisa, it does not have full diplomatic recognition.[12][13]

Somaliland is bordered by Ethiopia in the south and west, Djibouti in the northwest, the Gulf of Aden in the north, and by the Somalian region of Puntland in the east, covering most of the territory of the former British Somaliland protectorate.

In the northwest, there is the secessionist country of Somaliland with its capital in Hargeisa that declared its independence in 1991. This governing zone is not recognized by any major international organization or country, although it has remained more stable and certainly more peaceful than the rest of Somalia, neighboring Puntland notwithstanding.

Puntland in the northeast also remains autonomous but supports the Transitional Government and, unlike Somaliland, still considers itself a part of the Somali Republic. Abdullahi Yusuf Ahmed, Puntland's original president, ruled until mid-2001. In November 2001, a convention of elders, in a process disputed by Yusuf, selected Col. Jama Ali Jama to succeed him. Forces loyal to Yusuf, who had retreated to Galkayo, attacked Garowe in November, resulting in a de facto division of Puntland. As many as 30 other factions vie for some degree of authority in the country.

Main article: Disarmament in Somalia

Efforts at mediation of the Somali internal dispute have been undertaken by many regional states. In the mid-1990s, Ethiopia played host to several Somali peace conferences and initiated talks at the Ethiopian city of Sodere, which led to some degree of agreement between competing factions. The Governments of Egypt, Yemen, Kenya, and Italy also have attempted to bring the Somali factions together. In 1997, the Organization of African Unity and the Intergovernmental Authority on Development (IGAD) gave Ethiopia the mandate to pursue Somali reconciliation. In 2000, Djibouti hosted a major reconciliation conference (the 13th such effort), which in August resulted in creation of the Transitional National Government, with a 3-year mandate to pursue national reconciliation. In early 2002, Kenya organized a further reconciliation effort under IGAD auspices.

On October 10, 2004, the Transitional Federal Parliament elected Abdullahi Yusuf Ahmed, president of Puntland, to be the next President and formed a new Transitional Federal Government. Because of the situation in Mogadishu, the election was held in a sports centre in Nairobi. The government located for a time to Baidoa. It has suffered internal crises, such as ministers quitting and a no confidence vote, but has survived.

The flag of the Supreme Islamic Courts Council

Main articles: Rise of the Islamic Courts Union (2006) and War in Somalia (2006–present)

In 2006 there emerged the Islamic Courts Union, supported by local businessmen who wanted to reclaim the country from factions of warlords, which effectively ruled it. Sharia Islamic law was briefly enforced in areas controlled by the Islamic Courts Union. They steadily widened the area they controlled and stopped just short of Baidoa, where the transitional government with support by Ethiopia managed to check their advance. Subsequent fighting resulted in the complete oust of the ICU.

The absence of a functioning central government in Somalia since 1991 has allowed outside forces to become more influential by supporting various groups and persons in Somalia. Djibouti, Eritrea, and Arab states have supported the Transitional Federal Government but, following the emergence of the Islamic Courts Union, and the intercession of its regional rival, Ethiopia, Eritrea switched support.

Ethiopia has provided political support to Somaliland and for a time assisted a group of southern warlords organized as the Somalia Reconciliation and Restoration Council (SRRC), which opposed the TFG. The warlords were also supported by the United States.

Ethiopia and the United States strongly opposed the Islamic Courts Union and both now support the nascent federal government. Ethiopian forces are located throughout southern and central Somalia, including the capital Mogadishu.

Since the end of the war with the ICU, Puntland has been under enormous economic and political pressures due to renewed feuding with Somaliland, internal turmoil over the proceeds and land use rights of natural resource exploration especially in non-Majerteen territories in Sool and Sanaag, and support for the TFG in the south. This culminated in the breakaway of Puntland-administered Sanaag into a new state, Maakhir but now almost all that area is, since 2005, under control of the Somaliland Republic. Somaliland forces launched massive military operation and took over large parts of the remaining land of Sool and Sanaag including Las Anod, Sool headquarter.

In January 2009, the former chairman of the Islamic Courts Union movement, Sheikh Sharif Ahmed, was elected president of Somalia in the second round of balloting held in the capital of neighboring Djibouti. Sharif received 293 of the 421 votes cast.

In late February, 2009, fighting between Islamists & AU peacekeepers resulted in 69 dead.

Hassan Dahir Aweys, who lead the Islamic Courts along with Sharif Ahmed returned to Somalia from Eritrea in Spring 2009 still opposing the TFG. Intensive fighting resumed in Somalia in May 2009, where Al-Shabaab forces along with their allies, Hizbul Islam have fought the coalition government composed of Islamic Courts Union fighters still loyal to Sharif plus the various clan militias in Mogadishu, surrounding areas of Hiiraan, Galgaduud, and the Shabelle. AU Peacekeepers remain in Mogadishu guarding the port, Villa Somalia, and the airport.

Executive branch

Further information: Transitional Federal Government

Main office holders

Office	Name	Party	Since
The following persons are *de jure* office holders			
President	Sharif Ahmed		31 January 2009
Acting Prime Minister	Abdiwahid Elmi Gonjeh		24 September 2010

Cabinet

Cabinet Position	Office Holder
Minister of Planning	Abdirahman Abdishakur Warsame
Minister of Internal Affairs	Sheikh Abdiqadir Ali Umar
Minister of Higher Education	Prof. Ibrahim Hassan Addow †
Minister of Information	Dahir Mohammud Guelleh
Minister of Justice	Sheikh Abdirahman Janaqow
Minister of Defense	Abdalla Boss Ahmed
Minister of National Security	Abdullahi Mohammed Ali
Minister of Finance	Sharif Hassan Sheikh Aden
Minister of Foreign Affairs	Ali Jama Jangeli
Minister of Health	Qamar Aden Ali †
Minister of Agriculture	Hassan Mohammed Nur Shatigadud
Minister of Rural Development	Khadijo Mohammed Diriye
Minister of Women and Family Affairs	Fowsiyo Mohammed Sheikh
Minister of Ports and Marine Transportation	Mohammed Ibrahim Habsade
Minister of Fisheries	Prof. Abdirahman Aden Ibbi

minister of federalism & constitutional

```
affairs
Madobe Nunow mohamed
```

†Killed in the 2009 Hotel Shamo bombing.

Legislative branch

Further information: Transitional Federal Parliament

The Transitional Federal Parliament has 275 members, with each of Somalia's four major clans getting 61 seats in the parliament, while an alliance of minority clans was awarded 31 seats.

Political parties and elections

Main article: List of political parties in Somalia

Main article: Elections in Somalia

Administrative divisions

Somalia is divided in 18 regions (plural - NA, singular - gobolka); Awdal, Bakool, Banaadir, Bari, Bay, Galguduud, Gedo, Hiiraan, Jubbada Dhexe, Jubbada Hoose, Mudug, Nugaal, Sanaag, Shabeellaha Dhexe, Shabeellaha Hoose, Sool, Togdheer, Woqooyi Galbeed. The North-Western regions seceded as Somaliland

International organization participation

Somalia is member of ACP, AfDB, AFESD, AL, AMF, CAEU, ECA, FAO, G-77, IBRD, ICAO, ICRM, IDA, IDB, IFAD, IFC, IFRCS, IGAD, ILO, IMF, IMO, Intelsat, Interpol, IOC, IOM (observer), ITU, NAM, OAU, OIC, UN, UNCTAD, UNESCO, UNHCR, UNIDO, UPU, WFTU, WHO, WIPO, WMO, WTrO (observer)

See also

- Somali Civil War
- Factions in the Somali Civil War
- Kritarchy
- Anarchy in Somalia

External links

- BBC Country Profile [1] for Somalia
- report about Somalian Economy [2] (perhaps dated)

Economy of Somalia

Economy of Somalia	
Currency	Somali shilling (SOS)
Trade organisations	AL, AU, CEN-SAD, IGAD
Statistics	
GDP	$5.731 billion (2009)
GDP growth	2.6% (2009)
GDP per capita	$600 (2009)
GDP by sector	agriculture (65%), industry (10%), services (25%) (2005)
Labour force	3.447 million (2007)
Labour force by occupation	agriculture (71%), industry and services 29% (1975)
Main industries	sugar refining, textiles, livestock, money transfer, telecommunications
External	
Exports	$300 million (2006)
Export goods	livestock, bananas, hides, fish, charcoal, scrap metal
Main export partners	UAE 56.8%, Yemen 21.2%, Saudi Arabia 3.7% (2008)
Imports	$798 million (2006)
Import goods	manufactures, petroleum products, foodstuffs, construction materials
Main import partners	Djibouti 30.3%, Kenya 7.9%, India 7.7%, US 6.2%, Oman 5.8%, UAE 5.7%, Yemen 4.9% (2008)
Public finances	
Public debt	$3 billion (2001)
Main data source: CIA World Fact Book [3] *All values, unless otherwise stated, are in US dollars*	

According to the CIA and the Central Bank of Somalia, despite experiencing civil unrest, Somalia has maintained a healthy informal economy, based mainly on livestock, remittance/money transfer companies and telecommunications. Due to a dearth of formal government statistics and the recent civil war, it is difficult to gauge the size or growth of the economy. For 1994, the CIA estimated the GDP at $3.3 billion. In 2001, it was estimated to be $4.1 billion. By 2009, the CIA estimated that the GDP had grown to $5.731 billion, with a projected real growth rate of 2.6%. According to a 2007 British

Chambers of Commerce report, the private sector also grew, particularly in the service sector. Unlike the pre-civil war period when most services and the industrial sector were government-run, there has been substantial, albeit unmeasured, private investment in commercial activities; this has been largely financed by the Somali diaspora, and includes trade and marketing, money transfer services, transportation, communications, fishery equipment, airlines, telecommunications, education, health, construction and hotels. Libertarian economist Peter T. Leeson attributes this increased economic activity to the Somali customary law (referred to as *Xeer*), which he suggests provides a stable environment to conduct business in.

Agriculture and natural resources

See also: Mineral industry of Somalia

The Central Bank of Somalia indicates that the country's GDP per capita is $333, which is lower than that of Kenya at $350, but better than that of Tanzania at $280 as well as Eritrea at $190 and Ethiopia at $100. About 43% of the population live on less than 1 US dollar a day, with about 24% of those found in urban areas and 54% living in rural areas.

Cans of *Las Qoray* brand tuna fish made in Las Khorey.

As with neighboring countries, Somalia's economy consists of both traditional and modern production, with a gradual shift in favor of modern industrial techniques taking root. According to the Central Bank of Somalia, about 80% of the population are nomadic or semi-nomadic pastoralists, who keep goats, sheep, camels and cattle. The nomads also gather resins and gums to supplement their income.

Agriculture is the most important economic sector. It accounts for about 65% of the GDP and employs 65% of the workforce. Livestock contributes about 40% to GDP and more than 50% of export earnings. Other principal exports include fish, charcoal and bananas; sugar, sorghum and corn are products for the domestic market. According to the Central Bank of Somalia, imports of goods total about $460 million per year, and have recovered and even surpassed aggregate imports prior to the start of the civil war in 1991. Exports, which total about $270 million annually, have also surpassed pre-war aggregate export levels but still lead to a trade account deficit of about $190 million US dollars per year. However, this trade deficit is far exceeded by remittances sent by Somalis in the diaspora, which have helped sustain the import level.

With the advantage of being located near the Arabian Peninsula, Somali traders have increasingly begun to challenge Australia's traditional dominance over the Gulf Arab livestock and meat market, offering quality animals at very low prices. In response, Gulf Arab states have started to make strategic investments in the country, with Saudi Arabia building livestock export infrastructure and the United Arab Emirates purchasing large farmlands. Somalia is also a major world supplier of frankincense and myrrh. Additionally, fishing fleets from Europe and Asia have reached commercial fishing agreements in the northern Puntland region.

Manufacturing

The modest industrial sector, based on the processing of agricultural products, accounts for 10% of Somalia's GDP.

The new Coca-Cola bottling plant in Mogadishu, a sign of growing business confidence.

Prior to the outbreak of the civil war in 1991, the roughly 53 state-owned small, medium and large manufacturing firms were foundering, with the ensuing conflict destroying many of the remaining industries. However, primarily as a result of substantial local investment by the Somali diaspora, many of these small-scale plants have re-opened and newer ones have been created. The latter include fish-canning and meat-processing plants in the north, as well as about 25 factories in the Mogadishu area, which manufacture pasta, mineral water, confections, plastic bags, fabric, hides and skins, detergent and soap, aluminum, foam mattresses and pillows, fishing boats, carry out packaging, and stone processing.

According to the UNDP, investments in light manufacturing have expanded in Bosaso, Hargeisa and Mogadishu, in particular, indicating growing business confidence in the economy. To this end, in 2004, an $8.3 million Coca-Cola bottling plant opened in Mogadishu, with investors hailing from various constituencies in Somalia. The robust private sector has also attracted foreign investment from the likes of General Motors and Dole Fruit.

Airline industry

Air Somalia plane in Sharjah, United Arab Emirates. Somalia today has a thriving private airline industry.

Prior to the civil war, Somalia had only one national airline, Somali Airlines, that serviced the entire country. Due to the entrepreneurial spirit of the Somali people and a lack of strict regulatory frameworks, by 1997, up to 14 private airline firms operating 62 aircrafts were offering commercial flights to international locations. With competitively priced flight tickets, these companies have helped buttress Somalia's bustling trade networks.

Prominent Somali-owned private airlines include Air Somalia and Daallo Airlines, which serve several domestic locations including Bosaso and Hargeisa, as well as international destinations such as Dubai and Jeddah.

Hospitality

Somalia's hospitality sector has seen an unprecedented level of growth in the past few years. Much construction is taking place in Mogadishu and other major urban centers, encouraging the formation of new restaurants and hotels. Private-security militias are hired to ensure safety and the normal conduct of business.

Telecommunications and media

The Hormuud Telecom building in Mogadishu.

Somalia now offers some of the most technologically advanced and competitively priced telecommunications and internet services in the world. After the start of the civil war, various new telecommunications companies began to spring up and compete to provide missing infrastructure. Funded by Somali entrepreneurs and backed by expertise from China, Korea and Europe, these nascent telecommunications firms offer affordable mobile phone and internet services that are not available in many other parts of the continent. Customers can conduct money transfers and other banking activities via mobile phones, as well as easily gain wireless internet access.

After forming partnerships with multinational corporations such as Sprint, ITT and Telenor, these firms now offer the cheapest and clearest phone calls in Africa. Installation time for a landline is just three days, while in Kenya to the south, waiting lists are many years long. These Somali telecommunication companies also provide services to every city, town and hamlet in Somalia. There are presently around 25 mainlines per 1,000 persons, and the local availability of telephone lines (*tele-density*) is higher than in neighboring countries; three times greater than in adjacent Ethiopia. Prominent Somali telecommunications companies include Golis Telecom Group, Hormuud Telecom, Somafone, Nationlink, Netco, Telcom and Somali Telecom Group. Hormuud Telecom alone grosses about $40 million a year. Despite their rivalry, several of these companies signed an interconnectivity deal in 2005 that allows them to set prices, maintain and expand their networks, and ensure that competition does not get out of control.

Investment in the telecom industry is one of the clearest signs that Somalia's economy has continued to grow despite the ongoing civil strife in parts of the southern half of the country. Although in need of some regulation, the sector provides invaluable communication services, and in the process, greatly facilitates job creation and income generation.

As of 2005, there were also 20 privately-owned Somali newspapers, 12 radio and television stations, and numerous internet sites offering information to the public. Several local satellite-based television services transmit international news stations, such as CNN. In addition, one of Somalia's upstart media firms recently established a partnership with the BBC.

Finance

Main articles: Central Bank of Somalia and Somali shilling

The Central Bank of Somalia is the official monetary authority of Somalia. In terms of financial management, it is in the process of assuming the task of both formulating and implementing monetary policy.

Owing to a lack of confidence in the local currency, the US dollar is widely accepted as a medium of exchange alongside the Somali shilling. Dollarization notwithstanding, the large issuance of the Somali shilling has increasingly fueled price hikes, especially for low value transactions. This inflationary environment, however, is expected to come to an end as soon as the Central Bank assumes full control of monetary policy and replaces the presently circulating currency introduced by the private sector.

Although Somalia has had no central monetary authority for upwards of 15 years between the outbreak of the civil war in 1991 and the subsequent re-establishment of the Central Bank of Somalia in 2009, the nation's payment system is actually fairly advanced due primarily to the widespread existence of private money transfer operators (MTO) that have acted as informal banking networks.

A Dahabshiil franchise outlet in Columbus, Ohio.

These remittance firms (*hawalas*) have become a large industry in Somalia, with an estimated $1.6 billion USD annually remitted to the region by Somalis in the diaspora via money transfer companies. The latter include Dahabshiil, Qaran Express, Mustaqbal, Amal Express, Kaah Express, Hodan Global, Olympic, Amana Express, Iftin Express and Tawakal Express. Most are credentialed members of the Somali Money Transfer Association (SOMTA), an umbrella organization that regulates the community's money transfer sector, or its predecessor, the Somali Financial Services Association (SFSA). A unique feature of the Somali funds transfer companies is that they all charge the same low commission of 5% for sending amounts of up to approximately $1000, a fee range that encompasses the vast majority of household Somali remittances. For amounts greater than $1000, these companies charge commission fees of between 3%-4%, significantly lower than Western Union's 7.1% fee and MoneyGram's 7.2% fee for sending the same amount to Ethiopia. The bulk of remittances are sent by Somalis based abroad to relatives in Somalia, a practice which has had a stimulating effect on the country's economy.

Dahabshiil is the largest of the Somali money transfer operators (MTO), having captured most of the market vacated by Al-Barakaat. The firm has its headquarters in London and employs more than 2000 people across 144 countries, with 130 branches in the United Kingdom alone, a further 130 branches in Somalia, and 400 branches globally, including one in Dubai. The company provides a broad range of financial services to international organisations, as well as to both large and small businesses and private individuals. After Dahabshiil, Qaran Express is the largest Somali-owned funds transfer company. The firm has its headquarters in both London and Dubai, with 175 agents worldwide, 66 agents in Somalia and 64 in London, and charges nothing for remitting charity funds. Mustaqbal is the third most prominent Somali MTO, with 8 agents in Somalia and 49 in the UK. As with Dahabshiil and Qaran Express, it also has a notable presence internationally.

As the reconstituted Central Bank of Somalia fully assumes its monetary policy responsibilities, some of the existing money transfer companies are expected in the near future to seek licenses so as to develop into full-fledged commercial banks. This will serve to expand the national payments system to include formal cheques, which in turn is expected to reinforce the efficacy of the use of monetary policy in domestic macroeconomic management.

Energy

The World Bank reports that electricity is now in large part supplied by local businesses, using generators purchased abroad. By dividing Somalia's cities into specific quarters, the private sector has found a manageable method of providing cities with electricity. A customer is given a menu of choices for electricity tailored to his or her needs, such as evenings only, daytime only, 24 hour-supply or charge per lightbulb.

Somalia has untapped reserves of numerous natural resources, including uranium, iron ore, tin, gypsum, bauxite, copper, salt and natural gas. Due to its proximity to the oil-rich Gulf Arab states such as Saudi Arabia and Yemen, the nation is also believed to contain substantial unexploited reserves of oil. A survey of Northeast Africa by the World Bank and U.N. ranked Somalia second only to Sudan as the top prospective producer. American, Australian and Chinese oil companies, in particular, are excited about the prospect of finding petroleum and other natural resources in the country. An oil group listed in Sydney, Range Resources, anticipates that the Puntland province in the north has the potential to produce 5 billion to 10 billion barrels of oil. As a result of these developments, the Somali Petroleum Company was created by the federal government.

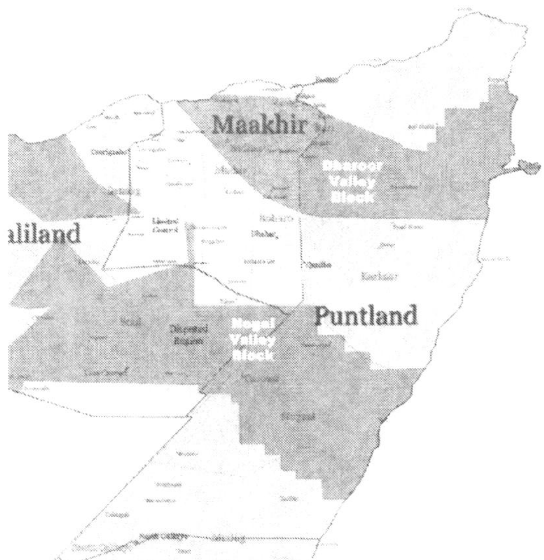

Oil blocks in Puntland.

According to surveys, uranium is also found in large quantities in the Buurhakaba region. A Brazilian company in the 1980s had invested $300 million for a uranium mine in central Somalia, but no long-term mining took place.

Additionally, the Puntland region under the Farole administration has since sought to refine the province's existing oil deal with Range Resources. The Australian oil firm, for its part, indicated that it looked forward to establishing a mutually beneficial and profitable working relationship with the region's new government.

In mid-2010, Somalia's business community also pledged to invest $1 billion in the national gas and electricity industries over the following five years. Abdullahi Hussein, the director of the just-formed Trans-National Industrial Electricity and Gas Company, predicted that the investment strategy would create 100,000 jobs, with the net effect of stimulating the local economy and discouraging unemployed youngsters from turning to vice. The new firm was established through the merger of five Somali companies from the trade, finance, security and telecommunications sectors. The first phase of the project is scheduled to start within six months of the establishment of the company, and will train youth to supply electricity to economic areas and communities. The second phase, which is slated to begin in mid-to-late 2011, will see the construction of factories in specially designated economic zones for the fishing, agriculture, livestock and mining industries.

According to the Central Bank of Somalia, as the nation embarks on the path of reconstruction, the economy is expected to not only match its pre-civil war levels, but also to accelerate in growth and development due to the Somalia's untapped natural resources.

See also

- Anarchy in Somalia

External links

- Economy of Somalia [1] at the Open Directory Project
- CIA World Factbook: Somalia [2]

Culture of Somalia

Culture of Somalia

Art
Architecture
Pottery · Textile
Music · Wood carving
Language
Literature · Mythology
Writing systems · Poetry
Other
Dance · Dress
Games · Cuisine
Society · History
Islam · Festivals · Institutions
Science and Technology
Maritime · Medicine · Astronomy · Media
Cinema · Coinage
See also
Education · Politics
Symbols · Military

The **culture of Somalia** is an amalgamation of traditions indigenously developed or accumulated over a timeline spanning several millennia of Somali civilization's interaction with neighbouring and far away civilizations such as Ethiopia, Yemen, India and Persia.

Languages

Main articles: Somali language and Languages of Somalia

The Somali language is the official language of Somalia. It is a member of the Cushitic branch of the Afro-Asiatic language family, and its nearest relatives are the Afar and Oromo languages. Somali is the best documented of the Cushitic languages, with academic studies of it dating from before 1900.

The Osmanya writing script.

Somali dialects are divided into three main groups: Northern, Benaadir and Maay. Northern Somali (or Northern-Central Somali) forms the basis for Standard Somali. Benaadir (also known as Coastal Somali) is spoken on the Benadir coast from Cadale to south of Merca, including Mogadishu, as well as in the immediate hinterland. The coastal dialects have additional phonemes which do not exist in Standard Somali. Maay is principally spoken by the Digil and Mirifle (Rahanweyn) clans in the southern areas of Somalia.

Since Somali had long lost its ancient script, a number of writing systems have been used over the years for transcribing the language. Of these, the Somali alphabet is the most widely used, and has been the official writing script in Somalia since the government of former President of Somalia Siad Barre formally introduced it in October 1972.

The script was developed by the Somali linguist Shire Jama Ahmed specifically for the Somali language, and uses all letters of the English Latin alphabet except *p*, *v* and *z*. Besides Ahmed's Latin script, other orthographies that have been used for centuries for writing Somali include the long-established Arabic script and Wadaad's writing. Indigenous writing systems developed in the twentieth century include the Osmanya, Borama and Kaddare scripts, which were invented by Osman Yusuf Kenadid, Sheikh Abdurahman Sheikh Nuur and Hussein Sheikh Ahmed Kaddare, respectively.

In addition to Somali, Arabic is an official national language in Somalia. Many Somalis speak it due to centuries-old ties with the Arab World, the far-reaching influence of the Arabic media, and religious education.

English is also widely used and taught. Italian used to be a major language, but its influence significantly diminished following independence. It is now most frequently heard among older generations. Other minority languages include Bravanese, a variant of Swahili that is spoken along the coast by the Bravanese people.

Religion

Main article: Islam in Somalia

Mosque in Borama, Somalia.

With few exceptions, Somalis are entirely Muslims, the majority belonging to the Sunni branch of Islam and the Shafi`i school of Islamic jurisprudence, although some are also adherents of the Shia Muslim denomination. Sufism, the mystical dimension of Islam, is also well-established, with many local *jama'a* (*zawiya*) or congregations of the various *tariiqa* or Sufi orders. The constitution of Somalia likewise defines Islam as the religion of the Somali Republic, and Islamic sharia as the basic source for national legislation.

Islam entered the region very early on, as a group of persecuted Muslims had, at Prophet Muhummad's urging, sought refuge across the Red Sea in the Horn of Africa. Islam may thus have been introduced into Somalia well before the faith even took root in its place of origin.

In addition, the Somali community has produced numerous important Islamic figures over the centuries, many of whom have significantly shaped the course of Muslim learning and practice in the Horn of Africa, the Arabian Peninsula, and well beyond. Among these Islamic scholars is the 14th century Somali theologian and jurist Uthman bin Ali Zayla'i of Zeila, who wrote the single most authoritative text on the Hanafi school of Islam, consisting of four volumes known as the *Tabayin al-Haqa'iq li Sharh Kanz al-Daqa'iq*.

Clan and family structure

Main article: Demographics of Somalia

The clan groupings of the Somali people are important social units, and clan membership plays a central part in Somali culture and politics. Clans are patrilineal and are often divided into sub-clans, sometimes with many sub-divisions.

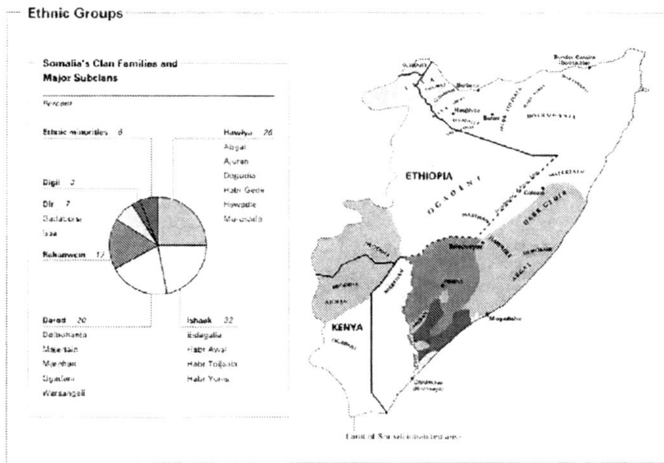

This 2002 CIA map shows the distribution of the various Somali clans.

Somali society is traditionally ethnically endogamous, so to extend ties of alliance, marriage is often to another ethnic Somali from a different clan. Thus, for example, a recent study observed that in 89 marriages contracted by men of the Dhulbahante clan, 55 (62%) were with women of Dhulbahante sub-clans other than those of their husbands; 30 (33.7%) were with women of surrounding clans of other clan families (Isaaq, 28; Hawiye, 3); and 3 (4.3%) were with women of other clans of the Darod clan family (Majerteen 2, Ogaden 1).

Major Somali clans include:

- Darod
- Dir
- Hawiye
- Isaaq
- Rahanweyn (Digil and Mirifle)

Attire

Men

When not dressed in Westernized clothing such as jeans and t-shirts, Somali men typically wear the *macawis* (ma'awiis), which is a sarong-like garment worn around the waist. On their heads, they often wrap a colorful turban or wear the *koofiyad*, an embroidered fez.

Due to Somalia's proximity to and close ties with the Arabian Peninsula, many Somali men also wear the jellabiya (*jellabiyad* in Somali), a long white garment common in the Arab world.

Somali man wearing a *macawis* sarong.

Women

During regular, day-to-day activities, women usually wear the *guntiino*, a long stretch of cloth tied over the shoulder and draped around the waist. In more formal settings such as weddings or religious celebrations like Eid, women wear the *dirac*, which is a long, light, diaphanous voile dress made of cotton or polyester that is worn over a full-length half-slip and a brassiere.

Married women tend to sport head-scarves referred to as *shash*, and also often cover their upper body with a shawl known as *garbasaar*. Unmarried or young women, however, do not always cover their heads. Traditional Arabian garb such as the jilbab is also commonly worn.

See also

- Music of Somalia
- Somali people
- Somaliwood

References

- *This article incorporates public domain material from websites or documents* [1] *of the Library of Congress Country Studies.*

External links

- Somali culture documentary [1]

Hannassa

Hannassa is a historic Somali settlement built on a promontory in Southern Somalia, containing ruins of houses with archways and courtyards as well as sites with pillar tombs, including a rare octagonal tomb. Excavations have retrieved sherds of Celadon and undecorated pottery. Amongst the ruins is a small mosque with a well preserved mihrab overlooking the Indian Ocean.

See also

- Gondershe

Maduna

Maduna(Somali: Maduuna) is an old Somali city 90 km southward of Erigavo. The structures consist of several hundred drystone buildings and a large retangular mosque whose walls were originally rendered with lime plaster. The city is said to date from the Golden Age of the Adal Sultanate, which was in the 15th and 16th centuries.

References

- An Archaeological Reconnaissance in the Horn: The British-Somali Expedition,1975 - Neville Chittick.

Overview of Mogadishu

Mogadishu

Mogadishu
مقديشو *Maqadīshū* ("The Seat of the Shah")

Nickname(s): Xamar

Mogadishu

Location of Mogadishu within Somalia

Coordinates: 2°02′N 45°21′E

Country	Somalia
Region	Benadir
Government	

- Mayor	Abdurisaq Mohamed Nor
Population (2006)	
- Total	2,000,000
Time zone	EAT (UTC+2)

Mogadishu (pronounced /ˌmɒɡəˈdɪʃuː/; Somali: *Muqdisho*, popularly *Xamar*; Arabic: مقديشو *Maqadīshū*; Italian: *Mogadiscio*, literally "The Seat of the Shah") is the largest city in Somalia and the nation's capital.

Located in the coastal Benadir region on the Indian Ocean, the city has served as an important port for centuries.

History

Early history

Main article: History of Mogadishu

Engraving of the 13th century Fakr ad-Din Mosque.

According to the *Periplus of the Erythraean Sea*, maritime trade connected Somalis in the Mogadishu area with other communities along the Indian Ocean coast as early as the 1st century CE. With Muslim traders from the Arabian Peninsula arriving circa 900 CE, Mogadishu was well-suited to become a regional center for commerce.

The name "Mogadishu" is held to be derived from the Arabic مقعد الشاه *Maq'ad-u-Shah* ("The seat of the Shah"), a reflection of the city's early Persian influence.

For many years, Mogadishu stood as the pre-eminent city in the بلاد البربر *Bilad-ul-Barbar* ("Land of the Berbers"), which was the medieval Arabic term for the Horn of Africa. Following his visit to the city, the twelfth century Syrian historian Yaqut al-Hamawi wrote that it was inhabited by dark-skinned Berbers, the ancestors of the modern Somalis.

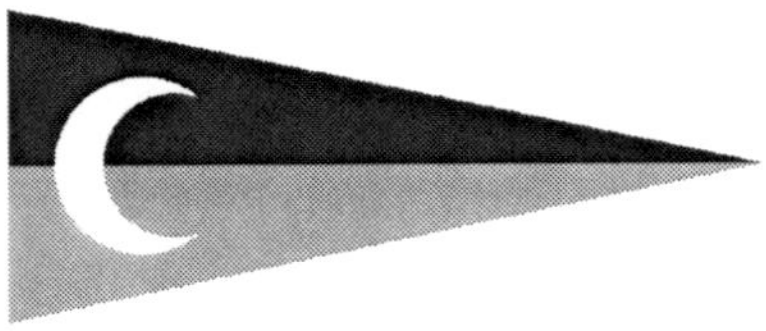

Flag of the Ajuuraan State, a Somali empire of which medieval Mogadishu was an important vassal.

The Sultanate of Mogadishu developed with the immigration of Emozeidi Arabs, a community whose earliest presence dates back to the 9th or 10th century. This evolved into the Muzaffar dynasty, a joint Somali-Arab federation of rulers, and Mogadishu became closely linked with the powerful Somali Ajuuraan State.

By the time of the Moroccan traveller Ibn Batuta's appearance on the Somali coast in 1331, the city was at the zenith of its prosperity. Batuta described Mogadishu as "an exceedingly large city" with many rich merchants, which was famous for its high quality fabric that it exported to Egypt, among other places. He added that the city was ruled by a Somali Sultan originally from Berbera in northern Somalia who spoke both Somali (referred to by Batutta as *Mogadishan*, the Benadir dialect of Somali) and Arabic with equal fluency. The Sultan also had a retinue of wazirs (ministers), legal experts, commanders, royal eunuchs, and assorted hangers-on at his beck and call.

The Portuguese would later attempt to occupy the city, but never managed to take it. The Hawiye Somali, however, were successful in defeating the Ajuuraan State and bringing about the end of Muzaffar rule.

1800s-1950s

By 1892, Mogadishu was under the joint control of the Somali Geledi Sultanate (which, also holding sway over the Shebelle region in the interior, was at the height of its power) and the Arab Sultan of Zanzibar.

In 1892, Ali bin Said leased the city to Italy. Italy purchased the city in 1905 and made Mogadishu the capital of the newly-established Italian Somaliland. After World War I, the surrounding territory came under Italian control with some resistance.

Thousands of Italian colonists moved to live in Mogadishu and founded small manufacturing companies. They also developed some agricultural areas around the capital such as the *Villaggio duca degli Abruzzi* and the *Genale*.

In the 1930s, new buildings and avenues were built. A 114 km narrow-gauge railway was laid from Mogadishu to Jowhar, then called "Villaggio Duca degli Abruzzi". An asphalted road, the *Strada Imperiale* was also constructed, intended to link Mogadishu to Addis Ababa.

Mogadishu remained the capital of Italian Somaliland throughout the existence of the latter, and became the capital of independent Somalia in 1960.

Modern history

Main articles: Somali Civil War, Battle of Mogadishu (1993), Battle of Mogadishu (2006), Fall of Mogadishu, Battle of Mogadishu (March–April 2007), Battle of Mogadishu (November 2007), Battle of Mogadishu (2008), Battle of South Mogadishu, Battle of Mogadishu (2009), and Battle of Mogadishu (2010)

A residential area of Mogadishu, with a U.S. Marine Corps helicopter in the foreground. (1992).

Rebel forces entered and took the city in 1990, forcing the then President of Somalia, Mohamed Siad Barre, to flee in 1991 to Kenya. One faction proclaimed Ali Mahdi Muhammad president, another Mohamed Farrah Aidid. A contingent of United States Marines landed near Mogadishu on December 9, 1992 to spearhead the United Nations peacekeeping forces during Operation Restore Hope, in which Pakistan, Italy and Malaysia also participated.

Skyline of Mogadishu. (2006).

In the wake of Operation Restore Hope, further US peacekeeping continued, until, on October 4, 1993, American forces were finally evacuated to the UN's Pakistani base by an armored convoy along the so-called "Mogadishu Mile". In that exercise alone, 19 U.S. soldiers died and 73 were injured, while two US Black Hawk helicopters were shot down and three further MH-60s put out of action. After the battle, one or more US casualties of the conflict were dragged through the streets of Mogadishu by crowds of local civilians and SNA forces. The Malaysian forces lost one soldier and had seven injured, while the Pakistanis suffered two injured. Casualties on the Somali side were heavy, with estimates on fatalities ranging from 500 to over 2,000 people. The Somali casualties were a mixture of militiamen and local civilians. Somali civilians suffered heavy casualties due to the dense urban character of that portion of Mogadishu. Two days later, a mortar round fell on the U.S. compound, killing one U.S. soldier, and injuring another twelve.

Mogadishu was subsequently run by competing warlords until 2006, when Islamists and businessmen formed a successful coalition government, which came to be known as the Islamic Courts Union(ICU). The ICU seized control of the entire country, except for the town of Baidoa, which was held by the Transitional Federal Government, the internationally recognized government of Somalia. Later that same year, the Ethiopian military ousted the ICU and restored the internationally-recognized government, which had long remained in exile in Kenya, with Baidoa being its only Somali foothold.

Mogadishu was the scene of bitter warfare and devastation caused by fighting between Ethiopian and Somali government troops, and Islamist guerrillas. Fighting escalated in March–April 2007, November 2007 and April 2008 with hundreds of civilian casualties. In October 2008, the BBC reported that the city had been "abandoned by at least half of its residents", and that there were "street after ruined street of bombed-out buildings in the center of Mogadishu".

As of 2008, a 2,700-strong African Union peacekeeping force is attempting to bring stability and security to the city, as well as providing medical aid to the population.

Since May 8, 2009, there has been an increase in violence reportedly leading to the displacement of more than 165,000 of the inhabitants. The violence has culminated in several suicide bomb attacks, normally rare occurrences in Somalia. The attacks have claimed many lives, amongst them Mohamed Hussein Addow, a legislative politician and the third high-profile public killing in as many days throughout the country. During 2009, Mayor Abdurisaq Mohamed Nor told civilians to seek refuge from the fighting outside the capital, advising to keep at least 2 km distance between themselves and the capital ahead of a government offensive. The more formidable nature of the al-Shabab fighters has been attributed to the training received from foreign fighters, veterans of the Iraq/Afghani conflict, who are to blame for the two explosions in Mogadishu on August 21, 2010. In August 2010, a round of heavy fighting in Mogadishu culminated in a suicide attack on a hotel near the presidential palace, in an area where the security is known to be 'tight'. The attack was followed by an hour of fighting and left 32 dead, including 6 Somali MPs and 5 government officials.

There is no effective police force in the city. The only hope for security is through the service of private guards for-hire.

Geography

Mogadishu is located at 2°4′N 45°22′E. The Shebelle River (*Webiga Shabelle*) rises in central Ethiopia and comes within 30 kilometers (19 mi) of the Indian Ocean near Mogadishu before turning southwestward. Usually dry during February and March, the river provides water essential for the cultivation of sugarcane, cotton, and bananas.

Features of the city include the *Hamarwein* old town, the Bakaara Market, and the former resort of Gezira Beach. The sandy beaches of Mogadishu are reported by the few Western travelers to be among the most beautiful in the world, offering easy access to vibrant coral reefs.

Climate

For a city situated so near the equator, Mogadishu has a dry climate. It is classified as hot and semi-arid (Köppen climate classification *BSh*). Much of the land the city lies upon is desert terrain. The city has a low annual rainfall of 427mm, most which falls in the wet season. The rains are very variable from year to year, and drought is a constant problem for the people living in Somalia.

Sunshine is abundant in the city, averaging eight to ten hours a day year-round. It is lowest during the wet season, when there is some coastal fog and greater cloud coverage as warm air passes over the cool sea surface.

Climate data for Mogadishu													
Month	**Jan**	**Feb**	**Mar**	**Apr**	**May**	**Jun**	**Jul**	**Aug**	**Sep**	**Oct**	**Nov**	**Dec**	**Year**
Record high °C (°F)	34 (93)	32 (90)	33 (91)	36 (97)	34 (93)	32 (90)	32 (90)	30 (86)	32 (90)	32 (90)	32 (90)	34 (93)	36 (97)
Average high °C (°F)	30 (86)	30 (86)	31 (88)	32 (90)	32 (90)	29 (84)	28 (82)	28 (82)	29 (84)	30 (86)	31 (88)	30 (86)	30 (86)
Average low °C (°F)	23 (73)	23 (73)	24 (75)	26 (79)	25 (77)	23 (73)	23 (73)	23 (73)	23 (73)	24 (75)	24 (75)	24 (75)	24 (75)
Record low °C (°F)	20 (68)	18 (64)	20 (68)	20 (68)	18 (64)	20 (68)	15 (59)	16 (61)	18 (64)	18 (64)	21 (70)	20 (68)	15 (59)
Precipitation mm (inches)	0 (0)	0 (0)	0 (0)	58 (2.28)	58 (2.28)	97 (3.82)	64 (2.52)	48 (1.89)	25 (0.98)	23 (0.91)	41 (1.61)	13 (0.51)	427 (16.81)
Source: BBC Weather													

Economy

Mogadishu serves as a commercial and financial center. The economy has recovered somewhat from the civil unrest although the Somali Civil War still presents many problems. The effective absence of government yields free trade without taxes or regulatory expenditures, but comes at the cost of civil society and infrastructure. Businesses have hired armed militias to provide security against gunmen, leading to a gradual reduction in open street violence [*citation needed*]. However, high levels of crime including frequent murders and occasional bombings are still found in the city.

Bakaara Market in the heart of Mogadishu. Somali marketplaces have thrived due to the fragility of the government.

Principal industries include food and beverage processing and textiles, especially cotton ginning. The main market offers goods from food to electronic gadgets.

A Coca-Cola bottling plant in Mogadishu

Hormuud Telecom, the largest telecommunications company in southern and central Somalia, has its headquarters in Mogadishu. Telcom is another telecommunications service provider based in the city.

Transportation

Road

Roads leading out of Mogadishu connect the city to other Somali locales and to Ethiopia and Kenya.

Air

Private airlines such as Jubba Airways service Mogadishu at airports within and around the city. The intense fighting largely destroyed the old Mogadishu International Airport (now renamed Aden Adde International Airport), which briefly reopened before the War in Somalia (2006-2009). As of 2007, K50 Airport serves Mogadishu.

The Port of Mogadishu in 1992. Three cargo ships, large, medium and small sized vessels are moored to the docks. A tugboat is heading out of the port.

Sea

Mogadishu leads Somalia in port traffic and still serves as a major seaport. International traders actively benefit from its de facto duty-free status. However, piracy is widespread around Somalia's coastal areas, making sea transport risky.

Railway

There were projects during the 1980s to reactivate the 114 km railway between Mogadishu and Jowhar, built by the Italians in 1926 but dismantled in WWII by British troops. The Mogadishu-Villabruzzi Railway was planned in 1939 to reach Addis Ababa.

Government

Since February 2009, the Transitional Federal Government, with the help of the African Union and the support of the United Nations , has started drafting a consitution to help *"shape [Somalias] destiny"*. Furthermore steps have been taken to counter the insurgency from groups such as al-Shabab through military means. This has incurred little success and, currently, up to a third of Mogadishu is held by insurgents. Attempts have been made to negotiate a diplomatic solution through either a cease fire or even appease the aggressive nature of al-Shabab, with the implementation of Shari'a law, neither method has been met with success.

Education

Despite the civil unrest, Mogadishu counts several institutions of higher learning.

The Hammar Jab Jab School in Mogadishu.

Mogadishu University (MU) is a non-governmental university that is governed by a Board of Trustees and a University Council. It is the brainchild of a number of professors from the Somali National University as well as other Somali intellectuals who sought to find ways to provide post-secondary education in the wake of the civil war. Financed by the Islamic Development Bank in Jeddah, Saudi Arabia, as well as other donor institutions, the university counts hundreds of young Somali graduates from its seven faculties, some of whom continue on to pursue Master's degrees abroad thanks to a scholarship program. Mogadishu University has established partnerships with several other academic institutions, including the University of Aalborg in Denmark, three universities in Egypt, seven universities in Sudan, the University of Djibouti, and two universities in Yemen. It has also been scored among the 100 best universities in Africa in spite of the harsh environment, which has been hailed as a triumph for grass-roots initiatives.

New Mogadishu University campus.

The Somali National University, founded in 1954 during the "Italian Trust Administration of Somalia" (AFIS), has been closed indefinitely due to extensive damage.

Benadir University (BU) was established in 2002 with the intention of training doctors. It has since expanded into other fields.

Due to human capital shortage in the country's private sector management, the Somali Institute of Management and Administration Development (SIMAD) has given priority to the fields of business administration, information technology and accountancy.

Sport

The city is home to Mogadiscio Stadium, which plays host to the Somalia Cup and to football teams from the Somalia League.

Notable Mogadishans

- Ayub Daud, professional footballer
- Fatima Siad, fashion model
- Hassan Abshir Farah, former Prime Minister of Somalia and Mayor of Mogadishu
- Ali Mohamed Ghedi, former Prime Minister of Somalia
- Iman, supermodel
- K'naan, award-winning musician
- Mo Farah, international track and field athlete
- Mustafa Mohamed, professional athlete
- Omar Abdirashid Ali Sharmarke, former Prime Minister of Somalia
- Rageh Omaar, award-winning journalist
- Saba Anglana, international singer and actress
- Said Sheikh Samatar, scholar and writer
- Yasmin Warsame, supermodel
- Zahra Bani, professional athlete

Born in Mogadishu, supermodel Iman was the first Somali woman to appear on the cover of Vogue in 1979 and to sign a cosmetics contract.

See also

- Mogadishu-Villabruzzi Railway

External links

- Mogadishu city portal [1]
- GlobalSecurity.org page on the city's history [2]
- Mogadishu at Google Maps [3]
- Map of Mogadishu (1997) [4]
- BBC articles:
    - "Inside Somalia's danger zone" [5], October 5, 2008 (videos)
    - "Somalian 'ghost city' wracked by war" [6], October 6, 2008
- Photos of Mogadishu taken between 1993 and 1995 [7]
- Chisholm, Hugh, ed (1911). "Mukdishu". *Encyclopædia Britannica* (Eleventh ed.). Cambridge University Press.

- Few Traces Of Past Glory In Mogadishu [8] - audio report by *NPR*

ace:Mogadishu pnb:موگادیشو

Banaadir

Benadir or **Banaadir** (Somali: *Banaadir*, Arabic: بنادر) is a region (*gobolka*) in southern Somalia. Its capital is Mogadishu, though the region itself is coextensive with the city and is much smaller than the historical region of Benadir. It is bordered by the Somali regions of Middle Shabele and Lower Shabele, as well as the Indian Ocean.

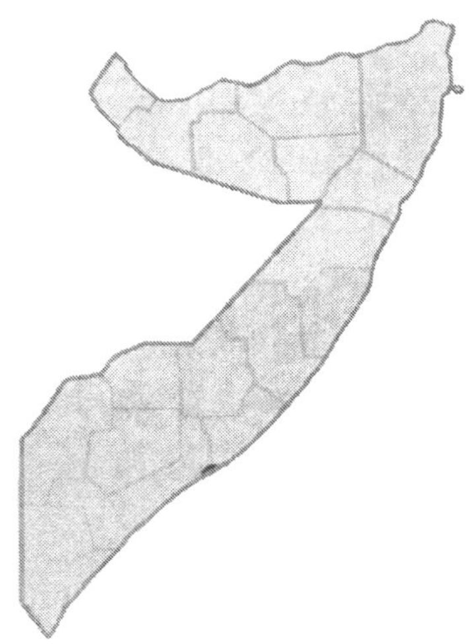

Red shading indicates location of Banaadir in Somalia

The Somali term *Banaadir* derives from the original Persian word *bandar*, meaning "port" or "harbour". It refers to the northern historical ports of Barawa and Mogadishu.

Geographical coordinates: 2°2′59″N 45°15′44″E

History of Mogadishu

History of Mogadishu

Mogadishu (pronounced /ˌmɒɡəˈdɪʃuː/; Somali: *Muqdisho*, popularly حَمر *Xamar* ; Arabic: مقديشو *Maqadīshū*; Italian: *Mogadiscio*, literally "The Seat of the Shah") is the largest city in Somalia and the nation's capital.

Mogadishu skyline circa 1993.

Located in the coastal Benadir region on the Indian Ocean, the city has served as an important port for centuries.

Medieval city-state

According to the *Periplus of the Erythraean Sea*, maritime trade connected Somalis in the Mogadishu area with other communities along the Indian Ocean coast as early as the 1st century CE. With Muslim traders from the Arabian Peninsula arriving circa 900 CE, Mogadishu was well-suited to become a regional center for commerce.

The name "Mogadishu" is held to be derived from the Arabic مقعد شاه *Maq'ad Shah* ("The seat of the Shah"), a reflection of the city's early Persian influence.

For many years, Mogadishu stood as the pre-eminent city in the بلد البربر *Bilad al Barbar* ("Land of the Berbers"), which was the medieval Arabic term for the Horn of Africa. Following his visit to the city, the twelfth century Syrian historian Yaqut al-Hamawi wrote that it was inhabited by dark-skinned Berbers, the ancestors of the modern Somalis.

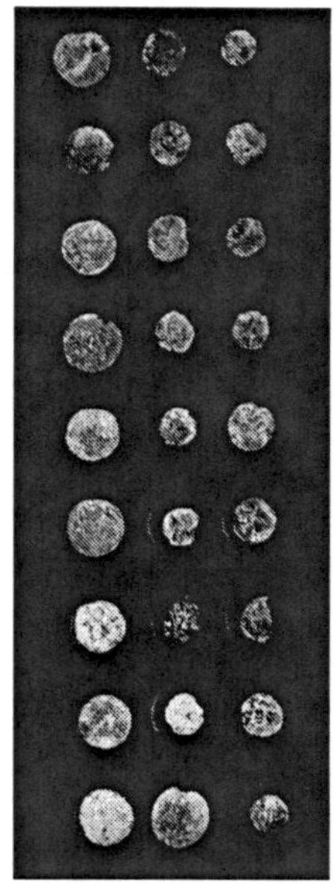

Mogadishan currency.

The Sultanate of Mogadishu developed with the immigration of Emozeidi Arabs, a community whose earliest presence dates back to the 9th or 10th century. This evolved into the Muzaffar dynasty, a joint Somali-Arab federation of rulers, and Mogadishu became closely linked with the powerful Somali Ajuuraan State.

By the time of the Moroccan traveller Ibn Batuta's appearance on the Somali coast in 1331, the city was at the zenith of its prosperity. Batuta described Mogadishu as "an exceedingly large city" with many rich merchants, which was famous for its high quality fabric that it exported to Egypt, among other places. He added that the city was ruled by a Somali Sultan who spoke both Somali and Arabic with equal fluency.

Archaeological excavations have recovered many coins from China, Sri Lanka, and Vietnam. The majority of the Chinese coins date to the Song Dynasty, although the Ming Dynasty and Qing Dynasty "are also represented," according to Richard Pankhurst.

In 1416, Mogadishu sent ambassadors to pay tribute to the Ming dynasty. The Yongle Emperor dispatched Admiral Zheng He to return ambassadors to the Somali city, with Zheng He revisiting Mogadishu in 1430.

Trading across the Arabian Sea enabled major ports like Mogadishu to prosper during the later Middle Ages. Ross E. Dunn describes Mogadishu and other East African Muslim settlements as "a kind of medieval America, a fertile, well-watered land of economic opportunity and a place of salvation from drought, famine, overpopulation, and war at home."

The Portuguese would later attempt to occupy the city, but never managed to take it. The Hawiye Somali, however, were successful in defeating the Ajuuraan State and bringing about the end of Muzaffar rule.

The Ajuran Period

After entering Muqdisho, the Darandoolle quarrelled with the Ajuran. They quarrelled over watering rights. The Ajuran had decreed: 'At the wells in our territory, the people known as Darandoolle and the other Hiraab cannot water their herds by day, but only at night"...Then all the Darandoolle gathered in one place. The leaders decided to make war on the Ajuran. They found the imam of the Ajuran seated on a rock near a well called Ceel Cawl. They killed him with a sword. As they struck him with the sword, they split his body together with the rock on which he was seated. He died immediately and the Ajuran migrated out of the country.'

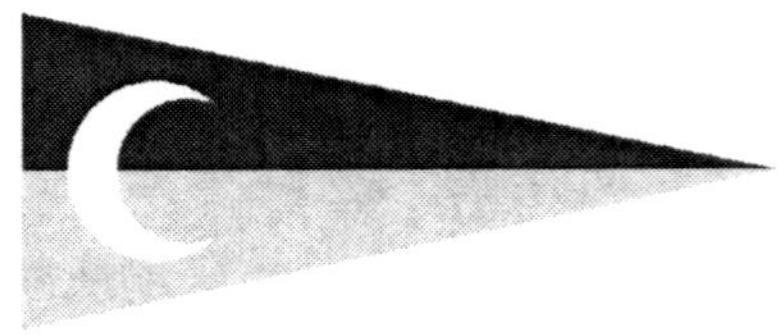

Flag of the Ajuuraan State, a Somali empire of which medieval Mogadishu was an important vassal.

The Darandoolle became as such the first group to rebel against the tyranny of Ajuran in the interior, and ever since this Ajuran defeat other groups would follow in the rebellion which would eventually bring down Ajuran rule of the inter-riverine region.

After the defeat of the Ajuran in the interior, the Darandoolle Mudulood established themselves around Mogadishu and Shabelle river valley, in which Wacdaan inhabited the environs of Afgoye, Hilibi in Lower Shabelle, Moobleen went part of the region now known as Middle Shabelle, while the Mataan established themselves in and around Mogadishu city, where 1720 Mataan collected tax and port tariffs of the city, and emerged as the authority of Mogadishu city.

Colonial era

By 1892, Mogadishu was under the joint control of the Somali Geledi Sultanate (which, also holding sway over the Shebelle region in the interior, was at the height of its power) and the Arab Sultan of Zanzibar.

In 1892, the sultan of Zanzibar leased the city to Italy. Italy later tried to purchase the city but couldn't succeed and in 1905 made *Mogadiscio* the capital of Italian Somaliland.

In 1926, after a bloody repression by governor Cesare Maria De Vecchi, southern Somalia was fully pacified and started to enjoy a period of economic development. The Somali colonial troops called Dubats (and the gendarmerie Zaptié) were extensively used by De Vecchi in this military campaign.

In the early 1930s, the new Italian governors, Guido Corni and Maurizio Rava, started a policy toward a friendly assimilation of the Somalis and their clans. Many Somalis of Mogadishu were enrolled in the Italian colonial troops.

Some thousands of Italian colonists moved to live in Mogadishu, which become a commercial centre with some small manufacturing companies, and in some agricultural areas around the capital (like the "Villaggio duca degli Abruzzi - Giohar" and "Genale").

Mogadishu in the late thirties was developed, by the 10,000 Italian Somalians living there, into a modern capital with new buildings and avenues such as the first avenue which they commemorated chief of the area Hassan Gedi Abtow. Also they did a connected 114 km railway to Jowhar and by a new-asphalted long road (called "Imperial Road") to Addis Abeba.

British forces operating from Kenya during World War II captured and occupied Mogadishu. The capital of Italian Somaliland fell to the British forces on February 26, 1941. The British continued to rule until Italy returned in 1950 to administer their former Somali protectorate. Education advanced with the 1954 establishment of the Somalia National University.

Somalia achieved independence in 1960 with the union of the territories of former Italian Somaliland and British Somaliland, and Mogadishu was proclaimed the capital.

Somali Civil War

Collapse of government and UN intervention

Rebel forces entered and took the city in 1990, forcing President Mohammed Siad Barre to resign and flee in January 1991 to Lagos, Nigeria. One faction proclaimed Mohammed Ali Mahdi president, another Mohammed Farah Aidid. The Somalia National University, which enrolled 4600 students before the war, closed as the educational system soon collapsed.

Intense battling between these rivals and other clan-based rebel factions damaged many parts of Mogadishu in 1991-1992 and led to tens of thousands of casualties as an intense drought-induced famine ravaged rural Somalia.

A contingent of United States Marines landed near Mogadishu on December 9, 1992 to spearhead United Nations peacekeeping forces. The United Nations sought to capture warlord Mohamed Farrah Aidid in 1993 to enable the establishment of a transitional government. Somalis loyal to him ambushed the peacekeepers and killed 24 Pakistanis.

Aerial view of a residential area of Mogadishu, with a U.S. Marine Corps helicopter in the foreground, December 1992.

On October 3, 1993, the United States Army Rangers and the Army's Delta Force went on a mission to capture two of Aidid's warlords, which lead to the Battle of Mogadishu. Although the mission was successful, five American army UH-60 Black Hawk helicopters were shot down during the battle (two in the city [Durant's "Super 64" and Wolcot's "Super 61"] and 3 at a safe area), causing about 100 United States Army Rangers and Delta Force operators to be pinned down in the city, trying to rescue survivors and recover the dead. In this Battle of

Mogadishu, the Somalis killed 18, one soldier three days later in a mortar strike and 1 Malaysian soldier and injured several dozen. Estimates put the number of Somali casualties at 500-1000 militia and civilians dead and 3000-4000 injured. The later nonfiction books Black Hawk Down: A Story of Modern War, In The Company Of Heroes, and motion picture *Black Hawk Down* dramatized the events of this battle.

With these casualties, United States President Bill Clinton withdrew American forces in 1994. Two factions in Mogadishu nevertheless reached a peace accord on January 16, 1994. Heavy fighting, however, intensified between numerous warlords and factions for control over the city after the March 3, 1995 withdrawal of the last international peacekeepers.

Mohamed Farrah Aidid declared himself president in June 1995 and by 1996 captured strategic neighborhoods in Mogadishu and some outlying territory. Rival militias renewed fighting in Mogadishu and Hoddur in 1996. Aidid ultimately died in July 1996 from gunshot wounds suffered in a street battle.

Second Battle of Mogadishu

Main article: Second Battle of Mogadishu

On 7 May 2006, fighting broke out between Islamist militias and an alliance of Somali warlords over control of Mogadishu. The opposing forces were the Alliance for the Restoration of Peace and Counter-Terrorism (ARPCT), and militia loyal to the Islamic Court Union (ICU). The conflict began in mid-February, 2006, when Somali warlords formed the ARPCT to challenge the emerging influence of the ICU. It has been alleged that the United States has provided funding for the ARPCT due to concerns that the ICU has ties to al-Qaeda. Most of the combat was concentrated in the Sii-Sii (often written "CC" in English) district in northern Mogadishu with both the Islamist militias and the secular warlords fighting for control of Mogadishu. On 5 June 2006, the ICU militia seized Mogadishu.

Fall of Mogadishu

Main article: Fall of Mogadishu

Mogadishu in 2006.

While the ICU consolidated control over Mogadishu, a UN-supported Transitional Government remained undefeated in Baidoa, despite a series of military setbacks. An attempt by the ICU to capture Baidoa prompted a military intervention by Ethiopia in support of the Transitional Government starting December 21, 2006. On December 25 Ethiopian jets bombed Mogadishu's main airport held by the ICU since June. Witnesses reported MiG fighter jets fired missiles into the airport twice. One person was killed and a number injured. Further north, Beledweyne was also bombed, according to witnesses. The fighting between the Ethiopian-backed TFG and the ICU became stretched to over 400 km (250 miles) of land.

Following a rapid advance, Ethiopian and pro-government militias surrounded Mogadishu. A spokesman stated that the troops would besiege the city but not attack it in order to avoid civilian casualties. On December 27, reports stated that the ICU was abandoning the city. On December 28, 2006, pro-government militias claimed to have taken control of key locations, including the former presidential palace.

Battle of Mogadishu (2007)

Main article: Battle of Mogadishu (2007)

In January 2007, an Islamic insurgency erupted in Mogadishu, targeting government and Ethiopian forces. A helicopter was shot down as battles engulf in the city on March 30, 2007. Two Ethiopian helicopters fired on a rebel stronghold before one was hit by a missile. In addition, Ethiopia told its forces had killed 200 insurgents in a two-day joint offensive with Somali troops against the Islamic Courts Union.

Transitional Federal Government

On December 29, 2008, Abdullahi Yusuf Ahmed announced before a united parliament in Baidoa his resignation as President of Somalia. In his speech, which was broadcast on national radio, Yusuf expressed regret at failing to end the country's seventeen year conflict as his government had mandated to do. He also blamed the international community for its failure to support the government, and said that the speaker of parliament would succeed him in office per the charter of the Transitional Federal

Government.

Over the next few months, a new President was elected from amongst the more moderate Islamists, and Omar Abdirashid Ali Sharmarke, the son of slain former President Abdirashid Ali Sharmarke, was selected as the nation's new Prime Minister. The Transitional Federal Government, with the help of a small team of African Union troops, also began a counteroffensive in February 2009 to retake control of the southern half of the country. To solidify its control of southern Somalia, the TFG formed an alliance with the Islamic Courts Union, other members of the Alliance for the Re-liberation of Somalia, and Ahlu Sunna Waljama'a, a moderate Sufi militia. Furthermore, Al-Shabaab and Hizbul Islam, the two main Islamist groups in opposition, began to fight amongst themselves in mid-2009.

As a truce, in March 2009, Somalia's newly established coalition government announced that it would re-implement Shari'a as the nation's official judicial system. However, conflict continues in the southern and central parts of the country between government troops and extremist Islamist militants with links to al-Qaeda.

National elections

While its institutions still have room for improvement, the Transitional Federal Government continues to reach out to both Somali and international stakeholders to help grow the administrative capacity of the Transitional Federal Institutions and to work toward eventual national elections in 2011, when the interim government's mandate expires.

Cities and Towns Nearby to Visit

Kismayo

Kismayo
Kismaayo
كيسمايو

Overview of Kismayo

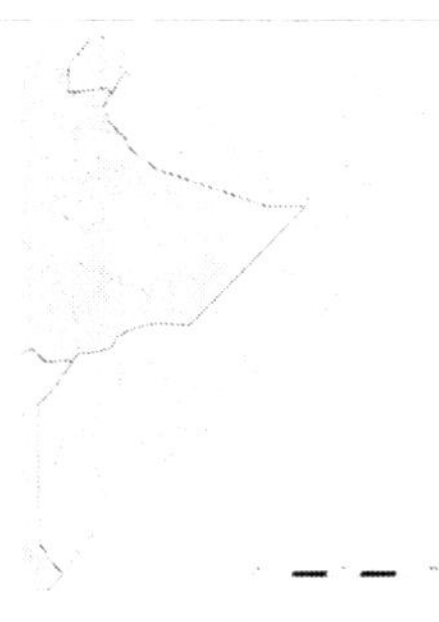

Kismayo
Location in Somalia

Coordinates: 0°21′37″S 42°32′55″E

Country	Somalia
Region	Jubbada Hoose
District	
Population (2007)	

- Total	70,000
Time zone	East Africa Time (UTC+3)

Kismayo or **Kismayu** (Somali: *Kismaayo*; Arabic: كيسمايو, Kīsmāyū; Italian: *Chisimaio*) is a port city in the Jubbada Hoose region of Somalia, and is the country's third largest city. It is situated 328 miles (528 km) southwest of Mogadishu, near the mouth of the Jubba River, where that river flows into the Indian Ocean. As of 2008, the population is estimated at 70,000 inhabitants.

History

Middle Ages and Early Modern period

The city, along with the surrounding region, was part of the Ajuuraan Empire in the medieval period and came under the rule of the Geledi Sultanate in 19th century during their struggle with the Zanzibaris and the Ottoman Khedive vassal state of Isma'il Pasha. In the late 19th century Somali merchants from Bandar Qassim equipped with several cannons conquered the city by storm before Sultan Ahmed Yusuf drove them out the city. It was part of Trans-Juba, which belonged to the British, from July 1, 1895, as part of the East Africa Company's East Africa Protectorate. On July 15, 1924, it was ceded to Italy and became part of the Colony of Trans-Juba (*Oltre Giuba*). In 1926, the area was incorporated into the Italian Somaliland, and became the capital of its Trans-Juba province.

Somali Civil War

Main article: Somali Civil War

After the former Somali President Siad Barre was overthrown, Kismayo became a city in constant turmoil, fought over by warring clans vying for control of the area. A prolonged struggle for control of the city took place among various clans, resulting in many innocent civilian casualties, including English UNICEF aid worker Sean Devereux who was assassinated in January 1993. By this time, control of Kismayo was being fought between supporters of Mohammed Said Hersi, known as General Morgan, and supporters of Col. Omar Jess of the Somali Patriotic Movement. In March 1993, a United States Marine amphibious group arrived in the city in an attempt to keep the peace as part of the United Nations intervention in Somalia.

By December 1993, General Mohammed Said Hersi Morgan's troops controlled Kismayo, despite the presence of peacekeepers. The last UN troops left Kismayo in December 1994. General Hersi Morgan declared Jubaland independent on September 3, 1998. but was ousted from Kismayo in June 1999. From June 1999 - June 2001, Kismayo was the headquarters for the Allied Somali Forces, which was contesting the area known as Jubaland with the Somali Patriotic Movement (SPM). The ASF renamed itself the Juba Valley Alliance in June 2001.

Government

A new district administration was established on 6 September 2008. Its members reportedly represented the ICU and Al-Shabaab (three members each) plus a local clan (one member) which had played a part in the military assault. Representatives of the Islamic Courts Union have questioned the legitimacy of the authority. On 1 October 2009, Al Shabaab took full control of the city, after Sheikh Ahmed Madobe, a senior commander of Ras Kamboni Brigade (a part of Hizbul Islam), challenged Al Shabaab's control.

Demographics

Besides Somalis, the district is home to a diverse group of people, including Indians, Benadiri, Bantus, Bravanese, Bajunis, and many other minorities.

Districts

Kismayo is divided into five *degmo*, or districts, of which Calanleey is the oldest:

- Farjano
- Faanoole
- Shaqaalaha
- Siinaay
- Calanleey

Airport

Kismayo Airport, which was formerly a Somali Air Force training base, is situated about 10 km from the city. It has a large abandoned and looted Administration building with a badly maintained 12000-foot-long (3700 m) runway. The airport was re-opened in October 2008, with the restriction that flights delivering khat were prohibited from landing at the airport. The airport was renamed after Imam Ahmed Gurey, a 16th century Somali warrior.

Port

Kismayo's large docks are situated on a peninsula on the Indian Ocean coast. Formerly one of the Bajuni Islands, the peninsula was subsequently connected by a narrow causeway when the port was built, with United States assistance, in 1964. The port served as a base for the Somali Navy as well as the Soviet Navy after a military coup in Somalia in 1969. The United States and Somalia jointly refurbished the port in 1984 after "extensive deterioration of the 2070-foot-long (630 m) four-berth, marginal wharf at the Port of Kismayo necessitated a major rehabilitation to maintain operations."

Education

Being Somalia's third largest city, Kismayo is home to a large population, which is served by a number of local high schools, skills training centers and institutions of higher education. Kismayo University, established in August 2005, is located about 1 km north, along the Kismayo-Mogadishu main road. In the larger Jubba region, there two additional tertiary schools, namely, the University of Gedo and Bardera Polytechnic. Both are situated in Bardera.

Climate

Kismayo

Climate chart (explanation)

J	F	M	A	M	J	J	A	S	O	N	D

average max. and min. temperatures in °C

precipitation totals in mm

Imperial conversion

J	F	M	A	M	J	J	A	S	O	N	D

average max. and min. temperatures in °F

precipitation totals in inches

The city of Kismayo is located in the fertile Juba Valley, and is known for its clean and beautiful beaches and tropical weather. The climate is hot year-round, with seasonal monsoon winds and irregular rainfall with recurring droughts. The *gu* rains, also known as the Southwest Monsoons, begin in April and last until June, producing significant fresh water and allowing lush vegetation to grow. The gu season is followed by the *hagaa* (xagaa) drought.

Economy

In October 2008, the daily labor rate was estimated at 157,500 Somali shillings ($4.50), up from 52,000 ($2.21) in January 2008, while kilogram of red rice rose from 14,170 ($0.61) to 46,000 ($1.31). A liter of diesel cost 43,000 shillings ($1.23) and a camel costs over 15 million shillings ($435). Total cereal production as of 2008 was estimated to be 780MT.

Before the war, there were a meat-tinning factory, as well as a tannery, and a modern fish factory. There were also two sugar refineries, one at Jowhar and another situated near Jilib As of January 2007, the market was bustling, although the city's infrastruction had incurred considerable damage.

See also

- Fall of Kismayo

External links

- Kismayo web portal [1]
- 1992 Map of Kismayu [2]

Geographical coordinates: 0°21′37″S 42°32′55.6″E

Afgooye

Afgooye أَفْجوِيي

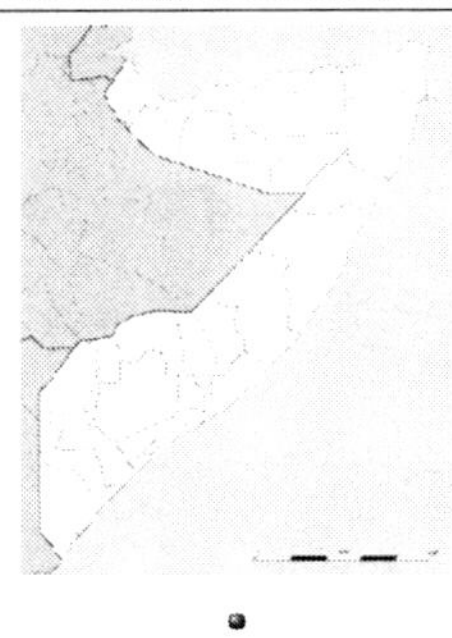

Afgooye أَفْجوِيي

Location in Somalia

Coordinates: 2°7′N 45°7′E

Country	Somalia
Somalia	Shabeellaha Hoose
District	

Afgooye (Arabic: أفجويي) is a town in the Shabeellaha Hoose region of southern Somalia. It is situated about 25 kilometres west of Mogadishu, the nation's capital. The Shabelle River passes through the middle of the town.

The Italians occupied this town in 1908, which led to both its incorporation into Italian Somalia and the end of its slave market.

Geographical coordinates: 2°07′N 45°07′E

Notes

this town has attracted the gulf investments at 1980s and kuwait king used to visit it at ramadan month. the main tribes in this town are as follows: Geledi, Wacdaan, Bagadi, Wadalaan and few Communites of Garre and Murusade

Dinsoor

Dinsoor

Dinsoor

Location in Somalia

Coordinates: 2°24′N 42°59′E

Country	Somalia
Region	Bay Region
District	
Time zone	East Africa Time (UTC+3)

Dinsoor is a town in Somalia. It was founded in 1805, when a group of nomads constructed a water well near a mountain area called *Bug*. It is the fourth largest city in Bay, a province in southwestern Somalia.

Dinsoor has one local airport called Mecca Boqol. The city also serves as a centre for business and trade in the region, and is the only district in Bay which shares borders with all of the districts in the region.

References

- Somalia. Waaxda Dhexe ee Istaatistikada (1981). *Report on the demographic survey of Banadir, Bay, and Lower Shebelle regions of Somalia, 1980-81* [1]. The Dept..

Geographical coordinates: 2°24′N 42°59′E

Jamaame

Jamaame

The Juba River downstream from Jamaame.

Jamaame

Location in Somalia

Coordinates: 0°4′N 42°45′E

Country	Somalia
Region	Jubbada Hoose
District	
Time zone	East Africa Time (UTC+3)

Jamaame, also spelt **Jamame** or **Giamame** and known in Italian as **Margherita**, is a densely populated town in southern Somalia.

Overview

Jamaame is situated in the Jubbada Hoose region, between the Indian Ocean in the east, the agricultural land along the Jubba river in the west, and in the south, the port city of Kismayo.

Demographics

The inhabitants of Jamaame are the Somali Sheekhaal, Tunni and Biyomaal clans, as well as Arabs who immigrated from Yemen, and Bantu minorities who live and work as farmers along the Jubba river.[*citation needed*] Geographical coordinates: 0°04′N 42°45′E

Xuddur

Huddur
Huddur Hadama
Hudur

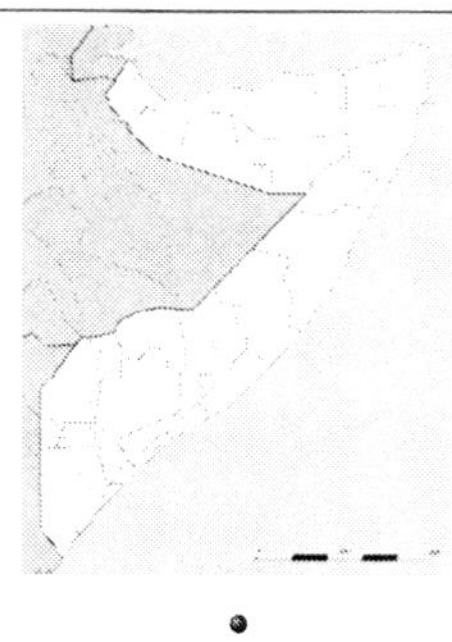

Location in Somalia

Coordinates: 4°7′12″N 43°53′16″E

somalia	Somalia
Region	Bakool
District	
Time zone	East Africa Time (UTC+3)

Huddur (also spelled **Xuddur**) is the capital city of Bakool, Somalia. It is located in the south-west of Somalia, around 4°7′12″N 43°53′16″E. The population belong predominantly to the Hadame clan and are religious. The main language spoken in Huddur is Af Maay. In the mid-1980s it became the first. capital city of the region and it has been a strategic place for the Somali Air Force. Since 1991 when Mohammed Siad Barre's regime was overthrown, the city has remained relatively peaceful.

Wajid, Somalia

Geographical coordinates: 3°48′28″N 43°14′56″E

Wajid

Location in Somalia

Coordinates: 3°48′28″N 43°14′56″E	
Country	Somalia
Region	Bakool
District	
Time zone	East Africa Time (UTC+3)

Wajid is a town and district in the Bakool region of Somalia. Wajid town is located approximately 302 kilometres (188 miles) north west of the national capital, Mogadishu, 78 kilometres (49 miles) south west of the district capital, Xuddur, and 69 kilometres (43 miles) south east of the Somalia-Ethiopia border.

In 2004, the population of the district was estimated at 36,995. Wajid district is a rural area with a semi-arid to arid climate. Many of the district's inhabitants derive their livelihood from pastoral activities, such as raising livestock, and agriculture, such as growing sorghum.

In July 2006, Wajid was occupied by Ethiopian forces during the Ethiopian military intervention in Somalia. Wajid has been the scene of clashes between various parties to the ongoing conflict in Somalia. In early August 2008, Wajid town was the scene of armed fighting between Al Shabaab fighters and local armed groups. Al Shabaab is reported to be in control of Wajid town.

Since 2006, Wajid has been severely affected by drought and the district currently faces a humanitarian crisis brought about by conflict and a lack of food security. In August 2008 it was reported that malnutrition rates in Wajid were among the highest in Somalia.

See also

- Bakool

External links

- 'Bakool region: Waajid district' (map) [1], from the Food Security Analysis Unit (FSAU) Somalia website.
- Photos of Wajid [2] hosted by Panoramio.

Jilib

Jilib جلب	
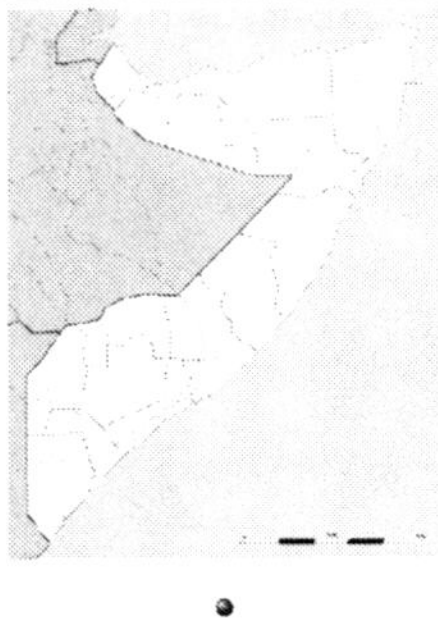 Jilib Location in Somalia	
Coordinates: 0°30′N 42°46′E	
Country	Somalia
Region	Middle Juba
District	
Population (2008)	
- Total	45,000 est.
Time zone	East Africa Time (UTC+3)

Jilib (other names: **Gilib, Gelib, Jillib, Jillio**; Arabic: جلب) is a town in Somalia, with an estimated population of approximately 45,000. . It is located on the main road from Mogadishu south to Kismayo and is the most populous town in the Middle Juba Region.

The Islamic Courts Union was defeated there in the Battle of Jilib December 2006 January 2007. The ICU recaptured the town on May 17, 2008.

References

Geographical coordinates: 0°30′N 42°46′E

Barawa

Barawa مدينة بَراوة
Baraawe
Brava Ierè

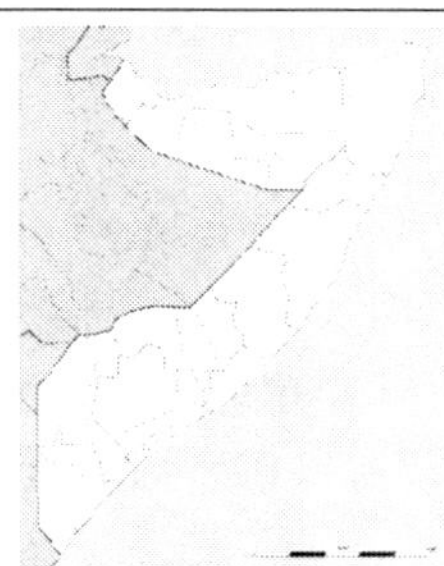

Barawa مدينة بَراوة
Location in Somalia

Coordinates: 1°12′N 44°02′E

Country	Somalia
Somalia	
District	Shabeellaha Hoose
Time zone	+3

Barawa or **Brava** (Somali: *Baraawe*, Arabic: مدينة براوة) is a port town on the south-eastern coast of Somalia. The traditional inhabitants are the Tunni Somalis and the Bravanese people, who speak Bravanese, a Swahili dialect.

History

In the 16th century, Barawa, which was then part of the Ajuuraan Empire, was sacked by the Portuguese during the *Battle of Barawa* but quickly recovered from the attack. In 1840, soldiers of the Bardheere Jama'a took the city under siege while attempting to discover a more direct sea route, and inflicted much damage. The town's inhabitants pleaded with Sultan Yusuf Mahamud Ibrahim of the Gobroon Dynasty for protection, with the Sultan's troops then invading Bardera and burned the city to the ground. Eventually, in 1889, Barawa was ceded to the control of the Italians when the Sultan of Zanzibar was forced to agree to the annexation of all the Banadir ports to the Italian Company already established in the Horn of Africa. The city, however, like the rest of the Benadir coast, was not under Zanzibari control but under Gobroon and Bimal rule, therefore making the Italian-Zanzibar agreement null and void. The Italians faced stiff resistance from many parts of the Benadir coast, and its inland regions and the slave trade of the Somali merchants would remain unchallenged for years to come.

Sheikh Uways al-Barawi organized an Ikhwaan and led the Banadir revolt, which was duly crushed in 1908. The Sheikh subsequently migrated to Biyoley to reorganize his Ikhwan, but was killed in 1909. One result of the unsuccessful revolt was the establishment of the Uwaysiyya order, named after the martyr Sheikh Uways, which succeeded in establishing jama'as in the riverine region of southern Somalia and neighboring regions, which acted as centres of charity and learning. In addition to the famous Sheikh Uways, Baraawe has produced numerous well respected Ulama including Sheikh Nureini Sabiri, Sheikh Qassim al-Baraawi, Sheikh Ma'llim Nuri and a female poet-saint, Dada Masiti.[*citation needed*] The city was the stronghold of the Hizbiya Digil-Mirifle (HDM) party, which was founded in 1947 and later became the Hizb al-Dastuur Mustaqil al-Somali (Somali Independent Constitutional Party, HDMS)

As of 2009, the Barawa area had come under the control of al-Shabab. In September 2009, a United States military raid killed Saleh Ali Saleh Nabhan, a suspected al-Qaida operative.

External links

- Bravanese [1]
- BravaOnLine [2]

Geographical coordinates: 1°12′N 44°02′E

Mandera

Mandera is a town in North Eastern Province, Kenya. It is capital of the Mandera District. The town is located at around 3°55′N 41°50′E, near the borders with Ethiopia and Somalia. It has a population of 30,433 (1999 census) [1]

It used to be one single district subdivided into the three constituencies of Mandera Central, Mandera East and Mandera west. However, in 2007, president Kibaki created two new districts called Mandera west and Mandera central in effect turning every constituency into a district.

It is located in an area prone to drought. From late 2005, there has been a severe famine. As with the other areas of the North Eastern Province, Mandera is inhabited almost exclusively by ethnic Somalis. The major three clans in the town are Murule, Garre and Degodiya. Other clans include Sheekhaal, Marehan, Sharmooge and Leysan clans.

Subdivison

Mandera as a whole used to be one district that was divided into three constituencies, namely Mandera East, Mandera Central and Mandera West. However, in 2007, president Kibaki ordered the creation of two more districts in the area which turned the area into three districts by creating two more districts of Mandera Central and Mandera West.

Climate

Mandera

Climate chart (explanation)

J	F	M	A	M	J	J	A	S	O	N	D

average max. and min. temperatures in °C

precipitation totals in mm

Imperial conversion

J	F	M	A	M	J	J	A	S	O	N	D

average max. and min. temperatures in °F

precipitation totals in inches

The Climate of Mandera is an arid climate under the Koppen climate classification. Temperatures tend to be hot throughout the year. Daily temperatures are typically above 30 °C (86 °F) while at night, temperatures can fall to 20 °C (68 °F). Precipitation is extremely low, with the area receiving very minimal amount of rain. Droughts are not unusual, often resulting in significant loss of livestock to the inhabitants of the rural towns, many of whom remain nomads.

Inter-Clan conflict

The region around Mandera, known as the Mandera triangle, is prone to conflicts between the Somali clans who dominate the area. Clan clashes between the Garre and Murule Somali clans in Mandera district has so far claimed at least 100 lives since they first erupted in December 2004.

The conflicts were triggered by the December 19th, 2004 murder of a Murulle relief worker by Garre gunmen at Fino-Elwak road junction. He was apparently suspected of being a spy working inside of Murule territory. This killing led to growing hostility between the two clans, which eventually degenerated into full-scale overt confrontation in January 2005.

A number of issues have been advanced to explain the cause and genesis of this clan conflict.

In 1988, Mandera Central constituency was carved out from the then larger Mandera East where Murule dominate following devastating clan clashes between Murule and Garre clans in early 1980's. This creation of a new constituency was envisaged at cooling growing tensions between the two clans over political representation.

With Mandera Central constituency formed, the issue of political representation was solved but another problem was born. There emerged growing hatred and suspicion between the two clans. Differences began to widen to an extent that the clan leadership and chiefs from both clans started to openly mobilise their clan members for the domination of the other.

And to worsen the already fragile situation, the KANU administration (especially between 1982-2002) created many administrative units (sublocations, locations and divisions) in hitherto community-grazing areas in the district, mainly for political mileage. The disputed Alango location (both clans claiming ownership of the two locations, one in Mandera East and the other in Mandera Central constituencies) is a good example of conflict arising from creation and or competition over administrative units. Chiefs and their assistants in the location and other neighbouring locations have been clamouring that their boundaries have been interfered with.

Murule and Garre clans have accused each other of harbouring and supporting foreign militia. Watering livestock at Alango Dam has often resulted in confrontations and armed violence.

Although the creation of additional administrative units was meant to make 'services closer to the people', it is important to point out that that has not been the case in Mandera and adjacent districts. These additional locations and sub locations have mainly contributed to the escalation of conflicts in the entire North Eastern province, because clans which felt they have an upper hand in the politics were "out manoeuvered" by others.

On the other hand, the power struggle between different factions in Somalia has spilled over to the Kenyan side. Each of the clan has been trying to forge military alliance with their counterparts in Somali.

The Murule have allegedly forged an alliance with the Ali Dera section of the larger Marehaan clan of Somalia, which are a power house in the Gedo region of Somalia.

The Garre, too, have allegedly forged an alliance with their Garre kinsmen in Ethiopia and Somalia. It is also rumoured that these alliances are being forged ahead of the 2007 general elections as each group intends to mobilize enough voters to sustain their political representation and or supremacy.

Competition over access to pasture and water resources in the district has been the traditional cause and trigger of conflict between the two clans. The Garre community wants herders to be confined to their traditionally designated grazing areas. Murulle community who happen to own substantial number of livestock including camels but have a smaller grazing area are of the opinion that the former's position is meant to confine them to a very small grazing area, which cannot sustain their huge camel herds and deny them access to pasture on the western flank of the district, which is mainly inhabited by the Garre.

Civil Action projects, supported through the Combined Joint Task Force - Horn of Africa (CJTF-HOA), a U.S. led multi-nation group based in Djibouti, has established a closer working relationships with local people of Arabia, Mandera East in order to end the threat of terrorism in the region.

Former U.S. Ambassador to Kenya William M. Bellamy on January 2004, presided the construction of the Arabia Secondary School in Mandera District of Kenya's North Eastern Province. He was hosted by the area M.P., the Hon. Shabaan Isaak.

The Arabia Secondary School project is by far the largest of many similar "Civil Action" projects in Kenya. Over the past year U.S. military and counterparts in the Kenyan Department of Defense Projects have worked together on projects at various locations in that area. U.S. soldiers and the Kenyan military cooperated over the past several months on that project to refurbish and expand facilities at the school, located some 70 km. south of Mandera town.

The Arabia Secondary School now has a library, a new dining hall and kitchen, and an additional classroom building. As a result, the number of students attending the school will increase from 160 to 240. The U.S. committed a total of 7.3 million Kshs. to underwrite the project, using local contractors and supplies.

Notable among personalities from Mandera include The Barclays Bank of Kenya Managing director, Adan Mohamed and former chairman of the Law Society of Kenya, Ahmed Nasser.

In the 2007 election, the former Assistant minister for Local Government Shaaban Issack has been defeated by ODM's Hussein after serving the area for almost three consecutive terms. However, he disputed the results, citing election malpractices and lodged a petition in the high court of Kenya before withdrawing it.

Rape and torture allegations

In 2008, there has again being an inter-clan conflict between Garre and Murulle. The government sent security forces, including the military, to quell the violence. They were sent to Elwak, an area largely inhabited by the Garre clan. The residents accused the forces of torture and rape. Human Rights Watch said its research showed that thousands of residents had being tortured and women raped and called for an inquiry into what it called collective punishment. The Police however maintain that there had neither been torture nor beatings.

External links

- Food distribution in Mandera district (Kenya) [2]

References

it is worth noting that the use of Heer system (traditional way of solving conflict among Somalis) play a significant role whereby elders were instrumental in mediating between waring clans which have been used in similar inter and intra clan conflict in North Eastern province.

th

Merca

Merca مركة *Marka*	
 Merca city	
 Merca مركة Location of Merca in Somalia	
Coordinates: 1°42.89′N 44°46.2′E	
Country	Somalia
Region	Lower Shabele
District	
Population	
- Total	350,000 est.
Time zone	East Africa Time (UTC+3)

Merca (Somali: *Marka*, Arabic: مركة) is a port city on the coast of southern Somalia, facing the Indian Ocean. It is the main town in the Lower Shabele region, and is located approximately 70 km (45 miles) southwest of the nation's capital, Mogadishu.

History

Minaret and moonrise in Merca.

Merca was established in the 5th century by the Biyomaal clan. The first Somalis arrived in the city in the 3rd century BC and gained control of the area and the local trade.

The Biyomaal and the Ashraaf of Merca fought against the Italian colonialists of Italian Somaliland in a twenty-year war known as the *Biyomaal and Ashraaf Revolt* in which many of their warriors assassinated several Italian governors. During the Biyomaal and Ashraaf Revolt, several prominent leaders were killed. Monuments erected in their memory can still be found in Merca.

In the late 20th century, the town gained a reputation as a beach resort, although it was subsequently severely damaged during the Somali Civil War. On 13 November 2008, Al-Shabaab took control of the city.

Art

Although visual art is not popular in Somalia due to prevailing beliefs that it contradicts Islam's proscription on all forms of idolatry, a lot of the known visual art in the country derives from the small historical town of Merca. Known for its beautiful white sandy beaches and orange dunes, the city's picturesque contrast of colors serves as an inspiration for local visual artists.

See also

- Mogadishu

External links

- Osmanart [1] - homepage of visual artist from Merca

Jowhar

Jowhar	
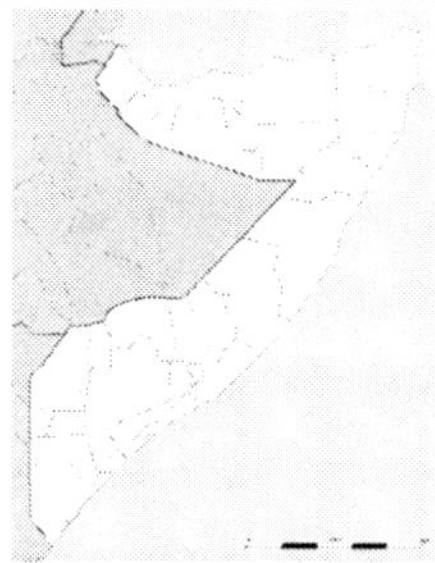 Jowhar Location in Somalia	
Coordinates: 2°47′N 45°30′E	
Country	Somalia
Region	Shabeellaha Dhexe
District	
Elevation	328 ft (100 m)
Population (2005)	
- Total	48,000
Time zone	East Africa Time (UTC+3)

Jowhar (Somali: *Jowhaar*, Arabic: جوهر, Italian: *Villaggio Duca degli Abruzzi*) is the capital town of the Shabeellaha Dhexe region of Somalia (located at 2°46.8′N 45°30.048′E), and, along with Baidoa, used to form the joint administrative capital of the Transitional Federal Government, which captured it from the Islamic Courts Union.

The town lies 90 km (50 mi) along a major road north of the nominal national capital of Mogadishu. There is an airport in the north of the town.

History

Jowhar was founded by an Italian Duke, Luigi Amedeo Savoia, who first came to the African continent in 1883 and liked the place. He raised funds to build dams, roads, a railroad, schools, hospitals, a Church, and a Mosque. He eventually married a Somali woman and died in his village.

Villaggio Duca degli Abruzzi

Italian explorer and nobleman Luigi Amedeo Savoia-Aosta founded in 1920 the eponymous *Villaggio Duca degli Abruzzi* as an agricultural settlement in Italian Somalia experimenting with new cultivation techniques. In 1926, the colony comprised 16 villages, with some 3,000 Somali and 200 Italian inhabitants.

Situated between the Darod and the Hawiye Somali clan strongholds, the area is of strategic importance. It is also of considerable economic value notably due to its banana, cotton and sugar plantations.

From 1911 in Jowhar (ex-Giohar), Italians like the Prince of Savoy, Luigi Amedeo, started to take the local farmers and resettle them in specific new villages in an attempt to improve the economy of Italian Somalia. The area around the *Villaggio Duca degli Abruzzi* was the most agriculturally developed of Somalia before World War II and had some food industries..

In the 1920s, during the construction of a new dam, the Italians forced the local population of the area to resettle, and in the process generated resentment.

In 1940, the *Villaggio Duca degli Abruzzi* (called even "Villabruzzi") already had a population of 12,000, of whom nearly 3,000 were Italian Somalians, and enjoyed a notable level of development as a small manufacturing area.

The Italians, who believed in the economic potential of the region, also built a railroad system that linked Jowhar to Mogadishu for the next thirty years, and was used mainly to export bananas and coffee to Europe.

At independence, the vacuum created by the outgoing Italians was not filled by the new Somali elites in charge, as the latter deemed the cattle trade and urban assets more profitable.

After WWII

Jowhar changed name from the Italian *Villaggio Duca degli Abruzzi* to the actual name in 1960, when Somalia gained its independence.

With a "socialist" regime in 1969, such a fertile land was nationalized and was only available to cultivators through fifty years leases. The government fixed the prices of agricultural products and could purchase up to 80% of the harvests. Under Co-operative Act n°70 of 1973, petty farmers were expropriated again to leave place for the State orientated Fanoole Rice Farm, Mogambo Irrigation Project and Juba Sugar Complex.

Jowhar only became the regional capital in the mid-1980s when Mogadishu was taken out of Shabeellaha Dhexe to form its own region, Banaadir.

Role in Transitional Federal Government

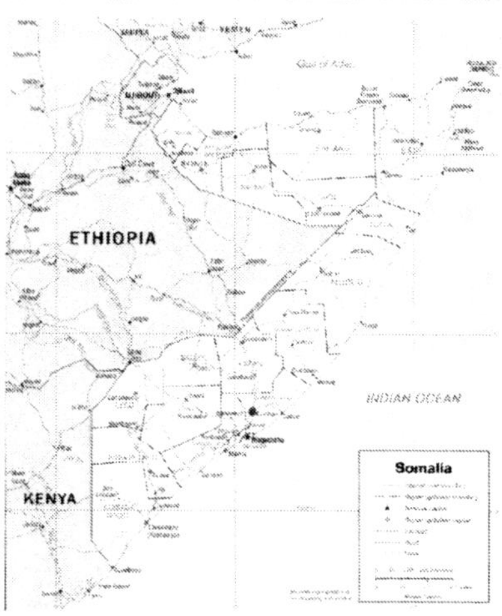

Political map of Somalia showing the location of Jowhar (here spelled "Giohar"), north of Mogadishu, with a red dot.

As part of a 2004 agreement, Jowhar and the town of Baidoa were to form a joint administrative capital of the Transitional Federal Government, sited away from Mogadishu for security reasons. Continued fighting has threatened to derail the peace process, but in July 2005, transitional president Abdullahi Yusuf Ahmed relocated to the town from his base in Bossaso, moving the process forward, and joining transitional Prime Minister Ali Mohammed Ghedi, already resident in the town one month. Part of the parliament became based in Jowhar, while some ministries were established in Mogadishu. By February 2006, despite Ghedi's security concerns[1], the two leaders had left to Baidoa, where it was decided the parliament would meet.

Recent fighting

Main article: Battle of Jowhar

On December 27, 2006, the internationally-backed transitional government forces, united with Ethiopian troops, recaptured Jowhar from the Islamic Courts Union.

On May 17, 2009, the Islamic al-Shabab militia took over the town.

External links

- Article with photos on a 2005 visit to 'Villaggio Duca degli abruzzi' and areas of former Italian Somalia (in italian) [2]
- 2°46′47″N 45°30′11″E

Bibliography

- VILLES EN GUERRE EN SOMALIE :MOGADISCIO ET HARGEISA Marc-Antoine PÉROUSE DE MONTCLOS (http://ceped.cirad.fr/cdrom/integral_publication_1988_2002/dossier/pdf/dossiers_cpd_59.pdf)

See also

- Italian Somalians
- Railway Mogadiscio-Villabruzzi

Hobyo

Hobyo	
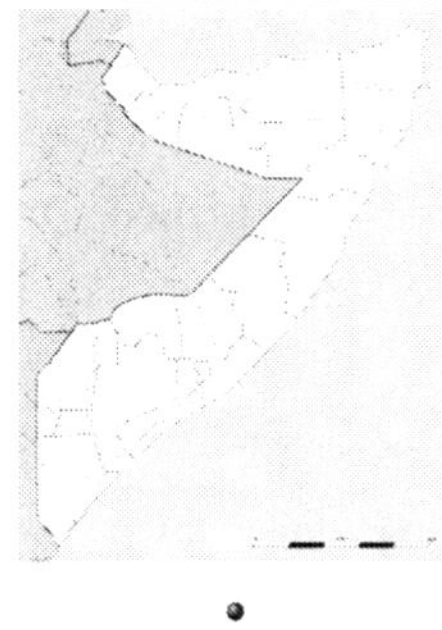 Hobyo Location in Somalia	
Coordinates: 5°21′N 48°32′E	
Country	Somalia
Region	Mudug
District	
Time zone	East Africa Time (UTC+3)

Hobyo (also spelled *Obbia* and *Hobyaa*) is an ancient harbor city in the Mudug region of Somalia. Hobyo literally means "here, water", and the plentiful fresh water to be had from the wells in and around the town (a rarity in this part of the world) has been the driving force behind Hobyo's ancient status as a favorite port-of-call for sailors.

Hobyo's Origins (12th century to 15th century)

Hobyo's history began as a place for sailors and caravans to get fresh water, thus its name. It only became a town of importance when the Muslim pilgrims departing for Mecca on their Hajj and the sea captains who would take them there began favoring the town as a point of departure because of its fresh water. This sea and land traffic soon led to Hobyo becoming something of a commercial center. Opone, the once-great entrepot, which had been the center of commerce, began its decline into obscurity.

The increasing importance and rapid settlement of more southernly cities such as Mogadishu further boosted the prosperity of Hobyo, as more and more ships made their way down the Somali coast and stopped in Hobyo to trade and replenish their water.

Hobyo in the Medieval World (15th century to 17th century)

Hobyo was the commercial centre of the Ajuuraan State, based in Qalafo (located in the present-day Ogaden). Commercial goods harvested along the Shabelle River (especially around the agricultural centers of Harardheere and El-Dheer) were brought to Hobyo for trade. The Ajuuraan rulers collected their tribute from the town in the form of sorghum (durra).

Hobyo's Ajuuraan rulers were allies with and occasionally overlords of the Mogadishu Sultanate, and trade between Hobyo and the Benadir coast flourished for some time. So vital was Hobyo to the prosperity of the Ajuuraan State that when the Hiraab (a lineage of closely related Hawiye clans) successfully revolted against the Ajuuraan and established an independent Hiraab Imamate, which included Hobyo, the Ajuran's might dwindled rapidly. This was not the only fragmentation of the Ajuuraan State, as the Warsengali also broke away to form their own sultanate in the north, and the Majerteen Sultanate shook off centuries of Ajuuraan hegemony. The Ajuuraan remained in their power base in Qalafo, but were a shadow of their former selves.

Hobyo in the Colonial Era (17th century to 20th century)

A Majerteen pretender to the throne, Yusuf Ali Keenadid, who had been exiled to Arabia by sultan Boqor Isman Mahamud after a failed coup d'etat, returned from Arabia and invaded Hobyo with an army of mercenaries from Hadramut in 1878. After conquering Hobyo from the Hiraab Imamate, he established himself as the Sultan of Hobyo.

The Hiraab Imam had become too involved in the politics and conflicts with other Hawiye clans, with the Sultan of Oman and with the Portuguese, which had drawn his attention south to Mogadishu, and little resistance to Yusuf Ali Keenadid could be mustered.

The rest of the Hiraab Imamate was rapidly snapped up by the Italians, though the Imam remained a powerful force due to his influence over Hiraab communities, and plays an important part in politics right up to the present day.

The people in and around Hobyo grew mainly sorghum and beans as their staple foods, supplementing this with herds of camels, cattle, goats and sheep. Livestock, hides and skin, aromatic woods and raisins were the primary exports, while rice, other foodstuffs and clothes were imported. Merchants looking for exotic goods came to Hobyo to buy textiles, precious metals and pearls.

Modern Hobyo (20th century to the present day)

With the defeat of the Sultanate of Hobyo at the hands of Fascist Italy 50 years later, Hobyo was annexed into Italian East Africa.

After its annexation by Italy, Hobyo's lifeblood, the trade routes that had passed through the town for 10 centuries, moved permanently south to Mogadishu. The town never recovered. The majority of the populace, who had been involved in said mercantile activities, followed the trade down to Mogadishu, establishing the link between these cities that has existed to this day, and the town has played no major role in any of the ensuing conflicts with Ethiopia either as part of Italian East Africa or independent Somalia. The governments of both have actively encouraged the town's decline in fact, as they increasingly centralized Hobyo's historical roles within Mogadishu. Hobyo is a shadow of its former importance and wealth.

Hobyo was captured by the Islamic Court Union (ICU) on August 16, 2006, after several days negotiation with leading figures in the town. ICU armed pickup trucks ("technicals") surrounded the town several days before, and sent in delegates to negotiate Hobyo's surrender. The city was apparently taken without firing a shot, as the unnamed warlord of Hobyo had fled days earlier upon hearing of the ICU's approach.

The ICU had taken the town in an unsuccessful attempt to end piracy on the Benadir Coast, and Hobyo was the last remaining major port south of Puntland.

Hobyo chose to join the newly formed Galmudug State as an alternative to annexation by the ICU, creating a buffer between the ICU and Puntland, but with the rise in conflict between Galmudug and the ICU, ICU forces took the city again on November 1.

Hobyo's present status is clear, as the clans Saad is Powerful around Hobyo controlling Hobyo, broke away from the ICU just before the Ethiopian offensive to the coast.At the moments Contralling Ahlusunna WalJaaca as they are Contrallars of Galmudug State.

Hobyo is also involved in piracy, serving as a location for pirates to anchor hijacked ships, such as the MV Faina, while demanding ransoms.

See also

- Galmudug

References

Geographical coordinates: 5°21′N 48°32′E

Hargeisa

Hargeisa
Hargaysa
هرجيسا

Central Hargeisa at dusk.

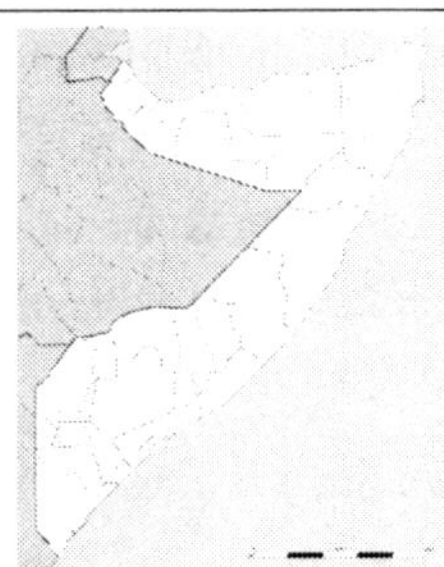

Hargeisa

Location of Hargeisa in Somalia

Coordinates: 9°30′N 44°0′E

***De facto* state**	Somaliland
***De jure* state**	Somalia (claims all of Somaliland)
Region	Somaliland
Sub-Region	Maroodi Jeex
Granted capital status	1941 (*British Somaliland*)
	1960 (*State of Somaliland*)
	1991 (*Somaliland*)
Government	

- Mayor	Mudane Hussain Mohammoud Jiciir
Elevation	1326 m (4350 ft)
Population	
- Total	1300000
- Density	15/km^2 (38.8/sq mi)
Time zone	EAT (UTC+3)
Languages	Somali, Arabic and English
Religion	Sunni Islam
Website	Hargeisa New Site [1] Old Site [2]

Hargeisa (Somali: *Hargaysa*, Arabic: هرجيسا) is the capital of the Woqooyi Galbeed region and the 2nd largest city in Somalia with a population of approximately 1.3 million. Hergesia is the capital of Somaliland, a *de facto* independent republic that is internationally recognized as a part of Somalia. It was the colonial capital of British Somaliland from 1941 to 1960 when it gained independence as the State of Somaliland and united with Italian Somaliland to form the Somali Republic.

History

Prehistoric inhabitants

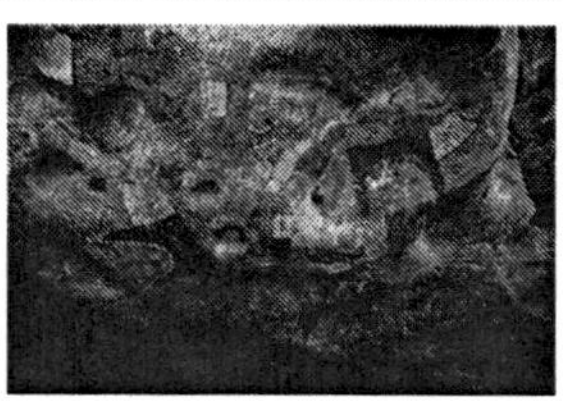

The Laas Geel rock art on the outskirts of Hargeisa.

The city is home to Neolithic cave paintings recently discovered named Laas Geel. The cave paintings are situated on the outskirts of the city, located around a plethora of granite alcoves and rocky mountains. The paintings show ancient inhabitants of the area worshipping cattle. It also shows animals which are commonly seen in the region primarily antelopes, camels and early dogs. The Laas Geel cave paintings were discovered in November 2002 by a French archaeological team. They contain some of the earliest known art in the Horn region and Africa in general, dating back to somewhere between 8,000 and 9,000 BCE.

British Somaliland

A civil war-era plane monument in the center of Hargeisa.

In 1888, after signing successive treaties with the then ruling Somali Sultans such as Mohamoud Ali Shire of the Warsangali Sultanate, the British established a protectorate in the region referred to as British Somaliland. The British garrisoned the protectorate from Aden in present-day Yemen, and administered it from their British India colony until 1898. British Somaliland was then administered by the Foreign Office until 1905 and afterwards by the Colonial Office.

Berbera, a major trading harbour on the Red Sea, was the protectorate's first capital due to its strategic importance. However, the capital was moved from Berbera to Hargeisa, and the city was granted capital status in 1941. During the East African Campaign, the protectorate was occupied by Italy in August 1940, but recaptured by the British in March 1941. The protectorate gained its independence on 26 June 1960. Days later, the country was unified with Italian Somaliland to form a new Somali Republic (Somalia) on 1 July 1960.

1980s events

Due to the Barre regime's violent repression, Somalis in the northwestern part of the country (particularly the Isaaq clan), encouraged by Ethiopia in opposition to Somalia, took up arms and formed the Somaliland National Movement (S.N.M.) in 1981 to resist Barre. In the late 1980s, Barre virtually lost control of the province and ordered the air force to bomb Hargeisa, today's capital of Somaliland. The bombing and subsequent raids of government troops claimed tens of thousands of casualties.

A war memorial in the form of a MiG fighter jet was erected in Hargeisa to mark this event.

Reconstruction

As control of Mogadishu shifted in favor of the United Somali Congress (USC) in 1991, a power struggle between the leaders had led to the city's destruction. While Mogadishu and the rest southern Somalia were being destroyed, the opposite was happening in Hargeisa and the rest of northwestern Somalia. By 18 May, 1991, secessionists in the Somaliland region had declared independence and reconstruction had begun.

Small section of Hargeisa.

Since 1991, the city has undergone a massive facelift and over 99% of devastated commercial and residential homes have now been rebuilt and in better condition than before the war. Remittance money sent from overseas relatives contributed tremendously in the reconstruction of the city as well as entrepreneurial spirit of local residents and citizens throughout the Somaliland region.

Hargeisa has working traffic lights and traffic laws are respected. All residents entitled to drive must hold a photo driving license. All cars bear Somaliland license plates.

Geography

Hargeisa countryside

Hargeisa is located in a valley in the western section of the country. The city is in a mountainous area because it is situated in an enclosed valley of the Galgodon (Ogo) highlands, at an elevation of 1,334 meters (4,377 ft) above sea level. This altitude gives Hargeisa and the surrounding area a milder climate than the Gulf of Aden coastal area (one of the hottest areas on earth) and the Hargeisa region has a fairly equable climate. The temperature ranges between 13 and 32 degrees Celsius (55 and 89 degrees Fahrenheit).

Hargeisa receives larger amounts of rain, and used to be surrounded by forest when the city was smaller but the countryside around the city still has small juniper forests. Near Hargeisa are the fertile Sheikh and Daallo mountains, which also receive large amount of rain. South of Hargeisa is the Sahaley Savannah which attracts many different animals to graze in the area

Hargeisa is also close to another town in northwestern Somalia called *Arabsiyo*. It is a major farming and agricultural area and it falls into the main boundaries of Hargeisa.

Great Kudus

Wildlife

Due to its fertility and greenery, wild animals (e.g. zebras) come to the Hargeisa area to either breed or graze on the grassland savannah. Animals that can be found in Hargeisa include the Kudu, wild boar, Somali Wild Ass, warthogs, antelopes, the Somali sheep, wild goats, camels and many different types of birds. South of Hargeisa is a grassland savannah, which attracts many types of wildlife to the area including lions and leopards.

Economy

A shopping mall in downtown Hargeisa.

Hargeisa is the financial hub to many entrepreneurial industries ranging from food processing, gem stonecutters, construction, retail, import and export, Internet cafes, and companies that process remittances from relatives abroad who send money. Some families have moved back to the city, living in mansions in the hills during the summer.

Hargeisa city is the namesake of Hargeisa Minerals & Resources Company and contains many of Somaliland's business Headquarters in its city limits.

The city also has a private and public menageries, it houses animals from the region including lions, leopards, antelopes, birds and reptiles.

Transport

The city is home to Hargeisa International Airport, with flights to Addis Ababa, Djibouti City, Dubai and many other cities across Africa and Somalia. All foreigners are required to exchange 50 US Dollars to local currency (which is the Somaliland Shilling. (1 USD=6700 Somaliland Shillings in Open market as of April 2009, Official rate is almost half of the open market). There are local bus services in Hargeisa. There are also other buses and shared taxis that goes to other cities in Somaliland.

Hargeisa International Airport

Paved roads are available in Hargeisa, however most have been badly damaged by tanks and shelling during the war. The vast majority of the roads were paved by the British, during colonial rule. The local government has repaired some of the roads but many others are still awaiting repair.

Buses are the most commonly used form of public transport in the city. They travel on a number of routes serving nearly all districts of the city. Intra-city bus services are available connecting the major towns and cities like Burao, Berbera and Borama to Hargeisa.

Taxis are available, but are a less common form of public transport.

Education

School classroom

In Hargeisa, there are several colleges and some universities; the main ones includes University of Hargeisa, Admas University College, Somaliland University of Technology, Gollis University and Hope University

The Edna Adan Maternity Hospital offers nursing programmes.

There are also several state-run and privately owned secondary and high schools including Abaarso Tech, the premiere secondary school in the capital region. In addition, many primary schools and nurseries are dispersed all around the city.

Students receive instruction from teachers who have studied abroad or from teachers who were educated prior to the Somali Civil War.

Communication

Hargeisa has a modern telephone system and nearly everyone in the city enjoys a telephone and some with access to the internet. Internet cafes are dotted all around Hargeisa and many youngsters and adults benefit from this. Mobile communication services are available in Hargeisa. The main mobile communication services in Hargeisa are operated by Telesom, Nationlink Somaliland, Soltelco Telcom and Somtel.

See also

- Arabsiyo
- Salahlay
- Toon

External links

- Hargeisa City Gov New Site [1]
- Hargeisa City Government Old Site [2]

Geographical coordinates: 9°30′N 44°0′E

Attractions In and Around the City

Mogadishu Cathedral

Cattedrale di Mogadiscio Mogadishu Cathedral	

Basic information	
Location	Somalia
Geographic coordinates	2°2′8″N 45°20′29″E
Affiliation	Roman Catholic
Year consecrated	1928
Ecclesiastical or organizational status	Cathedral
Architectural description	
Architectural style	Norman Gothic
Completed	1928

Mogadishu Cathedral was a Roman Catholic cathedral located in Mogadishu, Somalia, and seat of the Roman Catholic Diocese of Mogadiscio. It was built in 1928 in accordance with the Italian plan for the development of Mogadishu as capital of Italian Somaliland. It was built in a Norman Gothic style, and based on Cefalù Cathedral. The last Bishop of Mogadishu, Salvatore Colombo, was killed while saying mass in this cathedral by armed insurgents in 1989.. After some years, the building was completely destroyed by Muslim fundamentalists..

References

Based on Italian article

Mosque of Islamic Solidarity

Mosque of Islamic Solidarity	
 The Mosque of Islamic Solidarity in Mogadishu, overlooking the Indian Ocean.	
Basic information	
Location	Mogadishu Somalia
Affiliation	Islam
Architectural description	
Architectural type	Mosque
Completed	1987
Specifications	
Minaret(s)	1

The **Mosque of Islamic Solidarity** (Somali: *Masjidka Isbaheysiga*) is a mosque located in Mogadishu, Somalia.

History

The Mosque of Islamic Solidarity was constructed in 1987 with financial support from the Saudi Fahd bin Abdul Aziz Al Saud Foundation. It is the main mosque in Somalia's capital city, and an iconic building in Somali society.

For 16 years following the outbreak of the Somali Civil War, the mosque had been closed down. However, in 2006, with the rise to power of the Islamic Courts Union, it was reopened once again.

Capacity and location

Capable of accommodating up to 10,000 worshippers, the Mosque of Islamic Solidarity is the single largest masjid in the Horn of Africa. The mosque also overlooks the Indian Ocean.

Maintenance

While parts of the mosque have collapsed since the start of the civil war in Somalia in 1991, the Islamic Courts Union has attempted to restore it. The deputy chairman of the ICU's executive committee has also called on Somali merchants and businessmen to assist in the restoration efforts.

See also

- Islam in Somalia
- Architecture of Somalia
- Timeline of Islamic history
- Islamic architecture
- Islamic art
- List of mosques

References

- Somalia Largest Mosque Opens [1] - *Islamonline.net*
- Shaul Shay, *Somalia between jihad and restoration*, (Transaction Publishers: 2008)

Fakr ad-Din Mosque

Fakr ad-Din Mosque مسجد فخر الدين زنكي	
 The 13th century Fakr ad-Din mosque in Mogadishu, Somalia.	
Basic information	
Location	Mogadishu Somalia
Affiliation	Islam
Architectural description	
Architectural type	Mosque
Completed	1269
Specifications	
Dome(s)	2

The **Fakr ad-Din Mosque** (Arabic: مسجد فخر الدين زنكي) is the oldest mosque in Mogadishu, Somalia. It is located in *Hamar Weyne* (literally "Big Town"), the oldest part of the city.

Description

The mosque was built in 1269 by the first Sultan of Mogadishu. Stone, including Indian marble, and coral were the primary materials used in the construction of the mosque, which displays a compact rectangular plan with a domed mihrab axis. Glazed tiles were also used in the decoration of mihrab, one of which bears a dated inscription.

Photographs of the Fakr ad-Din mosque feature in drawings and photographs of central Mogadishu from the late 19th century onwards. The mosque can be identified amidst other buildings by its two cones, one round and the other hexagonal.

External links

- Description of mosque at ArchNet. [1]
- 1882 [2]
- 1882 - Behind the market [3]
- 1910 [4]
- 1930's - immediate left [5]
- 1936 - on the middle left [6]
- 1981 [7]
- 1986 - lower centre [8]

Villa Somalia

Villa Somalia is the presidential palace of Somalia, which sits on high ground near the shores of the Indian Ocean in Mogadishu, with access to both the harbor and airport.

The complex was the residence of the first president of Somalia, Aden Abdullah Osman Daar of the Somali Youth League (SYL); and of Siad Barre, president until his ouster in 1991. The compound was subsequently captured by the forces of Mohamed Farrah Aidid's United Somali Congress (USC) after a fierce battle for control of the capital.

By the time a United Nations relief mission, UNOSOM I, was launched to quell the fighting in Mogadishu, a Somali reconciliation conference had taken place in Djibouti. At this meeting, Ali Mahdi Mohamed was elected President by Somali politicians and clan leaders. However, political player and warlord Mohamed Farah Aidid rejected Ali Mohamed's selection by the conference and refused to submit to his rule. This resulted in four months of continued fighting between Mohamed and Aidid, the latter declaring himself Interim President. Aidid took control of Villa Somalia while both warlords fought for control of the city.

In 2006, Villa Somalia was held for eight weeks by clan forces loyal to Hussein Mohamed Farrah, following the Second Battle of Mogadishu. In late July, the compound was turned over to the Islamic Courts Union. ICU leader Abdirahman Janaqaw announced the complex would host an Islamic Sharia court. The Islamists held onto Villa Somalia until the complex was taken over on December 28, 2006, by forces loyal to the Transitional Federal Government (TFG), which is governed by the Transitional Federal Parliament (TFP) of Somalia. The ICU had previously fled the capital due to an impending TFG and Ethiopian attack.

On January 1, 2007, in a move towards disarmament and reconciliation, the government announced a weapons turn-in. All collected arms were to be registered at Villa Somalia; Villa Baidoa was also mentioned as an arms collection point. An amnesty to Islamists was also extended.

On January 8, 2007, as the Battle of Ras Kamboni raged, TFG President Abdullahi Yusuf Ahmed entered Mogadishu for the first time since being elected. It was announced that the government would be relocated to Villa Somalia from its interim location at Baidoa.

In August 2009, Garowe Online reported some of the 40 tonsWikipedia:Manual_of_Style of arms given by the U.S. government in military aid to the Transitional Federal Government stored at Villa Somali were now on sale in the *Cirtoogte* ("Sky Shooter") market, where they were fetching a high price when resold to members of the opposition Islamist fighters of al Shabaab.

Links

2°2′27″N 45°20′7″E - Geo Links

References

Geographical coordinates: 2°02′23″N 45°20′05″E

Gezira Beach

Gezira Beach (also known as Jezira Beach) is a former tourist attraction of the city of Mogadishu, the capital of Somalia.

In July 1989 Gezira beach was the site of a mass extrajudcial execution by security forces of 47 members of the Isaaq.

Shebelle River

Shebelle River

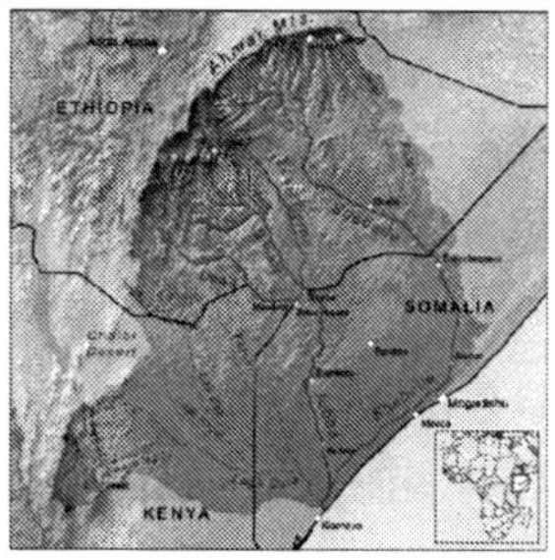

Map of the Jubba/Shebelle drainage basin

Origin	near 7°13′12″N 39°27′59″E
Mouth	Dries up near 0°09′57″N 42°46′22″E, occasionally continues into the Jubba River
Basin countries	Ethiopia, Somalia

The **Shebelle River** (Somali: *Webi Shabeelle*) begins in the highlands of Ethiopia, and then flows southeast into Somalia towards Mogadishu. Near Mogadishu, it turns sharply southwest, where it follows the coast. Below Mogadishu, the river becomes seasonal. During most years, the river dries up near the mouth of the Jubba River, while in seasons of heavy rainfall, the river actually reaches the Jubba and thus the Indian Ocean.

The Shebelle river's name is derived from the Somali term *Wabi Shabeelle*, meaning "Leopard/Tiger River". According to materials published by the Ethiopian Central Statistical Agency, the Shebelle is 1130 kilometers long, extending for 1000 km inside Ethiopia and 130 km inside Somalia. The Somali administrative regions consisting of Shabeellaha Dhexe and Shabeellaha Hoose are also named after the river.

Tributaries

The Shebelle has a number of tributaries, both seasonal and permanent rivers. They include:

- Erer River
- Galetti River
- Wabe River

The Fafen only reaches the Shebelle in times of heavy rainfall; its stream usually ends before reaching the main river.

History

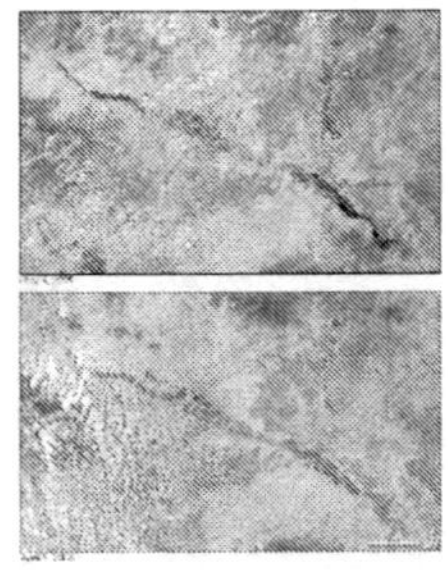

Satellite pictures showing the Shebelle valley in southern Somalia and Ethiopia before (below) and during (above) floods in 2005.

The source of the Shebelle River is venerated by both the Arsi Oromo and the Sidamo people. It is surrounded by a sacred enclosure wooded with juniper trees, which as of 1951 was under the protection of a Muslim member of the Arsi.

In 1989, with the help of Soviet engineers, the Melka Wakena dam was built on the upper reaches of the Shebelle River in the Bale Mountains. Producing 153 megawatts, this dam is Ethiopia's largest hydroelectric generator.

The recent history of the Shabelle is marked by frequent destructive flooding. The Shabelle is said to have flooded every other year prior to the 1960s; that decade had only two devastating floods, the *hidigsayley* in 1965, and the *soogudud* in 1966. In the 1970s, the most devastating flood was the *kabahay* of 1978. In 1996, floods devastated three woredas in Ethiopia. On 23 October 1999, the river unexpectedly flooded in the middle of the night, destroying homes and crops in 14 out of the 117 kebeles in Kelafo woreda, as well as 29 of the 46 kebeles in neighboring Mustahil woreda. According to the local authorities, 34 people and an estimated 750 livestock died, with 70,000 affected by the floods and in need of assistance. Two more recent floods was the *dawdle* in 2003, when about 100 livestock and 119 people were washed away, and the flood of April 2005, when about 30,000 persons were surrounded by floodwaters and 2000 camels and 4000 shoats had been washed away by flood; some locals consider this the worst flood in 40 years.

See also

- Geography of Ethiopia
- Geography of Somalia

External links

- ReliefWeb: Somalia Integrated Phase Classification Maps (as of Sep 2008) [1]
- Bale Mountains National Park [2]
- Map of the Shebelle River basin at Water Resources eAtlas [3]
- Hydropolitics in the Horn of Africa [4]

National Library of Somalia

The **National Library of Somalia** is, as its name suggests, the national library of Somalia. Established in 1975, it is located in Mogadishu. It came under the responsibility of the Ministry of Culture and Higher Education until the collapse of the government in 1991.

In 1983, it held approximately 7,000 books, little in the way of historical and cultural archival material, and was open to the general public. It was described in a UNESCO report as having "no regular acquisition budget", unqualified staff, unsuitable premises, and as being, on the whole, "little developed".

Bakaara Market

The **Bakaara Market** (Somali: *Suuqa Bakaaraha*) is an open market in Mogadishu, Somalia, and the largest in the nation. The name *Bakaaraha* derives from the Somali word for grain silo or storage, **baqaar.**

The market was created in late 1972 during the reign of Mohamed Siad Barre. Proprietors sold and still sell daily essentials (including staples such as maize, sorghum, beans, peanuts, sesame, wheat and rice), petrol and medicine, but it also largely expanded during the civil war and had has become notoriously known as a market of small arms and other weapons, including rocket propelled grenades (RPGs), mortars (80mm and 120mm), 23mm and 30mm antiaircraft guns, and ammunition of all types.

Bakaara Market in the heart of Mogadishu. Due to the fragility of the government, Somali marketplaces have thrived.

It is also famous for other illicit activities, such as forged Somali passports processed within minutes, including Ethiopian and Kenyan passports, and other forged documents, including but not limited to birth certificates and university diplomas. This illicit sub-market is famously known as *Cabdalle Shideeye,* named after one of its first proprietors.

The Bakaara Market is a focus of ongoing arms control efforts for the disarmament in Somalia, and has caught fire a few times in recent years.

Gunfire is commonly heard, as shoppers fire weapons into the air to test them before purchase, hence giving the sub-gun market the nickname *cirtoogte* (sky shooter). Anti-aircraft guns and mortars are tested at a further distance from the market. In 2001, a rough estimate by aid agencies placed the number of assault rifles in Mogadishu at somewhere near 1 million, for a city population of 1.5 million.

Battle of Mogadishu

In October 1993, the market was the site where one of the two Black Hawk helicopters were downed in the Battle of Mogadishu, which led to a fierce firefight in the area for the following hours as stated in the nonfiction book, *Black Hawk Down: A Story of Modern War.*

Violence, Fires, Counterfeit Currency

In 1997, a dispute arose over the control of the collection of taxes in the market. As a result of the confrontation, an RPG was fired into a fuel tank (which are above ground in the market, not stored underground). Several civilians were injured.

In March 1999 hundreds fled the market after fighting erupted. Fighting continued between Islamic Courts and secular militias through April.

On January 26, 2000, the market was the site of the shooting of Ahmed Kafi Awale, a radio commentator for Hussein Mohamed Aidid's Radio of the Somali People. Awale was there covering the market. Three others were killed and seven badly injured.

On January 5, 2001, a fire broke out in the market, caused by two fighting militias. The vegetable section of the market was destroyed, as was part of the milk section. Islamic Courts Union (ICU) militia forces broke up the fighting.

In February 2001, an influx of counterfeit currency led to the shutting of the market for a time. The Somali shilling collapsed. Traders only accepted U.S. dollars for a time. Not only the cost of arms were affected—the cost of food and essentials doubled during the crisis.

On April 10, 2004, another fire broke out in the market. According to a report to the UN Security Council:

> On the night of 10 April [2004], a serious fire in the main Bakaara market in Mogadishu resulted in at least eight people killed and more than 30 wounded. Armed looters shot indiscriminately into the crowd. The incident caused widespread insecurity in the areas surrounding the market.

On October 2, 2007, another raging fire started in the market, spreading rapidly. The fire reportedly was caused by a fired shell during a brief fight between the resistance forces against Ethiopian occupiers and their allied transitional government forces nearby.

On October 15, 2009, Al-Shabab insurgents shelled the Bakara Market with mortars, killing 20 people and wounding 58.

On May 1, 2010, two bombs detonated at a mosque near the market, killing 39 people and wounding 70.

Security Checkpoints

The security checkpoint for the market was controlled for a long while by Mohamed Qanyare Afrah, a Mogadishu warlord who was appointed Minister of National Security by the Transitional Federal Government. The checkpoints for the market were to be taken down in June 2005 as part of the Green Leaf for Democracy (GLED) initiative of a "Global Week against Small Arms."

Recent Activities

Main article: Disarmament in Somalia

The arms trading in the Bakaara Market was closed by the Islamic Courts Union (ICU) after they took control of the capital following the Second Battle of Mogadishu.

A fire broke out December 6, 2006, beginning at a charcoal storage facility and then spreading to nearby shops.

On December 11, the Islamists announced they planned to impose a tax on the market to raise funds for their movement. Before they could effect their plans, the ICU left the capital. On December 28, 2006, the market closed during the uncertainty of the Fall of Mogadishu.

Arms tradings recently re-opened with the ousting of the ICU by the Transitional Federal Government. However, Somali Prime Minister Ali Mohamed Gedi has ordered a disarmament of the populace, calling the future of the Bakaara Market into question.

A particular worry are the reports that children, armed with AK-47's and whips, are being used by the militant group al-Shabab as a method of enforcing their interpretation of Sharia law on the populace.

Istunka

Focus	Weapons
Country of origin	Somalia
Creator	Ajuuraans
Olympic sport	no

Culture of Somalia

Art
Architecture
Pottery · Textile
Music · Wood carving
Language
Literature · Mythology
Writing systems · Poetry
Other
Dance · Dress
Games · Cuisine
Society · History
Islam · Festivals · Institutions
Science and Technology
Maritime · Medicine · Astronomy · Media
Cinema · Coinage
See also
Education · Politics
Symbols · Military

Istunka is an annual martial arts festival held in the town of Afgooye, Somalia during the Somali new year. It traces itself back to the medieval Ajuuraan State and was centralized under Sultan Ahmed Yusuf during the 19th century Gobroon Dynasty. The tournament consists of several teams engaging each other in stick-combat.

Origin

The Istunka tournament was developed in the Ajuuraan period and was celebrated subsequently each year during the Somali new year along side other festivals such as Nowruz. It was not until the Gobroon Dynasty and the reign of Sultan Ahmed Yusuf that the martial art festival became a centralized tournament with separate teams each supported by an assembly of poets, female vocalists and dance groups throughout the duration of the contest.

Modern

In the modern era the festival became a popular tourist attraction in Somalia, particularly during the 1970s and 80s. It is still practiced annually in the Afgooye region.

See also

- Culture of Somalia
- Martial arts
- Stick fighting

Gelbis

Gelbis is a Somali Wedding Celebration where the bride and the groom are taken to the streets, especially on horses or on cars with people singing and dancing in happy moods.

Badbaado

Full name	Badbaado Football Club
Ground	Badbaado Mogadishu, Somalia (Capacity: 35000)
Chairman	
Manager	
League	Somalia League

Badbaado FC is a Somali football club based in Mogadishu, Somalia.

Banadir Stadium

Banadir Stadium	
Full name	Banadir Stadium
Location	Mogadishu, Somalia
Opened	1956
Renovated	2009
Expanded	1980's
Capacity	15,000
Tenants	

Banadir Stadium is a multi-use stadium in Mogadishu, Somalia . It is currently used mostly for football matches. It was opened in 1956 by the Italian National Olympic Committee . It is currently being rebuilt by FIFA's Win in Africa with Africa program.

External links

- Stadium information [1]

Mogadiscio Stadium

Mogadiscio Stadium is the national stadium of Somalia. It is located in the nation's capital, Mogadishu.

History and usage

The stadium was constructed during the Siad Barre administration, with the assistance of Chinese engineers. Mogadiscio Stadium was used for other purposes besides hosting sporting events; presidential addresses and political rallies, among other events, were also held there.

Capacity and facilities

Mogadiscio Stadium has a capacity of 35,000 spectators. It features a tournament ground, as well as grounds for track and field, football, basketball, volleyball and tennis.

Geographical coordinates: 2°4′3.1″N 45°20′7.7″E

References

- Daily report: People's Republic of China, Issues 53-61, (National Technical Information Service: 1986)

Music and Cuisine

Music of Somalia

Culture of Somalia

Art
Architecture
Pottery · Textile
Music · Wood carving
Language
Literature · Mythology
Writing systems · Poetry
Other
Dance · Dress
Games · Cuisine
Society · History
Islam · Festivals · Institutions
Science and Technology
Maritime · Medicine · Astronomy · Media
Cinema · Coinage
See also
Education · Politics
Symbols · Military

The **music of Somalia** generally refers to the music of the Somali people, as Somalia has the distinction of being one of the few countries in Africa that is almost entirely composed of one ethnic group.

Overview

Somalia has a rich musical heritage centered on traditional Somali folklore. Most Somali songs are pentatonic; that is, they only use five pitches per octave in contrast to a heptatonic (seven note) scale such as the major scale. At first listen, Somali music might be mistaken for the sounds of nearby regions such as Ethiopia, Sudan or Arabia, but it is ultimately recognizable by its own unique tunes and styles. Somali songs are usually the product of collaboration between lyricists (*midho*), songwriters (*lahan*), and singers (*'odka* or "voice"). Native instruments include the batar drum and the *kaban* or oud. Bands such as Waaberi and Horseed have gained a small following outside of the country. Others, such as Ahmed Cali Cigal and Maryam Mursal, have fused traditional Somali music with rock and roll, bossa nova, jazz, and other modern influences.

History

The first major form of modern Somali music began in the mid-1930s, when northern Somalia was a part of the British Somaliland Protectorate. This style of music was known as Xer-Dhaanto, an innovative, urban form of Somali folk dance and song. This period also saw the rise of the Xaaji Baal Baal Dance Troupe, which became very influential over the course of its long career.

Somali popular music began with the *balwo* style, which was created by Abdi Sinimo. This style began in Dilla, and then spread throughout the area. It was a mixture of modern poetry and Somali dance music.

Cabdillahi Qarshe rose to fame in the early 1940s as part of the qaraami style. Many qarami songs from this era are still extremely popular today. This musical style is mostly played on the *kaban* (oud). The first Somali kaban players were: Ali Feiruz, Mohamed Nahari, and others in 1950s.

During the Siad Barre regime, music was suppressed except for a small amount of officially-sanctioned music. There were many protest songs produced during this period.

Music institutions

The first radio station in Somalia to air popular Somali music was Radio Somali, based in Hargeisa. Nowadays, Somali music is also available for download on popular online Somali music portals.

List of Somali singers, songwriters and instrumentalists

- Abdi Sinimo
- Gulled ahmed
- Farhia Fiska
- Waaberi
- Jama Dhoodi

- Ahmed 'Hudeydi' Ismail Hussein.
- Hibo Mohamed Hudoon (Hibo Nuura)
- Kinsi Xaji Aden
- saado ali warsame
- Hussein Ali Kahin
- Abdikadir Moalin Yusuf Jubba
- Mohamed Ahmed kuluc
- Mohamed Nuur Giriig
- Omar Dhuule
- Mohamed Mooge
- Ahmed Ga`ayte
- Ali Roble Subagleh
- Ismail Abdi Guled " Ismail Yare"
- Mohamud Jama " Ali Dhere"
- Daud Ali Mas-haf
- Mohamed Suleman Tube`
- Haliimo Khaliif Magool
- Maryam Mursal
- Madar Ahmed Mohamed (Madar Yare)
- K'naan
- Hasan Adan Samatar
- Ahmed Mooge Liban
- Mohamed Mooge Liban
- Abdiqadir Sheikh Ali Sanka
- Yusuf Jamac Ganey
- Mohamed Saleebaan
- Mahamoud Mohamed Cige (Buuse)
- Mohamed Yusuf
- Amina Abdilahi
- Aar Maanta
- Muslimo Qasim Hilowle (Pianist)
- Fadumo Qasim
- Abdihakim Mohamed Warsame (Calaacal)
- Hassan Ganey
- Siraad Abdulle Ugas
- Ismail Sh.Ahmed Cagaf
- Mohamed Aden Dacar
- Ahmed Saleeben Bide

- Ali Saleban Bide
- Ahmad Ali Igaal
- Ahmed Mooge Liibaan
- Maxamed Nuur Giriig
- Salaaad Maxamed Shardi (Salaad Darbi)
- Mohamed Nur Shareco
- Barre Mohamed Fiidow (Barre Leento)
- Hasan Shiekh Muumin
- Huseen Aw Faarah
- Mohamed Ali Kaariye
- Mohamed Cabdulahi Sangub
- Mohamed Ibraahim Hadrawi
- Sahal Macalim Ciise
- Cabdi Adan Qays
- Hasan Haji Abdilahi (Hasan Ganay)
- Bashir Mahamed Idiris Baatil Taffare)
- Roda Cabdulahi Jamac (Roda Wacan)
- Maxamed Ahmed Shimbir
- Nuur Eebo
- Abdoulkader Juba
- Mahamed Jeesto
- Mohamed Omar Huryo

References

- Abdullahi, Mohamed Diriye (2001). *Culture and customs of Somalia* [1]. Greenwood. ISBN 9780313313332.

External links

- Somali Music [2]
- Heesta.com [3]
- Maalmo Somali Social music site [4]
- SomaliOZ Network - Somali music portal [5]
- Bclub19.com [6]
- Music lyrics from Somalia [7]
- Ahmed 'Hudeydi' Ismail Hussein [8] at BBC Radio 3's "World on Your Street"
- Somali Songs [9]

Somali cuisine

Culture of Somalia

Art
Architecture
Pottery · Textile
Music · Wood carving
Language
Literature · Mythology
Writing systems · Poetry
Other
Dance · Dress
Games · Cuisine
Society · History
Islam · Festivals · Institutions
Science and Technology
Maritime · Medicine · Astronomy · Media
Cinema · Coinage
See also
Education · Politics
Symbols · Military

Somali cuisine varies from region to region and is a mixture of native Somali, Ethiopian, Yemeni, Persian, Turkish, Indian and Italian influences. It is the product of Somalia's tradition of trade and commerce. All food is halal.

Breakfast

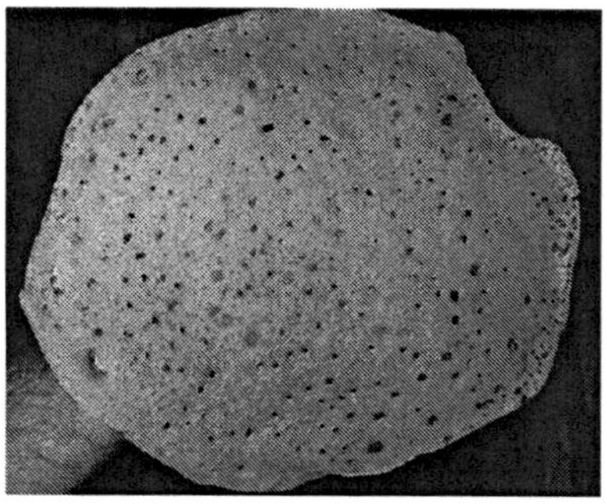
Somali *canjeero*.

Breakfast (*quraac*) is an important meal for Somalis. who often start the day with some style of tea (*shaah*). The main dish is typically a pancake-like bread (*canjeero*) similar to Ethiopian injera but smaller and thinner.

Canjeero is eaten in different ways, it may be broken into small pieces and ghee (*subag*) and sugar added. For children it is mixed with tea and sesame oil (*macsaaro*) until mushy. There may be a side-dish of liver (*beef*), goat meat (*hilib ari*), diced beef cooked in a bed of soup (*suqaar*) or jerky (*oodkac* or *muqmad*), which consists of small dried pieces of beef, or goat or camel meat, boiled in ghee.

Polenta (*mishaari* or *boorash* porridge) with butter and sugar is popular in Mogadishu.

In the north, bread (*rooti*) is popular. In Somalia a sweeter and oilier version of canjeero called *malawax* is a staple of most home-cooked meals.

Lunch

Lunch (*qado*) is often an elaborated main dish of rice (*bariis*) spiced with cumin (*kamuun*), cardamom (*heyl*), cloves {*qaranfuul*) and sage.

In the south, a hotpot of rice, vegetables, and sometimes meat, called *Iskudhexkaris* is common. Beyond the many styles of stew (*maraq*), rice is also served with meat on the side. In Mogadishu, steak (*busteeki*) and fish (*kaluun*) are widely eaten.

Cornmeal (*soor*) is popular. Unlike the ugali of Kenya, Somalis have a softer cornmeal mashed with fresh milk, butter and sugar or with a well in the soor filled with maraq.

A variation of the Indian chapati is the *sabaayad*. Like the rice, it is served with *maraq* and meat on the side. The sabaayad of Somalia is often somewhat sweet, and is cooked in a little oil.

Pasta (*baasto*) is popular often served with a heavier stew than the Italian pasta sauce, more distinctively, it is often served with a banana.

The most popular drinks at lunch are *balbeelmo* (grapefruit), *raqey* (tamarind) and *isbarmuunto* (lemonade). In Mogadishu, *cambe* (mango), *seytuun* (guava) and *laas* (Lassi) are popular as well. In Hargeisa in the north, the preferred drinks are *fiimto* (Vimto) and *tufaax* (apple).

Dinner

Various types of popular Somali dishes.

Somali people serve dinner as late as 9 pm. During Ramadan, supper-time often follows Tarawih prayers, sometimes even as late as 11 pm. *Cambuulo*, a favorite dish come dinnertime, is made of well-cooked azuki beans mixed with butter and sugar. The beans, which on their own are referred to as *digir*, can take up to five hours to finish cooking when left on the stove at a low temperature.

In 1988, the Somali newspaper *Xiddigta Oktoober* conducted a survey in which it found that 83% of Mogadishu's residents preferred cambuulo as their main dinnertime meal. It was a startling discovery since the dish is considered to be somewhat "low class" due to its flatulence-inducing after-effects caused by the natural sugars (known as oligosaccharides) in its beans.

Likewise, *qamadi* (wheat) is used. Cracked or uncracked, it is cooked and served just like the azuki beans.

Rooti iyo xalwo, slices of bread served with a gelatinous confection, is another popular dinnertime dish.

Muufo, a variation of cornbread, is a dish made of maize and is baked in a *foorno* (clay oven). It is eaten by cutting it into small pieces , adding *macsaro* (sesame oil), sugar and then mashing the whole with black tea.

And before bed, a glass of milk spiced with cardamom is often consumed.

Snacks

Sambuusa, a Somali version of the samosa, is probably the most popular form of a snack in Somalia. It is especially popular during Ramadan, as it is the dish of the *afur* (iftar). The Somali version is spiced with hot green pepper, and the main ingredient is often ground meat.

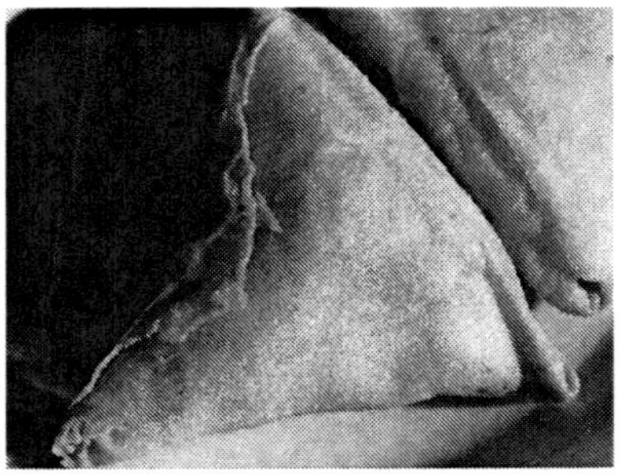

Sambuusa, or samosa, is a popular snack in Somalia.

Bajiye, a variation of the Indian pakora, is a popular snack in southern Somalia. The Somali version is a mixture of maize, vegetables, meat, spices, which is then deep fried. It is eaten by dipping it in *bisbaas*, a hot sauce.

Kabaab similar to that of Persia is not that widespread, but a few Somalis in the diaspora eat it.

Fruits such as mango, guava, banana and grapefruit serve as snacks throughout the day.

Sweets

Gashaato, a very popular coconut-based confection, set here to a backdrop of the Somali national flag.

Xalwo or halva is a fairly popular confection served during special occasions such as Eid celebrations or wedding receptions. *Xalwadii waad qarsatey!* ("You hid your *xalwo*!") is the phrase that follows a person who has eloped or has a small, private wedding. Xalwo is made from sugar, cornstarch, cardamom powder, nutmeg powder, and ghee. Peanuts are also sometimes added to enhance texture and flavor.

Gashaato or *qumbe*, made of coconut, oils and sugar, and spiced with cardamom, is a much-loved sweet. The sugar is brought to boil with a bit of water, then the cardamom is added followed by shredded coconut.

Lows iyo sisin is a favorite sweet in the south, made of a mixture of peanuts (*lows*) and sesame seeds (*sisin*) in a bed of caramel. It sticks together to form a delicious bar.

Jalaato, similar to the American popsicle, is made by freezing naturally sweet fruits with a stick in the middle. More recently in Mogadishu, it has grown to include *caano*/milk jalaato, which then requires sugaring up. The word *jalaato* comes from gelato, which is Italian for "frozen".

Buskut or *Buskud* comprise many different types of cookies, including very soft ones called *daardaar* (literally "touch-touch" due to its smooth, delicate texture).

Doolshe encompass many delectable styles of cakes.

After-meal

Somalis traditionally perfume their homes after meals. Frankincense (*lubaan*) or a prepared incense (*cuunsi*), which in countries in the Arabian Peninsula is known as *bukhoor*, is placed on top of hot charcoal inside an incense burner or censer (a *dabqaad*). It then burns for about ten minutes. This keeps the house fragrant for hours. The burner is made from soapstone found in specific areas of Somalia.

A *dabqaad* incense burner.

References

- Ali, Barlin (2007). *Somali Cuisine* [1]. AuthorHouse. ISBN 1425977065.

External links

- My Somali Food [2]
- Recipe & Cook Book:Somali Tea & Treats [3]
- Somali Recipes [4]
- Tammy's Somali Home [5]

Transportation

Aden Adde International Airport

Aden-Adde International Airport			
IATA: MGQ – ICAO: HCMM			
Summary			
Airport type	Joint (Civil and Military)		
Owner	{{{owner}}}		
Operator	{{{operator}}}		
Serves	{{{city-served}}}		
Location	{{{location}}}		
Hub for	{{{hub}}}		
Coordinates	02°00′49″N 45°18′17″E		
Website	{{{website}}}		
Runways			
Direction	**Length**		**Surface**
	ft	**m**	
05/23	9,901	3,018	Paved

Aden-Adde International Airport (IATA: **MGQ**, ICAO: **HCMM**), (formerly **Mogadishu International Airport**), is the international airport for Mogadishu, the capital of Somalia. It is named after Aden Abdullah Osman Daar, the first President of Somalia. The Somali civil war and the Ethiopian invasion have caused continual disruptions to the airport's operations.

In 2008, due to high risk on civilian aircraft, most airlines decided to land and depart from K50 Airport, about 50 km from Mogadishu in Lower Shabelle.

History

Mogadishu airport was created by the Italians in the 1940s. When Somalia became independent the Italians left the airport in good condition. The Somali government then agreed to use the airport as Mogadishu International Airport. The first few aircraft landing at Mogadishu were Somali Airlines DC-3. However, the Somali government had ideas to expand the airport but the idea was never put into action.

Mogadishu's airport was the site where the *Landshut Hijacking* was terminated on 18 October 1977. Lufthansa Flight 181 was a Lufthansa Boeing 737-230 Adv aircraft named Landshut that was hijacked on 13 October 1977 by four members of the P.F.L.P. Popular Front for the Liberation of Palestine (who called themselves Commando Martyr Halime), in the last major event of the German Autumn of 1977. On 18 October, the aircraft was stormed by the West German counter-terrorism group GSG 9 and all 86 passengers rescued. The rescue operation was codenamed "Feuerzauber" (German term for "Fire Magic", also known as "Zauberfeuer" or Magic Fire).

Mogadishu airport was also used by the Somali air force. The Somali Air Force had an airlift wing stationed at Mogadishu. The Somali air force also maintained an military academy at airport used by all members of Somali armed forces.

After reopening, African Express Airways was the first international airline to land at Mogadishu International Airport on August 3, 2006. The flight had departed from Nairobi..

On June 8, 2007, the Transitional Federal Government announced that the airport would be renamed for the first president of Somalia, Aden Abdullah Osman Daar, who died in Nairobi on June 8, 2007.

Airlines and destinations

Airlines	Destinations
Daallo Airlines	Djiboutii, Hargeisa
Jubba Airways	Djibouti, Hargeisa, Dubai, Jeddah
African Express Airways	Aden, Berbera, Dubai, Nairobi-Jomo Kenyatta, Sharjah

Previous Airlines

Airlines	Destinations
Somali Airlines	Hargeisa, Kismayo, Djibouti, Frankfurt, Rome, Jeddah, Dubai, Aden, Nairobi, Berbera, Sharjah, Damascus, Cairo, Khartoum, Paris, Amsterdam, London, Tripoli, Sanaa, Dar es Salaam
Alitalia	Rome, Athens, Addis Ababa, Asmara
Pakistan International Airlines	Karachi, Dubai, Nairobi, Lagos [suspended in 1996]
Saudi Arabian Airlines	Jeddah
Lufthansa	Frankfurt
Air France	Victoria, Port Louis
Kenya Airways	Nairobi
Djibouti Airlines	Djibouti
Aeroflot	Cairo, Dar es Salaam, Hodeida, Moscow

Accidents and incidents

- On 6 May 1970, Vickers Viscount 6O-AAJ of Somali Airlines caught fire on approach to Mogadishu International Airport. The nosewheel collapsed in a heavy landing and the aircraft was burnt out. Five of the 30 people on board were killed.

See also

- War in Somalia (2006–2009).

Mogadishu-Villabruzzi Railway

The **Mogadiscio-Villabruzzi Railway** was the railway of Italian Somalia, and connected the capital of Somalia with the Shebelle river agricultural areas from 1914 to 1941.

"Ansaldo 442" steam locomotive, built in 1938 and similar to those used in the Somalian railway

History

It was built initially for the surrounding area of Mogadishu (*Mogadiscio* in Italian) after World War I. In the 1920s the Italian nobleman Luigi Amedeo, Duke of the Abruzzi had the railway extended to the Shebelle river colonial villages he was then developing.

The line, 114 km long, reached Villabruzzi (then in full "Villaggio Duca degli Abruzzi", now "Jowhar") in 1928. The original proposal was for the railway to go on from Villabruzzi to the Somali border with Ethiopia and into the Ogaden, but the Second Italo-Abyssinian War in 1936 stopped further construction.

In 1939 the Italian leader Benito Mussolini planned road and rail connections between Mogadiscio and Addis Ababa, but only the road ("La Strada Imperiale") was built before World War II destroyed the Italian Empire.

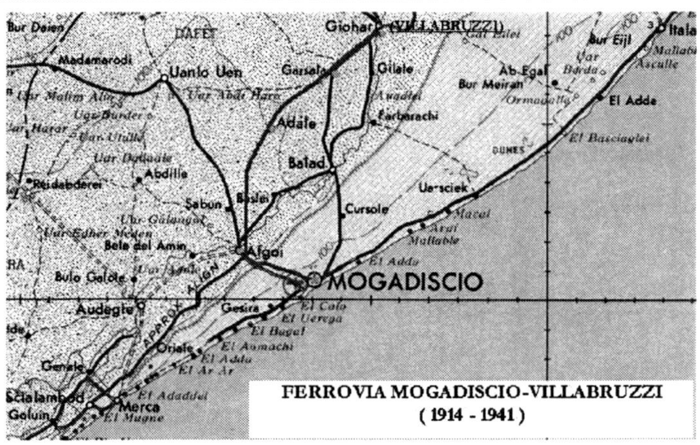

In green the Railway Mogadiscio-Villabruzzi (1914-1941)

In 1941 the railway was dismantled by the British troops when they conquered the "Africa Orientale Italiana". Since then the railway, except for a few tracks within Mogadishu harbour, was no longer used. In 1942 some diesel locomotives and related materials were moved by the British government to Eritrea, to be used on the Massawa-Asmara railway.

In the 1980s the Somalian president Siad Barre proposed the reactivation of the railway, but his fall in 1991 stopped the possible reconstruction.

Statistics

The railway in 1930 moved 19.359 passengers, and was used by even for tourism. In the same year 43.467 tons of products (mainly agricultural) were transported, with earnings up to 1.591.527 Lira somala. Most products transported were bananas and coffee, from farm plantations of the area of Villabruzzi, to be exported through the port of Mogadishu.

It was administered by the *Ferrovie Somale*, a government company.

The single track railway had a 950 mm gauge, as established in 1879 by an Italian law on minor gauges.

Equipment

The equipment of the Somalian railway was similar to the one used in the Eritrean Railway.

Steam locomotives

Three classes of steam locomotive were used: one design of 0-4-0 shunter and two designs of 0-4-4-0 Mallet for line service.

202 Series

These small 0-4-0 tank engines were and are the standard shunter locomotives of the system, built between 1927 and 1937 by the firm of Breda in Milan. They have short side tanks, a rear coal bunker, and a unified, oval dome containing the steam dome inside a larger sand dome - this arrangement, popular worldwide in nations that favored the sand dome, helped both to insulate the steam dome and to keep the sand dry with the warmth. Large, prominent builder's plates adorn the domes. They use Walschaerts valve gear with piston valves and superheating.

A pair of class 202 locomotives, similar to those used in the Somalian railway

440 Series

One of these early Mallet locomotives, which is a true Mallet and thus a compound, still exists in storage at the Asmara railway Station. It was a 1915 product of Ansaldo in Genova.

442 Series

These later, and much larger, compound Mallet locomotives were built by Ansaldo in Genova in 1938 to largely replace the earlier types, both the 440 Series and the unsuccessful 441 Series, which were simple locomotives (i.e., non-compound) and found liable to run out of steam on the heavy grades of the line. Like the other locomotives they are tank engines with large side tanks and a rear coal bunker, under cover of the cab roof in this design. These are quite hefty machines, as required by the tough demands of the terrain.

A class 440 locomotive, similar to those used in the Somalian railway

Railway stations

Name	Distance	Altitude
Mogadiscio	0 km (0.0 mi)	0 m (0 ft)
Ponte sullo Shebelle	30 km (18.6 mi)	18 m (59 ft)
Afgoi	50 km (31.1 mi)	64 ft (20 m)
Adalei	66 km (41.0 mi)	78 m (256 ft)
Garsala	80 km (49.7 mi)	88 m (289 ft)
Moico	90 km (55.9 mi)	91 m (299 ft)
Ponte sullo Shebelle	111 km (69.0 mi)	96 m (315 ft)
Villaggio Duca degli Abruzzi (Jowhar)	114 km (70.8 mi)	108 m (354 ft)

Bibliography

- Antonicelli, Franco. *Trent'anni di storia italiana 1915 - 1945*. Mondadori Editore. Torino, 1961.
- Del Boca, Angelo. *Una sconfitta dell'intelligenza. Italia e Somalia*. Laterza Editore. Bari, 1993.
- Tripodi, Paolo. *The Colonial Legacy in Somalia*. St. Martin's P Inc. New York, 1999.

See also

- Eritrean Railway
- Italian Somalia
- Transport in Somalia
- Italian Somalians

Article Sources and Contributors

Somalia *Source*: http://en.wikipedia.org/?oldid=390466444 *Contributors*:

History of Somalia *Source*: http://en.wikipedia.org/?oldid=388853383 *Contributors*: Woohookitty

Geography of Somalia *Source*: http://en.wikipedia.org/?oldid=383765502 *Contributors*:

Politics of Somalia *Source*: http://en.wikipedia.org/?oldid=387805957 *Contributors*: Therequiembellishere

Economy of Somalia *Source*: http://en.wikipedia.org/?oldid=380109562 *Contributors*: Middayexpress

Culture of Somalia *Source*: http://en.wikipedia.org/?oldid=386575933 *Contributors*: Gyrofrog

Hannassa *Source*: http://en.wikipedia.org/?oldid=371165434 *Contributors*:

Maduna *Source*: http://en.wikipedia.org/?oldid=378126262 *Contributors*: Mandarax

Mogadishu *Source*: http://en.wikipedia.org/?oldid=390427903 *Contributors*: Redthoreau

Banaadir *Source*: http://en.wikipedia.org/?oldid=385524219 *Contributors*:

History of Mogadishu *Source*: http://en.wikipedia.org/?oldid=381948681 *Contributors*: Middayexpress

Kismayo *Source*: http://en.wikipedia.org/?oldid=381482884 *Contributors*: WereSpielChequers

Afgooye *Source*: http://en.wikipedia.org/?oldid=387578371 *Contributors*: 1 anonymous edits

Dinsoor *Source*: http://en.wikipedia.org/?oldid=375117460 *Contributors*: 1 anonymous edits

Jamaame *Source*: http://en.wikipedia.org/?oldid=383383157 *Contributors*:

Xuddur *Source*: http://en.wikipedia.org/?oldid=363930125 *Contributors*:

Wajid, Somalia *Source*: http://en.wikipedia.org/?oldid=382932791 *Contributors*:

Jilib *Source*: http://en.wikipedia.org/?oldid=379447291 *Contributors*:

Barawa *Source*: http://en.wikipedia.org/?oldid=373832002 *Contributors*: Gyrofrog

Mandera *Source*: http://en.wikipedia.org/?oldid=390634319 *Contributors*: 1 anonymous edits

Merca *Source*: http://en.wikipedia.org/?oldid=383866494 *Contributors*:

Jowhar *Source*: http://en.wikipedia.org/?oldid=369436993 *Contributors*:

Hobyo *Source*: http://en.wikipedia.org/?oldid=390421873 *Contributors*: Tbhotch

Hargeisa *Source*: http://en.wikipedia.org/?oldid=383255867 *Contributors*: Marcassmith

Mogadishu Cathedral *Source*: http://en.wikipedia.org/?oldid=389703134 *Contributors*: Stoigniew

Mosque of Islamic Solidarity *Source*: http://en.wikipedia.org/?oldid=348005909 *Contributors*: 1 anonymous edits

Fakr ad-Din Mosque *Source*: http://en.wikipedia.org/?oldid=380244653 *Contributors*:

Villa Somalia *Source*: http://en.wikipedia.org/?oldid=349826500 *Contributors*: Gene Nygaard

Gezira Beach *Source*: http://en.wikipedia.org/?oldid=382580983 *Contributors*: Ronhjones

Shebelle River *Source*: http://en.wikipedia.org/?oldid=389036504 *Contributors*: Pfly

National Library of Somalia *Source*: http://en.wikipedia.org/?oldid=384037437 *Contributors*: Emijrp

Bakaara Market *Source*: http://en.wikipedia.org/?oldid=385541383 *Contributors*: Δ

Istunka *Source*: http://en.wikipedia.org/?oldid=378531508 *Contributors*: Eugene-elgato

Gelbis *Source*: http://en.wikipedia.org/?oldid=333303609 *Contributors*: 1 anonymous edits

Badbaado *Source*: http://en.wikipedia.org/?oldid=300234660 *Contributors*:

Banadir Stadium *Source*: http://en.wikipedia.org/?oldid=331326055 *Contributors*: LilHelpa

Mogadiscio Stadium *Source*: http://en.wikipedia.org/?oldid=384570304 *Contributors*: 1 anonymous edits

Music of Somalia *Source*: http://en.wikipedia.org/?oldid=390244795 *Contributors*: 1 anonymous edits

Somali cuisine *Source*: http://en.wikipedia.org/?oldid=374676079 *Contributors*: Xiglofre

Aden Adde International Airport *Source*: http://en.wikipedia.org/?oldid=390289790 *Contributors*: LobStoR

Mogadishu-Villabruzzi Railway *Source*: http://en.wikipedia.org/?oldid=375528577 *Contributors*: Hugo999

Image Sources, Licenses and Contributors

File:Flag of Somalia.svg *Source*: http://bibliocm.bibliolabs.com/mwAnon/index.php?title=File:Flag_of_Somalia.svg *License*: unknown *Contributors*: Anakin101, Anime Addict AA, Anonymous101, Flad, Fry1989, Gdgourou, Homo lupus, JLogan, Klemen Kocjancic, Mattes, Permjak, SKopp, ThomasPusch, Trijnstel, Tvdm, Ultratomio, Vzb83, احمد.علي1, 12 anonymous edits

File:Coat of arms of Somalia.png *Source*: http://bibliocm.bibliolabs.com/mwAnon/index.php?title=File:Coat_of_arms_of_Somalia.png *License*: Public Domain *Contributors*: User:Giuseppe Ricci

File:Somalia (orthographic projection)-Blue version.svg *Source*: http://bibliocm.bibliolabs.com/mwAnon/index.php?title=File:Somalia_(orthographic_projection)-Blue_version.svg *License*: Creative Commons Attribution 3.0 *Contributors*: Martin H., The Emirr

File:Amud, Somalia.jpg *Source*: http://bibliocm.bibliolabs.com/mwAnon/index.php?title=File:Amud,_Somalia.jpg *License*: Creative Commons Attribution-Sharealike 2.5 *Contributors*: A.T Curle - British Government Officer & Surveyor

File:LaasGeel.jpg *Source*: http://bibliocm.bibliolabs.com/mwAnon/index.php?title=File:LaasGeel.jpg *License*: Creative Commons Attribution-Sharealike 3.0 *Contributors*: User:MuusaHersi

File:Silk route.jpg *Source*: http://bibliocm.bibliolabs.com/mwAnon/index.php?title=File:Silk_route.jpg *License*: Public Domain *Contributors*: User:Splette

File:Qableh1.JPG *Source*: http://bibliocm.bibliolabs.com/mwAnon/index.php?title=File:Qableh1.JPG *License*: Creative Commons Attribution-Sharealike 3.0 *Contributors*: Abdirisak

File:Zayla.jpg *Source*: http://bibliocm.bibliolabs.com/mwAnon/index.php?title=File:Zayla.jpg *License*: Creative Commons Attribution-Sharealike 3.0 *Contributors*: User:Vascoscream

File:Fakr Ud Din Mosque.jpg *Source*: http://bibliocm.bibliolabs.com/mwAnon/index.php?title=File:Fakr_Ud_Din_Mosque.jpg *License*: unknown *Contributors*: Original uploader was RoboRanks at en.wikipedia

File:Mogadishan ship.JPG *Source*: http://bibliocm.bibliolabs.com/mwAnon/index.php?title=File:Mogadishan_ship.JPG *License*: unknown *Contributors*: Regio Governo Della Somalia

File:Hafun, Somalia.jpg *Source*: http://bibliocm.bibliolabs.com/mwAnon/index.php?title=File:Hafun,_Somalia.jpg *License*: Public Domain *Contributors*: Scoobycentric

File:Somali warriors board British naval batilla.jpg *Source*: http://bibliocm.bibliolabs.com/mwAnon/index.php?title=File:Somali_warriors_board_British_naval_batilla.jpg *License*: Public Domain *Contributors*: Middayexpress

File:Taleh Castle.jpg *Source*: http://bibliocm.bibliolabs.com/mwAnon/index.php?title=File:Taleh_Castle.jpg *License*: Creative Commons Attribution-Sharealike 3.0 *Contributors*: User:Scoobycentric

File:SYL-Freedom.jpg *Source*: http://bibliocm.bibliolabs.com/mwAnon/index.php?title=File:SYL-Freedom.jpg *License*: Public Domain *Contributors*: RoboRanks

File:Mogadishu.jpg *Source*: http://bibliocm.bibliolabs.com/mwAnon/index.php?title=File:Mogadishu.jpg *License*: Creative Commons Attribution-Sharealike 3.0 *Contributors*: User:Maxamad

File:Somalia map states regions districts.png *Source*: http://bibliocm.bibliolabs.com/mwAnon/index.php?title=File:Somalia_map_states_regions_districts.png *License*: Public Domain *Contributors*: User:Ingoman

File:Abdullahi Yusuf Ahmed 2.jpg *Source*: http://bibliocm.bibliolabs.com/mwAnon/index.php?title=File:Abdullahi_Yusuf_Ahmed_2.jpg *License*: unknown *Contributors*: U.S. Air Force photo by Tech. Sgt. Jeremy T. Lock

File:Somalian embassy in Paris.jpg *Source*: http://bibliocm.bibliolabs.com/mwAnon/index.php?title=File:Somalian_embassy_in_Paris.jpg *License*: GNU Free Documentation License *Contributors*: User:Pymouss44

File:Bakaara Market.jpg *Source*: http://bibliocm.bibliolabs.com/mwAnon/index.php?title=File:Bakaara_Market.jpg *License*: Creative Commons Attribution-Sharealike 1.0 *Contributors*: Ijo

Image:BosasoCity.jpg *Source*: http://bibliocm.bibliolabs.com/mwAnon/index.php?title=File:BosasoCity.jpg *License*: Creative Commons Attribution-Sharealike 3.0 *Contributors*: User:Scoobycentric

Image:Kismayo.jpg *Source*: http://bibliocm.bibliolabs.com/mwAnon/index.php?title=File:Kismayo.jpg *License*: Public Domain *Contributors*: Original uploader was Abdirisak at en.wikipedia

Image:Rays Hotel in Borama.jpg *Source*: http://bibliocm.bibliolabs.com/mwAnon/index.php?title=File:Rays_Hotel_in_Borama.jpg *License*: Creative Commons Attribution-Sharealike 1.0 *Contributors*: licensed from World66

File:Hargeisacitycentre.jpg *Source*: http://bibliocm.bibliolabs.com/mwAnon/index.php?title=File:Hargeisacitycentre.jpg *License*: Public Domain *Contributors*: Fdama

Image:Marka,Somalia.jpg *Source*: http://bibliocm.bibliolabs.com/mwAnon/index.php?title=File:Marka,Somalia.jpg *License*: Creative Commons Attribution-Sharealike 3.0 *Contributors*: User:Scoobycentric

File:Barawa.jpg *Source*: http://bibliocm.bibliolabs.com/mwAnon/index.php?title=File:Barawa.jpg *License*: Creative Commons Attribution-Sharealike 3.0 *Contributors*: User:Vascoscream

File:Presidentialres.jpg *Source*: http://bibliocm.bibliolabs.com/mwAnon/index.php?title=File:Presidentialres.jpg *License*: Public Domain *Contributors*: Original uploader was SmartBrainz at en.wikipedia

File:Almadow Overview.JPG *Source*: http://bibliocm.bibliolabs.com/mwAnon/index.php?title=File:Almadow_Overview.JPG *License*: Public Domain *Contributors*: Abdirisak

File:Juba river downstream Jamaame.jpg *Source*: http://bibliocm.bibliolabs.com/mwAnon/index.php?title=File:Juba_river_downstream_Jamaame.jpg *License*: Creative Commons Attribution-Sharealike 2.0 *Contributors*: Sylvie Doutriaux

File:Horses3.jpg *Source*: http://bibliocm.bibliolabs.com/mwAnon/index.php?title=File:Horses3.jpg *License*: Public Domain *Contributors*: Abdirisak

File:Edna-adan-maternity-hospital-hargeisa.jpg *Source*: http://bibliocm.bibliolabs.com/mwAnon/index.php?title=File:Edna-adan-maternity-hospital-hargeisa.jpg *License*: Public Domain *Contributors*: User:Chuckupd

File:Somali boy receives a polio vaccination.jpg *Source*: http://bibliocm.bibliolabs.com/mwAnon/index.php?title=File:Somali_boy_receives_a_polio_vaccination.jpg *License*: Public Domain *Contributors*: PV2 Andrew W. McGalliard

File:Mogadishu university.jpg *Source*: http://bibliocm.bibliolabs.com/mwAnon/index.php?title=File:Mogadishu_university.jpg *License*: Creative Commons Attribution-Sharealike 3.0 *Contributors*: User:Siphon

File:Hammar Jab Jab School.jpeg *Source*: http://bibliocm.bibliolabs.com/mwAnon/index.php?title=File:Hammar_Jab_Jab_School.jpeg *License*: Public Domain *Contributors*: USAID

File:Amoud University.jpg *Source*: http://bibliocm.bibliolabs.com/mwAnon/index.php?title=File:Amoud_University.jpg *License*: Creative Commons Attribution-Sharealike 1.0 *Contributors*: licensed from World66

File:Air Somalia Tupolev Tu-154.jpg *Source*: http://bibliocm.bibliolabs.com/mwAnon/index.php?title=File:Air_Somalia_Tupolev_Tu-154.jpg *License*: unknown *Contributors*: Leonid Faerberg (transport-photo.com)

Image:Laasqoray30.jpg *Source*: http://bibliocm.bibliolabs.com/mwAnon/index.php?title=File:Laasqoray30.jpg *License*: Public Domain *Contributors*: Abdirisak

File:Bosaso port.jpg *Source*: http://bibliocm.bibliolabs.com/mwAnon/index.php?title=File:Bosaso_port.jpg *License*: Creative Commons Attribution-Sharealike 3.0 *Contributors*: User:Siphon

File:Dahabshiil.jpg *Source*: http://bibliocm.bibliolabs.com/mwAnon/index.php?title=File:Dahabshiil.jpg *License*: Creative Commons Attribution 2.0 *Contributors*: geocam20000

Image:Puntland oil.png *Source*: http://bibliocm.bibliolabs.com/mwAnon/index.php?title=File:Puntland_oil.png *License*: Public Domain *Contributors*: User:Ingoman

File:Hormuud.jpg *Source*: http://bibliocm.bibliolabs.com/mwAnon/index.php?title=File:Hormuud.jpg *License*: Creative Commons Attribution-Sharealike 3.0 *Contributors*: User:Maxamad

File:P12.jpg *Source*: http://bibliocm.bibliolabs.com/mwAnon/index.php?title=File:P12.jpg *License*: Public Domain *Contributors*: GYSGT W. R. HOWER

File:Somcoralreef.jpg *Source*: http://bibliocm.bibliolabs.com/mwAnon/index.php?title=File:Somcoralreef.jpg *License*: Public Domain *Contributors*: National Oceanic and Atmospheric Administration (NOAA)

File:Fatima Jibrell.jpg *Source*: http://bibliocm.bibliolabs.com/mwAnon/index.php?title=File:Fatima_Jibrell.jpg *License*: Public Domain *Contributors*: Tom Sponheim

File:Little Somali girl.jpeg *Source*: http://bibliocm.bibliolabs.com/mwAnon/index.php?title=File:Little_Somali_girl.jpeg *License*: Public Domain *Contributors*: USAID

File:Ciismaniya.jpg *Source*: http://bibliocm.bibliolabs.com/mwAnon/index.php?title=File:Ciismaniya.jpg *License*: unknown *Contributors*: Original uploader was RoboRanks at en.wikipedia

File:Somaliamosque11.jpg *Source*: http://bibliocm.bibliolabs.com/mwAnon/index.php?title=File:Somaliamosque11.jpg *License*: Creative Commons Attribution-Sharealike 3.0 *Contributors*: Original uploader was RoboRanks at en.wikipedia

File:Somali food.jpg *Source*: http://bibliocm.bibliolabs.com/mwAnon/index.php?title=File:Somali_food.jpg *License*: Creative Commons Attribution-Sharealike 1.0 *Contributors*: adar saqadhi

File:Aar maanta.jpg *Source*: http://bibliocm.bibliolabs.com/mwAnon/index.php?title=File:Aar_maanta.jpg *License*: unknown *Contributors*: User:Xaawotaako

File:Eyl Castle.jpg *Source*: http://bibliocm.bibliolabs.com/mwAnon/index.php?title=File:Eyl_Castle.jpg *License*: Creative Commons Attribution-Sharealike 3.0 *Contributors*: User:MuusaHersi

Image:Mogadishan currency.JPG *Source*: http://bibliocm.bibliolabs.com/mwAnon/index.php?title=File:Mogadishan_currency.JPG *License*: Creative Commons Attribution-Sharealike 2.0 *Contributors*: Regio Governo Della Somalia

File:Ancient-Almnara.jpg *Source*: http://bibliocm.bibliolabs.com/mwAnon/index.php?title=File:Ancient-Almnara.jpg *License*: Creative Commons Attribution-Sharealike 3.0 *Contributors*: User:Vascoscream

File:Ahmed Gurey Mogadishu Monument.jpg *Source*: http://bibliocm.bibliolabs.com/mwAnon/index.php?title=File:Ahmed_Gurey_Mogadishu_Monument.jpg *License*: Public Domain *Contributors*: Original uploader was RoboRanks at en.wikipedia

File:Ottoman cannon end of 16th century length 385cm cal 178mm weight 2910 stone projectile founded 8 October 1581 Alger seized 1830.jpg *Source*: http://bibliocm.bibliolabs.com/mwAnon/index.php?title=File:Ottoman_cannon_end_of_16th_century_length_385cm_cal_178mm_weight_2910_stone_projectile_founded_8_October_1581_Alger_s *License*: Creative Commons Attribution-Sharealike 3.0 *Contributors*: User:PHGCOM

File:Medieval Mombasa.jpg *Source*: http://bibliocm.bibliolabs.com/mwAnon/index.php?title=File:Medieval_Mombasa.jpg *License*: unknown *Contributors*: BRAUN AND HOGENBERG

File:Sayyid Mohammed Abdullah Hassan.jpeg *Source*: http://bibliocm.bibliolabs.com/mwAnon/index.php?title=File:Sayyid_Mohammed_Abdullah_Hassan.jpeg *License*: unknown *Contributors*: Somali government

File:Sultan Yusuf Ali Kenadid.jpg *Source*: http://bibliocm.bibliolabs.com/mwAnon/index.php?title=File:Sultan_Yusuf_Ali_Kenadid.jpg *License*: unknown *Contributors*: Somali Government

File:Africa Orientale Italiana.gif *Source*: http://bibliocm.bibliolabs.com/mwAnon/index.php?title=File:Africa_Orientale_Italiana.gif *License*: Public Domain *Contributors*: .anaconda, Kimdime

File:HawoTakoFreedom.jpg *Source*: http://bibliocm.bibliolabs.com/mwAnon/index.php?title=File:HawoTakoFreedom.jpg *License*: unknown *Contributors*: Original uploader was RoboRanks at en.wikipedia

File:General Kediye.jpg *Source*: http://bibliocm.bibliolabs.com/mwAnon/index.php?title=File:General_Kediye.jpg *License*: Creative Commons Attribution-Sharealike 2.0 *Contributors*: Somali Government

File:Black Hawk Down Super64 over Mogadishu coast.jpg *Source*: http://bibliocm.bibliolabs.com/mwAnon/index.php?title=File:Black_Hawk_Down_Super64_over_Mogadishu_coast.jpg *License*: Public Domain *Contributors*: AEMoreira042281, Beta16, D.W., Maksim, Sven-steffen arndt, Tafkas, 4 anonymous edits

Image:Somalia-CIA WFB Map.png *Source*: http://bibliocm.bibliolabs.com/mwAnon/index.php?title=File:Somalia-CIA_WFB_Map.png *License*: unknown *Contributors*: Benchill, Hoshie, Jonathan Harker, Spangineer, Timeshifter, Wolfman, 1 anonymous edits

Image:Somalia sat.png *Source*: http://bibliocm.bibliolabs.com/mwAnon/index.php?title=File:Somalia_sat.png *License*: unknown *Contributors*: Cwolfsheep, Lokal Profil, Martin H.

Image:Somalia Topography en.png *Source*: http://bibliocm.bibliolabs.com/mwAnon/index.php?title=File:Somalia_Topography_en.png *License*: Public Domain *Contributors*: User:Sadalmelik

Image:Naasa Hablood2.jpg *Source*: http://bibliocm.bibliolabs.com/mwAnon/index.php?title=File:Naasa_Hablood2.jpg *License*: Creative Commons Attribution-Sharealike 2.5 *Contributors*: Original uploader was Abdullah Geelah at en.wikipedia

File:Coat_of_arms_of_Somalia.png *Source*: http://bibliocm.bibliolabs.com/mwAnon/index.php?title=File:Coat_of_arms_of_Somalia.png *License*: Public Domain *Contributors*: User:Giuseppe Ricci

Image:Somalia map states regions districts.png *Source*: http://bibliocm.bibliolabs.com/mwAnon/index.php?title=File:Somalia_map_states_regions_districts.png *License*: Public Domain *Contributors*: User:Ingoman

Image:Flag of Somalia Sky Blue.svg *Source*: http://bibliocm.bibliolabs.com/mwAnon/index.php?title=File:Flag_of_Somalia_Sky_Blue.svg *License*: Public Domain *Contributors*: User:SKopp

Image:Flag of the Islamic Courts Union.svg *Source*: http://bibliocm.bibliolabs.com/mwAnon/index.php?title=File:Flag_of_the_Islamic_Courts_Union.svg *License*: Public Domain *Contributors*: User:Ingoman

Image:MogadishuCoke.jpg *Source*: http://bibliocm.bibliolabs.com/mwAnon/index.php?title=File:MogadishuCoke.jpg *License*: GNU Free Documentation License *Contributors*: Original uploader was RJII at en.wikipedia

File:Somali Culture.jpg *Source*: http://bibliocm.bibliolabs.com/mwAnon/index.php?title=File:Somali_Culture.jpg *License*: Creative Commons Attribution-Sharealike 3.0 *Contributors*: Scoobycentric

File:Borama mosque.jpg *Source*: http://bibliocm.bibliolabs.com/mwAnon/index.php?title=File:Borama_mosque.jpg *License*: Creative Commons Attribution-Sharealike 1.0 *Contributors*: licensed from World66

File:Somalia ethnic grps 2002.jpg *Source*: http://bibliocm.bibliolabs.com/mwAnon/index.php?title=File:Somalia_ethnic_grps_2002.jpg *License*: Public Domain *Contributors*: Davepape, Gyrofrog, Mikm, Petri Krohn, Stannered, Str4nd, Túrelio, 10 anonymous edits

File:Old man in Harar.jpg *Source*: http://bibliocm.bibliolabs.com/mwAnon/index.php?title=File:Old_man_in_Harar.jpg *License*: Creative Commons Attribution 2.0 *Contributors*: Gusjer

Image:PD-icon.svg *Source*: http://bibliocm.bibliolabs.com/mwAnon/index.php?title=File:PD-icon.svg *License*: Public Domain *Contributors*: User:Duesentrieb, User:Rfl

File:Mogadishu Montage.jpg *Source*: http://bibliocm.bibliolabs.com/mwAnon/index.php?title=File:Mogadishu_Montage.jpg *License*: Creative Commons Attribution-Sharealike 3.0 *Contributors*: User:Scoobycentric

File:Somalia location map.svg *Source*: http://bibliocm.bibliolabs.com/mwAnon/index.php?title=File:Somalia_location_map.svg *License*: GNU Free Documentation License *Contributors*: User:Sting

File:Red pog.svg *Source*: http://bibliocm.bibliolabs.com/mwAnon/index.php?title=File:Red_pog.svg *License*: Public Domain *Contributors*: User:Andux

File:Muzzaffar (Mogadishu area) flag according to 1576 Portuguese map.svg *Source*: http://bibliocm.bibliolabs.com/mwAnon/index.php?title=File:Muzzaffar_(Mogadishu_area)_flag_according_to_1576_Portuguese_map.svg *License*: Public Domain *Contributors*: User:Scoobycentric

Image:Aerial view of a US helicopter as it flies over a Mogadishu residential area.JPEG *Source*: http://bibliocm.bibliolabs.com/mwAnon/index.php?title=File:Aerial_view_of_a_US_helicopter_as_it_flies_over_a_Mogadishu_residential_area.JPEG *License*: unknown *Contributors*: TSGT PERRY HEIMER

File:Mogadishu 2006.jpg *Source*: http://bibliocm.bibliolabs.com/mwAnon/index.php?title=File:Mogadishu_2006.jpg *License*: Creative Commons Attribution-Sharealike 3.0 *Contributors*: User:Scoobycentric

Image:Bakaara Market.jpg *Source*: http://bibliocm.bibliolabs.com/mwAnon/index.php?title=File:Bakaara_Market.jpg *License*: Creative Commons Attribution-Sharealike 1.0 *Contributors*: Ijo

File:MogadishuCoke.jpg *Source*: http://bibliocm.bibliolabs.com/mwAnon/index.php?title=File:MogadishuCoke.jpg *License*: GNU Free Documentation License *Contributors*: Original uploader was RJII at en.wikipedia

Image:Aerial view of the port of Mogadishu.JPEG *Source*: http://bibliocm.bibliolabs.com/mwAnon/index.php?title=File:Aerial_view_of_the_port_of_Mogadishu.JPEG *License*: unknown *Contributors*: TSGT PERRY HEIMER

Image:Iman (model).jpg *Source*: http://bibliocm.bibliolabs.com/mwAnon/index.php?title=File:Iman_(model).jpg *License*: Creative Commons Attribution-Sharealike 2.0 *Contributors*: Arthur from Westchester County north of NYC, USA, at Arthur@NYCArthur.com

File:Wikisource-logo.svg *Source*: http://bibliocm.bibliolabs.com/mwAnon/index.php?title=File:Wikisource-logo.svg *License*: logo *Contributors*: Nicholas Moreau

Image:Somalia regions map Banaadir.svg *Source*: http://bibliocm.bibliolabs.com/mwAnon/index.php?title=File:Somalia_regions_map_Banaadir.svg *License*: Public Domain *Contributors*: Budelberger, Lencer, Sven-steffen arndt

Image:Pictures from an armed convoy trip in Mogadishu.jpg *Source*: http://bibliocm.bibliolabs.com/mwAnon/index.php?title=File:Pictures_from_an_armed_convoy_trip_in_Mogadishu.jpg *License*: Creative Commons Attribution 2.0 *Contributors*: Béka, Orlovic

File:Mogadishan currency.JPG *Source*: http://bibliocm.bibliolabs.com/mwAnon/index.php?title=File:Mogadishan_currency.JPG *License*: Creative Commons Attribution-Sharealike 2.0 *Contributors*: Regio Governo Della Somalia

Image:Somali05.jpg *Source*: http://bibliocm.bibliolabs.com/mwAnon/index.php?title=File:Somali05.jpg *License*: GNU Free Documentation License *Contributors*: Aaker, Kilom691

File:Kismayo.jpg *Source*: http://bibliocm.bibliolabs.com/mwAnon/index.php?title=File:Kismayo.jpg *License*: Public Domain *Contributors*: Original uploader was Abdirisak at en.wikipedia

File:Afgoye, Somalia.JPG *Source*: http://bibliocm.bibliolabs.com/mwAnon/index.php?title=File:Afgoye,_Somalia.JPG *License*: unknown *Contributors*: Charles Guillain

File:Merca,_Somalia.jpg *Source*: http://bibliocm.bibliolabs.com/mwAnon/index.php?title=File:Merca,_Somalia.jpg *License*: Public Domain *Contributors*: Bacciy (talk). Original uploader was Bacciy at en.wikipedia

Image:Merca minaret moonrise.jpg *Source*: http://bibliocm.bibliolabs.com/mwAnon/index.php?title=File:Merca_minaret_moonrise.jpg *License*: Creative Commons world66 *Contributors*: tahir turk

Image:Political map of Somalia showing Jowhar.png *Source*: http://bibliocm.bibliolabs.com/mwAnon/index.php?title=File:Political_map_of_Somalia_showing_Jowhar.png *License*: Public Domain *Contributors*: Jeffrey Finkelstein

File:Flag of Somaliland.svg *Source*: http://bibliocm.bibliolabs.com/mwAnon/index.php?title=File:Flag_of_Somaliland.svg *License*: Creative Commons Attribution-Sharealike 2.5 *Contributors*: User:B1mbo

Image:Laas Geel.jpg *Source*: http://bibliocm.bibliolabs.com/mwAnon/index.php?title=File:Laas_Geel.jpg *License*: Creative Commons Attribution-Sharealike 2.5 *Contributors*: Abdullah Geelah

Image:Hargeysa memorial.jpg *Source*: http://bibliocm.bibliolabs.com/mwAnon/index.php?title=File:Hargeysa_memorial.jpg *License*: Creative Commons world66 *Contributors*: xirsi

Image:Calaamadaha area o galleryfull.jpg *Source*: http://bibliocm.bibliolabs.com/mwAnon/index.php?title=File:Calaamadaha_area_o_galleryfull.jpg *License*: Public Domain *Contributors*: Mokonono

Image:Hargeisa countryside.jpg *Source*: http://bibliocm.bibliolabs.com/mwAnon/index.php?title=File:Hargeisa_countryside.jpg *License*: Public Domain *Contributors*: Original uploader was Maaxdan at en.wikipedia (Original text : Maaxdan (talk))

Image:Kudu Kruger.jpg *Source*: http://bibliocm.bibliolabs.com/mwAnon/index.php?title=File:Kudu_Kruger.jpg *License*: GNU Free Documentation License *Contributors*: User:KlausF

Image:Shopping mall in Hargeisa.jpg *Source*: http://bibliocm.bibliolabs.com/mwAnon/index.php?title=File:Shopping_mall_in_Hargeisa.jpg *License*: Creative Commons Attribution-Sharealike 1.0 *Contributors*: Grip

Image:Hargeisa airport.jpg *Source*: http://bibliocm.bibliolabs.com/mwAnon/index.php?title=File:Hargeisa_airport.jpg *License*: unknown *Contributors*: Hersi

Image:Somaliclassroom.jpg *Source*: http://bibliocm.bibliolabs.com/mwAnon/index.php?title=File:Somaliclassroom.jpg *License*: GNU Free Documentation License *Contributors*: Original uploader was Blofeld of SPECTRE at en.wikipedia

File:Mogadischu Cathedral.jpg *Source*: http://bibliocm.bibliolabs.com/mwAnon/index.php?title=File:Mogadischu_Cathedral.jpg *License*: Public Domain *Contributors*: Courtesy R.W.S. Hudson

File:jubbarivermap.png *Source*: http://bibliocm.bibliolabs.com/mwAnon/index.php?title=File:Jubbarivermap.png *License*: Creative Commons Attribution-Sharealike 3.0 *Contributors*: User:Kmusser

Image:Shabeelle NASA.jpg *Source*: http://bibliocm.bibliolabs.com/mwAnon/index.php?title=File:Shabeelle_NASA.jpg *License*: Public Domain *Contributors*: NASA satellite

Image:Canjeelo.jpg *Source*: http://bibliocm.bibliolabs.com/mwAnon/index.php?title=File:Canjeelo.jpg *License*: Creative Commons Attribution-Sharealike 3.0 *Contributors*: Hadiyo1997

Image:Somali food.jpg *Source*: http://bibliocm.bibliolabs.com/mwAnon/index.php?title=File:Somali_food.jpg *License*: Creative Commons Attribution-Sharealike 1.0 *Contributors*: adar saqadhi

Image:Samosa 1.jpg *Source*: http://bibliocm.bibliolabs.com/mwAnon/index.php?title=File:Samosa_1.jpg *License*: GNU Free Documentation License *Contributors*: Svencb, Zantastik, 1 anonymous edits

Image:Gashaato.JPG *Source*: http://bibliocm.bibliolabs.com/mwAnon/index.php?title=File:Gashaato.JPG *License*: GNU Free Documentation License *Contributors*: Original uploader was Hadiyo1997 at en.wikipedia

Image:Dabqaad.jpg *Source*: http://bibliocm.bibliolabs.com/mwAnon/index.php?title=File:Dabqaad.jpg *License*: Creative Commons Attribution-Sharealike 2.5 *Contributors*: Original uploader was Abdullah Geelah at en.wikipedia

Image:Ansaldo 442 steam locomotive in Eritrea.JPG *Source*: http://bibliocm.bibliolabs.com/mwAnon/index.php?title=File:Ansaldo_442_steam_locomotive_in_Eritrea.JPG *License*: Creative Commons Attribution-Sharealike 3.0 *Contributors*: User:NoahHafra

Image:RailwayMogadiscioVillabruzzi.jpg *Source*: http://bibliocm.bibliolabs.com/mwAnon/index.php?title=File:RailwayMogadiscioVillabruzzi.jpg *License*: Public Domain *Contributors*: User:Duilmodena

Image:Eritrean Railway class 202 - Tivedshambo 2008-11-04.jpg *Source*: http://bibliocm.bibliolabs.com/mwAnon/index.php?title=File:Eritrean_Railway_class_202_-_Tivedshambo_2008-11-04.jpg *License*: Creative Commons Attribution-Sharealike 3.0 *Contributors*: Friedrichstrasse, Gugganij, Jameslwoodward, Optimist on the run, 1 anonymous edits

Image:Eritrean Railway class 440 - Tivedshambo 2008-11-04.jpg *Source*: http://bibliocm.bibliolabs.com/mwAnon/index.php?title=File:Eritrean_Railway_class_440_-_Tivedshambo_2008-11-04.jpg *License*: GNU Free Documentation License *Contributors*: Friedrichstrasse, Jameslwoodward, Optimist on the run, 1 anonymous edits

CPSIA information can be obtained at www.ICGtesting.com
Printed in the USA
LVOW11s1557041113

359953LV00008B/438/P

9 781249 224402